I Can't Believe
I'M STILL SINGLE

I Can't Believe

I'M STILL SINGLE

Sane, slightly neurotic (but in a sane way) filmmaker into good yoga, bad reality TV, too much chocolate, and a little kinky sex seeks smart, emotionally evolved . . . oh hell, at this point anyone who'll let me watch football

ERIC SCHAEFFER

Thunder's Mouth Press
New York

I CAN'T BELIEVE I'M STILL SINGLE

Sane, slightly neurotic (but in a sane way) filmmaker into good yoga, bad reality TV, too much chocolate, and a little kinky sex seeks smart, emotionally evolved . . . oh hell, at this point anyone who'll let me watch football

Thunder's Mouth Press
An Imprint of Avalon Publishing Group, Inc.
245 West 17th Street, 11th Floor
New York, NY 10011

AVALON
publishing group incorporated

Library of Congress Cataloging-in-Publication Data

Schaeffer, Eric, 1962-
I can't believe I'm still single: Sane, slightly neurotic (but in a sane way) filmmaker into good yoga, bad reality TV, too much chocolate, and a little kinky sex seeks smart, emotionally evolved . . . oh hell, at this point anyone who'll let me watch football / Eric Schaeffer. — 1st Thunder's Mouth ed.
p. cm.
Includes bibliographical references and index.
ISBN 978-1-56858-337-2 (trade pbk.)
1. Schaeffer, Eric, 1962- 2. Motion picture producers and directors--United States--Biography.
I. Title.
PN1998.3.S345A3 2007
791.4302'33092--dc22
[B]
2007005591

ISBN-13: 978-1-56858-337-2
ISBN-10: 1-56858-337-0

9 8 7 6 5 4 3 2 1

Printed in the United States of America
Distributed by Publishers Group West

To my mother and father. . . .

*To the Great Spirit in all things that make this human
experience so amazingly magical and divine. . . .*

*To women, without whom there would be no such thing as
love. . . .*

*And to all of us who believe in our heart of hearts that we
are, and forever will be, the fifth Beatle.*

Om bolo shri sad guru bhagavan ki. Jai!

Contents

either way i'm fucked

"I *want to acknowledge* something that I fear you are already aware of. But by doing so, I will alleviate the pressure for you not to stare at it and for me not to be obsessed with whether you are or are not staring at it . . . and that would be the final stages of this once-massive herpetic chancre on my lower lip."

"Yes, I've seen it."

"I'm not saying I'm going to, but did I want to . . . well, of course I want to; I've wanted to many times already even though I only met you two minutes ago . . . but if I were to *actually* kiss you at the end, or even in the middle of our date, you can rest assured you can't catch it from me."

"Of course, I can."

"No, you can't. It's almost finished. It's dead. If I kissed you in a more sensitive nether region there could be an issue, but your mouth is much stronger."

"Well I need to do some research on Web MD before any kissing occurs with that thing on your mouth. As fond of you as I am, I'm not willing to contract your herpes on our first date."

"Fair enough, but don't go on Hypochondriac MD. We won't be able to kiss until 2042, you'll freak yourself out so much."

We strolled along the running path that overlooks the Hudson River on the lower level of Riverside Park, chatting about whatever; I was lost in her sexy mouth. We sat on the benches above the baseball fields at 104th Street. They used to be dirt with patches of gray grass if you were lucky . . . now they're Astroturf. Sad, but at least they're not a Trump Tower.

A pause as the sun set, then . . .

"You know what I just realized?" She said, solemnly but with an edge of hopefulness.

"What?"

"Do you know what Valtrex is?" Was this the setup of a joke that had no chance of being funny, which concerned me, or did she really think I didn't know what Valtrex was, which also concerned me but in a cute and harmless way.

"Uhhhh, yeah. It's medicine to suppress herpes."

"Right. See, the thing is, I just realized, I've been taking it for the last five years."

"Sooooo, you have herpes."

"Yes."

"Upstairs or downstairs?"

"Upstairs."

"Right. Okay. So if I *had* kissed you, or if I *did* kiss you, it wouldn't matter what stage my cold sore was in because . . . "

"Right."

"And so why did you say that you had to look on Web M . . . ?"

"I don't know."

"Okay."

If my life were a bad car insurance commercial, this would have been the moment when that big black guy who played the assassinated president on 24 would have walked out from behind a bush, stood in front of our bench, and talked into the camera.

"We at Allstate know that you are a skillful, conscientious, and safe dater. But unfortunately, despite your best efforts, you can't control insane daters out there who might smash head-on into you, annihilating you in a moment's notice. We think you should be protected. That's Allstate's stand."

My new writer friend Lexi had set us up a week before. April (we'll call her that until we see how it all turns out, and whether out of love or spite she loses her anonymity) was a writer, too. I don't know why, but the day before I was to sit down and start writing my first book I fell into this group of female writer friends and possible love interests.

I actually thought it was endearing that April's nerves manifested in abject memory loss. If I were to dismiss a possible wife simply for committing a harmless pharmaceutical faux pas, then I would probably still be single at forty-four, which of course I am, but not because of eliminating ladies for such insignificant gaffes as that. No, I've dismissed girls for far less egregious errors to earn my bachelorhood at this mighty age.

Since I was seven years old, I have been starved for more. More sex, more money, more love, more drugs, more booze, more food, more excitement, more God. If it existed, I wanted more of it. The obsession for more rules me even though I hate it. It's the antithesis of how I want to live my life, but I feel powerless over it. My mind is like a pit bull, when it locks its jaws on an idea of how I can get something. Because if I can get some, I can get more. And I need to worry and figure and plan until I come up with a way to get it. I'm sure if I just keep thinking, against all odds, I'll find that perfect plan.

Try as I might, I rarely visit the world outside my head, which is sad to me. The few times I've been lucky enough to see it (I let myself out on unsupervised field trips every once in a while) it seems an amazing place.

It's my fantasy not to fantasize.

It's my dream to be present.

But it's very scary in the real world, so my mind convinces me I should instead worry about the certain impending disaster, and obsess on how everything I have is going to be taken from me and nothing I want will ever happen. See, by obsessing, I won't be in danger of its actually occurring. As if worrying about it will somehow control its outcome in my favor.

It's exhausting, my relentless mind. It's my enemy, an evil force led by a diabolical dictator whose grand scheme is my unmitigated ruination, yet I'm somehow possessed by its spell to keep obsessing when

I'd rather just be happy and watch the beautiful city walk by—why don't people know how to walk in New York City? I mean it was bad enough before cell phones and iPods and Blackberrys, the meandering purposelessness. This isn't a daffodil-laden hillside in *The Sound of Music* and you're not a whimsical whirling Julie Andrews! This is New York City, friend. There's no aimless Sufi dancing, singing, looking at birds that's supposed to go on. You walk in a fast, straight line to get to where you're going.

See, that's what I mean.

My brain sabotages me at every turn.

I don't set out to think like an asshole and luckily, my thoughts rarely inform my actual conduct, so I don't become the dick I would be if they did. For the record, I'm a very happy, loving, fair, compassionate human being who wants the best for everyone. I don't want to hold you down while a bus with an *Everyone Loves Earl* ad on its side drives over and crushes your head to death just because you suddenly veered a little to the right as you walked in front of me, causing me to have to alter my course by six inches. Yeah, I know a plane is off course 90 percent of the time and is constantly correcting its direction. That's a beautiful spiritual metaphor but, you know what, I'm not a plane, and I need to get home to check the barometer of my self-esteem, the blinking red light on the answering machine.

The machine will contain all the fabulous jobs and breathtaking women that will make my life perfect. Of course I have already checked my Blackberry for its blinking red light, having had my attention drawn to its upper right-hand corner countless times during the previous hour. And when not actually checking it, like Susan Lucci on pins and needles awaiting the opening of the Emmy envelope, I anticipate its ruby syncopated pulse with sublime expectation, usually only to be crucified when the truth is revealed . . . but there's the hope of that one victory every thirteen years that keeps me going.

There's also the chance that a lone renegade message might have been orphaned in a cyberspace crack or has yet to be transferred from my home computer e-mail to my Blackberry e-mail. Or maybe one of the seven people who have my home number has called with the perfect wife they can't believe they never thought of for me. Or someone, oh I don't know, Sheryl Crow, is a huge fan and called my agent in an effort to track me down and he's calling with her message. Or in some divine serendipitous accident, somehow someone somewhere happened upon my private line and is calling for my hand. So you see, my friends, many blinking red lights in many places that must be attended to, SO GET THE FUCK OUT OF THE WAY!!!

You think you're exhausted? You've been in my head for five minutes. I'm here 24/7.

In the old days before you could check your machine from the outside, even though I drove a cab and lived hand to mouth, I would go to Greece on my credit cards for two months every summer, mostly just to let the messages pile up so that the chances of my dream girl and dream job calling for me out of nowhere for no reason would exponentially increase. In ten years of summering on a Grecian rock, the only meaningful message I got upon my return in the fall was from a very, very angry Englishman who said he had spent three years in a Moroccan jail, knew where I lived, and was going to kill me if I didn't stay away from his girlfriend. I'm fairly sure it was a wrong number, as I had zero play that entire summer, but I took it to the police anyway. If I'm convinced the ConEd electricity company van parked out front has me under surveillance, you better believe an actual furious, obscenity-riddled message on my home machine threatening my life, whether accidental or not, is going to earn a trip to the DA.

When I'm finally able to finish worrying about the myriad of problems both real and imagined that are certain to ruin my life, I can get to the really important project.

Figuring out how to fix all my problems so I can get everything I want right now.

And for this, I am required to sit in a chair for hours and not move.

You may ask, "Why don't you get up out of the 'figuring out how to fix all my problems and get everything I want right now' chair and actually *do* something, instead of just sitting all day figuring?" Listen, I realize you're probably smarter than I am, but I *have* thought of that. It would be foolhardy, my well-meaning friend, to just jump up out of the figuring chair and recklessly attempt an action in the real world to try and manifest my goal until I have the perfect plan. It would definitely do more harm than good and set me back, possibly irreparably. I don't know this from actual experience, but in the marrow of my bones I feel it might be so, and I certainly don't want to test the theory lest I be right. Not that I'm not a fly-by-the-seat-of-my-pants fellow. I am. But I'm a pragmatist when it comes to self-destruction.

That I want to carefully plan.

So I sit. In the chair. On the bench. On the exercise bike at the gym, and think. Devise. Figure. For hours. Nothing can distract me. Unless of course I catch myself in the mirror that lurks behind that pretty girl who just did her runway walk down the aisle that leads from Equinox's front door to the locker room. This is the first moment the gym patrons who are already working out can glimpse you, their future wife or husband, so it's of utmost importance. Everyone utilizes different styles. The look-straight-ahead-with-shades-on-locked-jaw sprint. The power-Blackberry walk. The laid-back I'm-not-really-here-to-look-for-a-spouse-I-just-wanna-work-out saunter. And my favorite and personally most utilized, the "Upper-West-Side-kinda-down-to-earth-yet-still-kinda-cool-look-around-like-you-might-have-some-friends-on-various-machines-but-is-really-just-an-excuse-to-pose-in-many-different-angles" walk. It gives everyone a chance to see and subsequently, in my case, reject me because I'm not all lithe and cut up like some fucking Cirque de Soleil fire walker. I mean I'm not fat but I could lose, oh I don't know, forty pounds. Or thirty. Or twenty. Or ten. Or one. Depending on how *not* fat I am.

I've never ever looked exactly the way I wanted to. I once added up all the time I take to look at myself in the mirror. The glances in my

living room mirror on the way to the bathroom. The quick look in the
bathroom mirror while preparing for the toilet or the shower. The
looks while shaving that have nothing to do with the shaving. All the
peeks at my reflection in store windows, parked car windows, brass
elevator button panels, Irish people, anything shiny enough to produce
even a blurry silhouette of my frame and I'm there.

Even though they're just seconds at a time, so far they've added up
to two years, total. I know that sounds crazy, but do the math. Three seconds each time, a hundred times a day. That's three hundred seconds,
which is five minutes a day. That's thirty-five minutes a week. Two hours
and twenty minutes a month. One day a year times every year since I'm
seven, that's . . . thirty-seven days. Okay, so not two years, but you get
the point. That's thirty-seven days' worth of time that I could have been
doing something other than seeing myself not change. Do you ever
really look different from the first glance of the day to the fifty-fifth?
No, but the hope. The hope keeps you checking. Thirty-seven days. I
could have learned French, or at least enough to say, "Where's a
mirror?" So my question is—Wait, wasn't I worrying about something? I love that. As if it would be a bad thing to have forgotten and
moved on to something that might bring me pleasure. No, better
regurgitate that demon thought or it might get me when I least expect
it. I need to have it right where I can see it in the forefront of my mind.

My thinking may seem fragmented and nonsensical but like the
trillion maddening possibilities of a Rubik's Cube that for years of
trying add up to failure, frustration, and distraction, it's still safer than
being in the real world, and there's the hope of one day finding the
perfect combination. That last turn that locks in completion. Victory.
Perfection. And I'll be nailed to the gorgeous here and now. That's why
I must keep worrying and figuring and planning.

That hope.

Although, in Buddhist philosophy, hope is the enemy of the now.
So actually, either way, I'm fucked.

i've had three third dates in seven years

"So you're saying I'm not allowed to fuck that," I said dryly but since I'm not the Antichrist, obviously joking.

"I understand what you're saying. I mean, the hot pants, halter top, and makeup do make her look thirty instead of seventeen," April said with a breeziness that boded extremely well for our chances, like-minded non-PC comic sensibilities being crucial . . . and a lack of sexual abuse in her past.

"But no. You're not allowed to fuck that."

She passed the test . . . Or had she? I needed to be sure, so I burrowed subtly.

"I mean, where's her father when she's getting into that outfit?" I said with earnest condemnation.

"Dressing her in it. After he's fucked her." *She* wasn't joking. Serious trouble.

It's not that I minded that our conversation, while strolling back from the 108th Street basketball courts, had suddenly gotten that serious on the heels of my off-color joke, partially designed to act as a barometer of my date's sensibility (something I always investigate on the first date); I was concerned that my possible new wife had just revealed her own incestuous background.

It must be the most unimaginably heinous thing to live through. My sympathy and compassion for anyone who has and my rage at their abusers is endless—but it's a wound that, in my experience, often has difficulty healing in a way that allows women to get close to me. Except insofar as they want to draw me in to annihilate me as punishment for the hideous crime committed against them by some sick person in their past. But hey, I'm a recovering alcoholic-drug-addict-food-addict-single-at-forty-four-guy who's ravaged by sporadic insecurity, self-loathing, depression, envy, lust, greed, and a resulting hatred for everything and everyone in the world at times, so I'm no picnic either.

I figured I'd lighten the tone. "Your breasts are really, really nice." She laughed, bowed her head to stare at her black Converses, anywhere but my eyes, and turned beet red. If she could have choked out a word, it would have been "stop." I was scoring, so of course I continued.

"I mean, to the extent I can see them. You know, the tops of them, and the cleavage, and the shape of them in that really nice lacy thing you're wearing."

"How can you say something like that when I've only known you for an hour?"

I kept the pressure on. "How many times have you thought of kissing me so far?"

"Do you know how long I would have to know you before I would answer that question?"

"I love how you act all Spence prude when I know you're a freak. I mean you're half-Jew on both sides, right? What I love about the Jews is that they're not precious about bodily functions. They embrace the humanity of them. I had a girlfriend just like you, half-WASP, half-Jew. She would sit on my lap while I was taking a shit and rub my back, teaching me that that would help promote a nice movement."

She was caught in the undertow but not fully drowned yet. I had a few more precious seconds before I would have to revive her. I took them.

"See, most people think you rub your stomach, but your bowels are closer to your back than your front. Who knew?" She was out. I began resuscitation.

"See that building?" I pointed to a prewar that stood majestically guarding the park on 104th Street and Riverside.

"That's where I grew up. My mom still lives there. Let's go talk to her. She has to do your chart, anyway." She laughed. She was softening.

I pointed to the little park that separates upper and lower Riverside Drive. "I played in this park as a kid." She was nearly back. I had bought myself at least until the end of the walk in the park. But I might end up liking her, so I needed to give her a little more still.

"I saw this man crying on the subway before I met you today." And she started really listening to me for the first time.

I had been coming home from yoga on the uptown express. It was rush-hour crowded. I looked around for someone to give my seat to but no one standing was as old or tired as I felt, so I stayed. Through bags and hips I noticed a black woman sitting across from me. Concerned and fascinated, she was intently staring at someone on my side of the train. I turned to my left to try to see who she was looking at. Sitting at the end of my bench, slumped against the chrome hand rails, was a well-dressed middle-aged Puerto Rican man. He was quietly sobbing.

Like the woman across from me, people were perplexed at best, terrified at worst. Was he drunk? On drugs? A crazy man?

If you see a woman crying on the subway, you give her a handkerchief. If you see a man crying on the subway, you call the police. Women's tears are understood, expected even; men's, an aberration.

Had his mother just died? His son? Had he been fired from his dream job? Had the love of his life just left him? Or did he just feel like he couldn't take it anymore? I feel like that a lot. I was now fighting back tears. I couldn't say for this man but I often cry, though usually in private. If I get sad in public I'll find a bathroom stall somewhere in which to cry quietly for a few minutes. I didn't want to cause a never-ending chain reaction of weeping men in the subway, so I held it in. That's how he was crying. For every sadness every man had never cried for; wasn't allowed to, or felt too ashamed to.

I got off at Eighty-sixth Street and quickly walked home. I made it into the elevator and then broke down. The co-op board (of which I'm not a part, as I rent) just installed a camera in the fancy new wood-paneled elevator that replaced the sweet old manually operated tin one, and by doing so forced the elevator men to become doormen. All part of the board's grand scheme to turn our funky venerable Upper West Side building into a chichi Park Avenue one. Like putting a French poodle costume on a mutt. I've always preferred mutts.

If I were twenty years younger, as a little protest, I would have covertly keyed the expensive unblemished veneer just an inch or so. Not a huge gash. Just enough to say, "Hi. Fuck you." I could easily have done it with my right hand, concealed from the camera by my hip, as I pretended to read the mail in my left hand. Now though a citizen, I only wistfully imagined doing it.

I wondered if Jake, the Serbian elevator man turned doorman, was watching me cry as I rode up. I didn't care. He'd been privy to plenty of my private moments in there. My face being caressed by sweet girls. My face being slapped by hot dominatrices. You know, the usual stuff.

I entered my apartment. "Hi, house," I said softly. Beside animals, I also talk to inanimate objects. It's like having more friends and makes me feel like the whole world around me is alive instead of dead. I stood in my hallway and leaned my head against the bedroom doorjamb. That's where I do most of my crying. Standing up. I felt better. I wondered how far the Puerto Rican man's train ride was. And if he was still sad. That's when I suddenly remembered that I had the blind date with April. A stroll in the park at sunset.

I look like a fucking mess. I thought. Bloodshot eyes, puffy from just having cried, and the end of a cold sore. Great.

Man up you baby! You're forty-four, single, and waiting for you out there on the street corner is a lovely girl hoping you're going to be the best thing that ever happened to her. You can do this. Just don't talk about the crying or the cold sore and she'll never even notice you're all fucked up.

I splashed some water on my face and met April on West End, a couple of blocks from my house.

"April?"

"Hey, Eric."

"Hey. It's so nice to meet you."

"You, too. How are you?"

"Excellent."

"Great."

"And you?"

"Great."

"Perfect. Shall we walk to the park?"

"That would be lovely. Soooooo . . . " She looked at me and froze. She wanted to start the real conversation but it seemed she suddenly didn't know how or where to begin. This girl was so nervous she wouldn't have noticed if my ass had been transplanted onto my face, let alone a microscopic red bump on my lip. But at the end of the day, I am me.

"I want to acknowledge something that I fear you are already aware of. But by doing so, I will alleviate the pressure for you not to stare at it and for me not to be obsessed with whether you are or are not staring at it . . . and that would be the final stages of this once-massive herpetic chancre on my lower lip."

"Yes, I've seen it." And we were off.

Some people call it "oversharing." I call it being honest. Since second grade, I've always been that way.

Brooke Sweeny

"Hey, Harry!" Julio bellowed in a thick Puerto Rican accent while buttoning his pants and tucking in his blue button-down uniform shirt.

"Come here, I have something to show you." He beckoned toward the small back room at the other end of the huge marble lobby, where the doormen kept the packages, their lunches, and in Julio's case, the kiddy porn.

"Not now, Julio," I replied, like I always did on my way home after school, and headed for the elevator.

"I never seen a guy like you, Harry. You're the best guy here," he would always reply as he followed me in a fashion any casual observer would describe as menacing. But I liked and understood Julio and knew, even at seven, he was harmless, so I took it as a fun game we played every day. He gave me more affection and friendship than almost anyone. All the doormen did. Sanchez was big, red-faced, and Santa Clausian. He was how I imagined a grandfather would be. I never knew my grandfathers. One died of alcoholism before I was born. The other was struck by lightning on a golf course when I was one. Frank was the sweet toothless night guy. And Abe, the mean old white-haired one who yelled at us. I spent hours playing in that lobby, hiding underneath the stairwell, running fast and then sliding as far as I could in my socks on the smooth, slick floor before wiping out against the garbage room door. It was my playground and the doormen were my playmates.

"My name's Eric, not Harry. Learn to speak the language if you're gonna live in our country," I said, pretending to be mean as I boarded the elevator. Julio smiled.

"That's what I said. E-harr-ic. Harric." The elevator door was almost closed. Julio was walking faster and almost at the button, trying to catch me before I disappeared.

"Bye, Julio."

"Wait!" With an inch to go before I disappeared, suddenly, the door reopened. Julio, as he always did, had caught me just in time. He paused. His drunken mind darted with sick ideas he would never do, so I didn't hold against him. Even though I was only seven, I felt like a four-hundred-year-old man. I was very sexualized by that time, and understood Julio's predilections and perversions. If we were all held accountable for every thought that went through our minds, "twenty to life" would be a part of everyone's story.

He finished the game. "Just come over here, I want to show you something."

"See you later, Julio." I pressed the button and Julio let the door close, continuing to look at me through the round, chicken-wired-glass-paned, face-size hole in the black, metal elevator door as it shut.

"Okay, Harric. I'll see you in a little while." And he was gone. I was alone in the elevator. I loved being alone in the elevator. I played there when I wasn't playing in the lobby. Pressing buttons for no reason. Putting up signs advertising my magic shows or the home-made chocolate I sold door-to-door. Climbing up and standing on the brass handrails so I could get high enough to look in the light wells for money, convinced somehow that, like everywhere, money would just appear there. As if for some unknown reason people had thrown money at the ceiling of the elevator and it had gotten caught in the wooden trusses under the lights. It was 1969. There weren't any video games or MTV. These were the innocent ways we entertained ourselves as kids then.

Along with getting drunk, and butt-fucking and pissing on my little guy friends under the covers when we played "Bat Cave," of course.

Hey, they were the closest bodies around, since girls were still a couple of months away. Like everyone, once I realized it worked for more than peeing and felt really good when I rubbed it, I rubbed it anywhere on anything I could find. Wriggling like salamanders on the mats in gym class, moving it back and forth against the smooth sheets before I went to bed, humping teeter-totters, using vacuum cleaners to simulate vaginas. Whatever.

I liked womblike places. Insulated. Private. Under the stairwell in the lobby. The big closet in my room. A fort made out of brambles and cardboard boxes in Riverside Park. The elevator. The world felt dangerous to me, I felt safest away from people.

Alone.

I've always been very lonely. And felt like no one liked me. Of all the obsessions I've used not to feel that way, food was one of the first. And girls, of course. Which from my first memories went hand-in-hand. The first serious time spent on the planet was getting food from a breast (or a bottle masquerading as a breast), so it makes sense. Freud has nothing on me, kids. Sometimes a tower is just a tower and a tunnel just a tunnel, you know what I'm saying?

I was a colicky baby and cried a lot. My mother, who I love dearly, was crazy and would throw all my toys out the window and sit in the corner crying, overwhelmed, confused as to how to handle me. I was left to my own devices from an early age.

My mother had beautiful long black hair and a classic Irish face. She had deep blue eyes and looked like a teenager until she was thirty. As a child she had been locked in closets and left on street corners because her drunken parents lacked the ability to care for her in the manner she deserved. She didn't smile much.

On good days, she would scratch my back and we'd jump on her bed like a trampoline and she'd flash her kooky grin. On bad days, she was staving off a nervous breakdown one second at a time.

I was on the smallish side and thin, had long, gnarled dirty-blond hair and my dad's strong Pennsylvania Dutch nose; the dark blue eyes both my parents had but not their beauty. They looked like movie stars, I looked like a supporting player. I was sideways cute and, with my long hair, often mistaken for my mother's younger sister.

When I was one, I was blown across the room trying to perform cunnilingus on the electrical socket. My mom told me that's why I have a small scar above my upper lip on the left side. After that, even she, deranged as she sometimes was, somehow summoned the focus to keep me in the crib lest I be shocked to death. Was I trying to eat the outlet to satiate a food or a sexual hunger? Either way, it was a portent of things to come.

If I hadn't repressed most of my childhood I probably would have remembered that episode myself, but as it stands now, my first memory was when I was seven, after school, *Rubber Soul* on the old mono turntable in the living room. Our apartment was cluttered with an ordered chaos all rambling middle-class Upper West Side apartments had as a reflection of the like-minded single mothers who held on to their sanity through that frenetic yet comforting decorating style.

I opened the fridge, got my mom's bottle of red wine, half full because she didn't drink much, and poured a nice full glass, over ice, into a thick white coffee mug. I took it into her room because it had a better view of the river. I put my feet up on the windowsill and sat, drinking the cold red wine, looking out at the bright, sparkling, late-afternoon autumn-lit water, framed by the ugly postmodern prefab condos speckled on the beautiful Jersey cliffs, the din of the West Side Highway like a lullaby. My haven. My home.

After the cocktail came the feast. With boxes of Yodels, Ring Dings, and Devil Dogs, I settled down on my belly in front of *Batman* on the TV and slung my stupid night brace against the wall. Forget about wearing it in school. It was hard enough to negotiate hell without a birdcage jetting out of my face. They should be happy I was willing to slide that evil contraption anywhere near my head at all while in the safe anonymity of my home. I felt I had gone way past the call of duty by giving it two minutes of the required "all the time."

I made my mother take all my braces off a month after I got them anyway, convincing her rightfully that my "overbite," which was the scam of the century propagated by orthodontists of the '70s, was nothing more than the way God made everyone's jaw so your teeth wouldn't smash perfectly together on every bite. You were supposed to be able to slip your front teeth over your bottom ones. After some careful deliberation and self-testing she agreed, and "cool" Dr. Whatever-the-fuck-his-name-was unscrewed the painful metal from my mouth.

The Yodel box was wrapped in a perfectly thin dark blue and silver tinfoil, and made of good cardboard. Everything was made better then. Stronger, more real. The people. The bus drivers. The tokens. I opened the box and took out an individually wrapped Yodel. Being as I was already a full-on chocoholic, Willy Wonka was of course my favorite story. This was as close as I got to finding the golden ticket in the chocolate bar. Every day I opened countless Yodels hoping to find what I knew wasn't there. But it was there, so I kept opening them. And eating them. Then on to the Devil Dogs, Ring Dings, and Batman and Robin.

SPLAT!

POW!

And the sexiest creature in the world: Catwoman. The Julie Newmar Catwoman, of course. She always got me going. Since neither Dave from 101st Street, Larry from school, nor Michele, the Italian boy from the sixth floor were around to "play" with, I was left with the forbidden unconscious homoerotic tinglings produced by Batman and the Boy Wonder rolling around in S&M masks and latex suits, the heroin Yodels ramping through my veins, and self-sex until my mom got home at six. That was my after-school snack.

My day started with two packets of chocolate Carnation Instant Breakfast. Chocolate powder you dump in milk and, if you were smart, let coagulate at the bottom instead of stirring so you got chocolate pudding with a nice milk chaser instead of boring chocolate milk, which is what you got if you stirred. (A trick I use at the fat farm now, with my psyllium husk colon cleanser. Most people mix in the apple juice and drink it quickly before it gets thick. I, of course, let it congeal at the bottom and eat it like apple pudding, the closest thing to a real meal you get at fasting camp.) So, Instant Breakfast to begin, followed by two honey-dipped doughnuts from the doughnut shop by the bus stop on 103rd Street and Broadway, which was next to the Spanish porn theater. Another bit of festive culture destroyed by the yuppification of New York. Spanish porn. I used the twenty cents I had been given for bus money to buy the doughnuts. Yes, twenty cents; no, not in 1920; 1969, thank you very much. I snuck on the bus and got off at 120th Street and Broadway.

Before heading into school I stopped at the candy store and robbed them blind. Red hots, Jawbreakers, Reese's peanut butter cups. I needed a lot of candy to woo Brooke Sweeny's affections. Greg Valhala, my best friend but competition for her heart, might bring cash. I was also in love with two other women, my first-grade teacher Miss Kalawalawalki-something and Catwoman, of course. Brooke was my first choice, though; being neither thirty years my senior nor a TV star, and in my grade, she felt much more attainable. She had long brunette hair, a beautiful button-nosed Scottish face, a hint of hippie in her sundresses, and smelled like her smile: young and mischievous. I seriously dug her.

"Hey, Brooke. I brought you some candy."

"Thanks, Eric." Brooke batted her eyelashes like Ferdinand the bull's sister.

"But I brought you this!" Greg trumpeted triumphantly, and what seemed like a million dollars but was probably in the neighborhood of sixty cents poured from Greg's hands into Brooke's.

"Thank you, Greg."

Being the cagey second-grader Brooke was, she took our gifts and left us wanting, choosing neither of us as her boyfriend.

My whole life, I've been engaged in a battle of warring beliefs. On one hand, I've always felt, like when Brooke rejected me, that my lot in life is to inevitably be the odd man out and that it will always be that way for me. I'll get close but never be the winner. Winning is reserved for real people. Regular people. Good people. Not fucked-up imposters like me. But I've always also known deeply, with the same absolute, unequivocal belief, that it's only a matter of time until I get everything I want. That I have infinite possibilities. And that to find a wonderful woman to spend my life with is certainly no exception. They coexist, these two radically opposing beliefs. I live with them and many other battling fraternal twins but I don't let them stop me from moving forward in spite of their feuds.

To help widen my circle, creating a greater chance of meeting the love of my life, I recently enlisted the aid of the modern matchmaker. The Internet.

"Nerve Whoring"

I don't go on a lot of dates. I never have. The Great Spirit has graced us with this outrageously beautiful life and I feel it's a profane affront and sacrilegious waste of that gift to sit for even one second with someone

I don't like just so I can say I wasn't at Mission Impossible 6 by myself on a Friday night, thus avoiding an evening on my couch alone watching DVR'd reruns of Wife Swap while gorging on a six-pack of Entenmann's Assorted Doughnuts washed down with a pint of Ben and Jerry's New York Super Fudge Chunk, feeling if I was just one ounce less fat I would be man enough to possess the balls to drag myself to the balcony and hurl myself off the roof. As fun as the latter alternative sounds, I'd still rather take it or ANYTHING ELSE over having to suffer through the fake smiles and polite nodding-of-the-head associated with pretending that I find someone interesting that I never have and never will. But I hate being alone.

I'm an extroverted isolationist.

I seriously need my solitude, being Aquarian and a man, but I infinitely prefer sharing my life, albeit including necessary times of retreat, with a woman. Things aren't nearly as fun alone. I want a wife. I want to get married to a hot, funny, smart, wonderful, giving, stable, fabulous woman and make eleven or two babies with her. It's hard for me to meet women at work because I'm on either a film or television set where two kinds of girls exist: actresses and crew members. Crew members are out, since I'm their boss and, more important, can't lift as much cable as they can; and actresses are out because they're actresses. I don't want a woman to "act" as if she loves me, I want a woman who really will love me.

When not on a set, I'm either editing or writing, solitary jobs that go on for months. Since I don't drink or do drugs anymore, bars, parties, and clubs are out, so that leaves meeting women on the street on the way to the gym or yoga, or in the gym or yoga. Both have happened but, even for someone as fearless and forward as I am, it's still kind of awkward wooing in those venues. Blind dates and setups make me so sick to my stomach I rarely agree to them. The twelve minutes before your date arrives, hawking every woman that comes in the joint, scared to death it's her and then the subsequent relief it's not, only to have your hopes dashed anyway when she finally does arrive (twenty minutes late) makes having your gums filleted open and scraped because you were in the unfortunate three percentile for which the initial root canal didn't fix the problem, seem like an option you'd pray to experience with the sincerity of praying for a loved one to recover from cancer rather than suffer the "blind date wait."

I tried "It's Just Lunch," a dating service designed to match "busy professionals" with each other. Not that I consider myself a "busy professional" but, again, I'll try anything. I had an interview and told them all about myself and the kind of woman I'm looking for, and they said they had many perfect prospects. They don't show you pictures, though, which I thought was suspect. The idea is you just commit to a lunch or, in my case, an even more brief first date of "drinks." If you like each other, you take it from there yourselves. I met three women who were all perfectly nice, but didn't click with any of them.

I tried speed dating, which I thought would be right up my alley as they advertised an even shorter initial meeting then It's Just Lunch. I agreed that three minutes was plenty of time to decide if a girl was right enough for me to upgrade her to a real first date, so I thought it would be a great format. That's not to say I know if a woman is going to be my wife in three minutes, but I can definitely tell if there's no chance. If I'm attracted to a girl, all I need to do is quintessentially exist and I'll know based on her reaction in an instant. "I can't wait until the fashion cycle turns and you gals come down off your platform shoes. The whole universe of men, of which I'm a part, are gonna suddenly all be three inches taller." A semicute blond marketing researcher from Hoboken looked across the table at me, clueless. "You're still growing? I like my shoes. Wait. What are you talking about?" Luckily only another thirty-eight seconds to suffer through with her until the whistle would blow and, after secretly checking "no" next to her number 15 on my score sheet, I would get to move to the next table and quintessentially exist with the next possible love of my life. If both of you check "yes" next to each other's number on your score sheets, then at the end of the night your charges send you each other's e-mail address. Unfortunately, the only two women I liked at the speed dating I attended (a double session, of course: fifty women in three hours) were the wait-ress of the bar they threw the event in, and the moderator from the speed dating company itself. Both were unavailable.

Then there's the occasional random meet. I came home from a run once and, much to my surprise, right there in my elevator was Amanda, one of my favorite girls from a past season of *America's Next Top Model*. She was the gorgeous blond single mom from North Car-olina with the amazing wolf eyes, who was going blind? She was very sweet and open and nice to me. Apparently there's a famous hair colorist that lives in my building, and Amanda was there for an appointment to get her hair done. I asked her out before we got to her floor. She confessed that, although she was flattered, unfortu-nately her boyfriend, the father of their daughter, wouldn't go for that. Apparently the folks at the "reality show" thought she'd be slightly more enticing to the men of America as a single mom. She had been with her guy all along. *You mean it's not all real?!* I was crushed. But I still love the show and will continue to watch it reli-giously. Witnessing Tyra slowly losing her mind is a highlight of my week. She's divine. I like to silently repeat her most famous line with her as she does, "Congratulations. You're still in the running toward becoming America's Next Top Model." She's so magnifi-cently serious about it. Presidents, Nobeloriats, humanitarians, step aside, we have ANTM to crown! It's somehow comforting to watch the little pack of long-legged nubile Bambis running around doing . . . well, anything really. I mean we're men. We're wired to see a woman, smash her on the head with a bone, drag her unconscious body back to our apartment by the hair, and fuck her. I think you all should give us a break and, in fact, a little credit. We have suc-cessfully bucked that arcane evolutionary desire and have replaced it with the infinitely more civilized hour of ANTM every week. I think we've come a long way, baby.

With all of the aforementioned avenues exhausted, that leaves the chance that the person delivering my food is not a four foot ten non-English-speaking male immigrant, but a candidate for the love of my life and mother of my children. Hasn't happened yet. I have one place, and one place only, left to turn. The Internet.

When not in a committed relationship or if dating someone like April, whom I'm still figuring out if I want to commit to, "Nerve whoring" is what I do anywhere from one to twelve hours a day, depending on my schedule and ferocity. Match.com is too Middle American. It depresses me to have to look at all the pictures of girls with their Dorothy Hamill yearbook photos, who had not realized that hairstyle has been gone for a little while now. Or the chin-on-the-fist pose. Who ever told women that was attractive? And those strapless tube dresses? How outrageously unflattering are they? They make even nice-figured women look like circus freaks with jutting-tube tits tent-poling fabric under a scrunchy that has no business being anywhere other than in her hair, certainly not stretching around her chest to keep a dress up, defying gravity and leaving her breasts no alternative but to take on a job they shouldn't be requested to, contorting their natural elegant shape into one of a . . . I don't know. It's all just too unfortunate. And they're so "in" now. Those ugly dresses. Anyway, even though Match contains women who upset my sense of style, prohibiting me from even getting to their profile, of course I'm still on it. Craigslist doesn't work because I'm always seduced by the "Casual Encounters" and "Erotic" sections, and end up having cybersex with other sex addicts before I can make it to the personals. I even tried JDate. Being a lifetime Upper West Sider, I feel I've gained honorary adopted goy-Jew status and therefore qualify. And I like Jewish women. They're smart, straightforward, and sexy. But JDate was like a feeding frenzy. Fifty-five-year-old dyed redheads from Rosyln, Long Island, masquerading as thirty-five-year-old brunettes from the Upper East Side set on me like I was pickled herring at Shabbat. I felt as though they would climb through the computer and suck me through the ether straight to

Bergdorf's, to get married in the Prada shoe section. Nerve.com seemed just right. The girls were edgy but there was still the chance of meeting a wife. You fill out a "profile," a personality questionnaire designed to create an even playing field of data to base your decisions on. Questions like, "What's your favorite on-screen sex scene?" To which 90 percent of the women reply, *Betty Blue, The Lover,* and *Y Tu Mamá También.* While extremely rare, two women did list "Eric Schaeffer and the blond girl against the refrigerator in *Fall.*" Since they had the excellent taste to appreciate that sexy scene from one of my films, I had the excellent taste to fly to Des Moines and Santa Fe, respectively, and fuck them in Motel 6s against minifridges.

The two most important questions are "Why you should get to know me?" and "More about who I'm looking for." I just said in no uncertain terms that I'm brilliant, funny, perfect, crazy, and flawed, and am looking for a girl version of me. Though I only scan for women romantically, I have looked at the guys' profiles to see what I'm up against. Most of them are playing a guitar bare-chested in their pictures and spout the usual clichés, "I look good in both a tux and jeans, and can work either room." I'm not too worried.

My "cupid settings," the requirements for my prospective wife, are that she be single, no kids, between five foot five and six feet tall, height–weight proportionate, and a "yes to life" girl. (That doesn't mean she wants to blow Rush Limbaugh, knee-jerk liberals, it means she's a half-full not half-empty, happy, adventuresome kind of a lady.) She has to want kids and not be an active addict. There's wiggle room on the height. Hey, I'm reasonable. But not wanting kids or being a drunk are deal breakers. "What are the five things you can't live without?" "Lip gloss" seems to be most important to a lot of the gals, even the deep girls who still manage to find a place for it after "My family, love, animals, laughter . . . "

I search for girls between the ages of twenty-five and thirty-five. While I infinitely prefer the emotionally mature mind and relaxed disposition of women over forty, unfortunately, my wanting a bunch of babies but not wanting them for a couple of years precludes those women from my "search profile," and I must suffer the abject insanity of the twenty-nine-year-old woman. (And besides, by putting thirty-five as my limit, I still get women up to forty-five, which in all honesty I am happy to consider and would totally go for if I found one who blew my skirt up, but if I put forty-five as my top, I'd get fifty-five-year-old women writing to me, which is just unrealistic given what I'm looking for.) I view many profiles, send a few letters, and get back one or two responses. I try to get on the phone as quickly as possible, because tone in e-mail is hard to read and you can get fooled easily. A voice reveals so much more. And yes, I *can* know everything in a five-minute phone call, and no, I have never been wrong. I'm sure of this because I have tested it against my Jewish friends' collective theory of "Come on! How can you know from one phone call? You may be wrong" (for which they always seem to break out the heavy Yiddish accent, for some reason), and met a couple of these girls for a first date and had my initial suspicions confirmed.

Every morning, the first thing I do is walk past my little makeshift altar, not stopping to meditate because if I did I'd be too distracted by who might have "viewed me" while I was asleep, so I check that first. Three views. A forty-eight-year-old from Kentucky who "loved *If Lucy Fell*" and wonders why I'm using Eric Schaeffer's pictures on this Web site. A fat, fifty-five-year-old fisherwoman from Rhode Island who asks if I like to salsa dance, and a forty-four-year-old woman from Russia without a picture. Only three views and zero e-mails. I wrote six charming, funny notes to girls yesterday, and nothing. Next up is checking the "Most Popular People" list, the fifty most-viewed people, updated daily. "Taudry Hepburn" has been number one for ten months now, and it's clear why. Very Audrey Hepburn, five foot six, delicate frame, sexy shoes, and pretty feet. Wearing a classy short black dress as if she's on her way to the opera, she's turned in that posy, three-quarter, Miss America posture but pulls it off, being a Southern Jew. Just enough of her apartment is revealed so that you can see it's tasteful but not ostentatious. Clearly an attractive woman, thirty-three, but the picture isn't quite close enough for you to see her all that well. In her second photo, she's in a bikini, curled up in a beach chair on the porch of a beachy cottage, so she must summer in the Hamptons or Fire Island or something. Cool. But again, her face is obscured just enough by her floppy hat and shades. Her profile is flawless, as well. It entices without revealing too much. A "dirty but not too dirty" nurse kind of a thing. Priceless. Every man's dream. I wrote to her a couple of months ago and in her perfectly disarming TH way she said she was deluged with suitors and would "get back to me as quickly as possible." Could I please "wait my turn." After no response for two months, I wrote to her again last week:

> Dear Taudry Hepburn. I'm not being cheeky here, I really am fascinated. Seeing as you're the number one most popular girl on Nerve, conservatively you must receive 20 letters a day, which adds up to roughly 150 letters a week. Now, I understand many are from fat, old, balding, boring men but let's say two percent are from guys like me, and when I say like "me," I mean bad versions of me, but good enough to be in the realm of a first date possibility. That's 120 reasonably decent guys. That would be one date per weekend night for the last 10 months. So my question is this. What are you still doing here?

She viewed me within ten minutes but didn't write back.

Now I move to the guys list. "IM4U" has been number one for a couple of weeks. He was a newcomer to the list, entering at number twenty-six with a bullet. Unheard of, but he's model gorgeous, has a ripped body, and his "who I'm looking for" section is a bad country song he wrote. Not bad enough to be funny or clever even. Just bad. Tragic but you gotta love him. But wait! *He's suddenly gone! He found someone? Good for him.* And unlike Taudry Hepburn, he has the guts to delete his profile. It is a very sexy moment when, together, the new couple decides to delete all their Internet profiles. It's the new saying "I love you" for the first time. *Oh no, wait*, since IM4U has moved on, everyone moves up by attrition. That means fucking "Namaste" is number one again! Shit! Namaste means "the divine in me honors the divine in you" in Sanskrit. A beautiful sentiment lost on this particular bitch, if you ask me. I'm sorry, forgive me, Namaste, I'm just jealous. Namaste, Namaste.

Namaste held the top honor for the entire year, before being briefly unseated by IM4U. Namaste's the male Taudry Hepburn, diamond perfect in his execution. Good looking enough, forty, and separated. Perfect for all the dysfunctional codependent women of New York. He's available, sort of, but still married. His profile is painfully self-effacing

"I'm not really cool enough to be number one. I don't even answer all the questions on the profile like Taudry Hepburn does." Yeah. He plays the Taudry Hepburn card. And you're really not gonna believe this:

"Thanks for all the notes when Frankie my cat passed away last week." Gross, right? But that's not even the clincher. Brace yourself. As skillfully as Jeffrey Dahmer's convincing guys to give him permission to cut their dicks off and eat them, Namaste finishes the kill, now actually taking a page from his female doppelgänger, Taudry Hepburn.

"Since I've moved up this silly little list, I've been getting so many letters. Forgive me if it takes a little time to get to you all." He slays low self-esteem hearts yet gives them hope, and for the self-centered chicks, he's too busy, which makes them wet as well. *A master. I hate him. I must to do something, but what?*

Oh my god! I'm a genius!!!

I will launch a clandestine operation of obsessive random viewing, which will garner me enough view-backs to topple Namaste and make ME number one!

See, when a girl clicks on the "Who's viewed you" feature and sees you've viewed her, she clicks on your profile, viewing you back. These "view-backs" are how you get viewed unless a girl just happens to view you, which is not often because the girls, unlike the boys, are assaulted with letters and don't have time for random viewing. They barely have time for view-backs. The boys get so few e-mails and unsolicited views, we're forced to go trolling. The only problem is, I've been "hiding my profile" so I can continue to view girls anonymously, unbeknownst to this girl I dated a month ago. I just don't want her to see me back in the game so fast. It might hurt her feelings. Also, even though it didn't work out, I still kind of like her and do the "drive by her house" Internet equivalent and check out her profile to try and gauge what she's up to, you know, just because I'm curious, not because I'm jealous or anything. Yeah, that's right. The rule is, even if I break up with you, you can never go out with anyone ever again, even though I can. Life is tough, shorty.

But that all has to change now, as my entire plan hinges on girls seeing that I've viewed them. A good day for me is if six girls randomly view me. To beat Namaste, I'm going to have to garner, who knows, hundreds of views a day? The plan is this:

I will systematically click on and view *every single female* on Nerve, hoping for a high enough percentage of view-backs to catapult me to the top.

I've spent eight hours every day for six days clicking on women. I do morning, afternoon, and marathon evening sessions. I have a friend who offered up her profile as a view-laundering factory but, alas, the friendly customer support team at Nerve informed me that only one viewing per girl counts toward my weekly tally, so her plan to click on me over and over wouldn't work. I think I was cagey enough that the Ecuadorian lad who fielded my question didn't red-flag me. I continue undaunted.

A fat, black, sixty-year-old from Cleveland.

Click. *Can I really be doing this?*

Forty-four, dentures, a pet store worker from Michigan.

Click. *No, really. Who have you become?*

Sometimes in the midst of my rapid-fire clicking, I catch a woman's "headline," a single sentence we all must provide as a bit of flair.

"Debbie143 Looking for an honest man."

Click. *I am the horned one.*

"Shiva. Yoginis do it better."

Click. *I'm going to hell, just after Shiva, the Hindu God of Destruction, decapitates me and sticks an elephant's head on my bloody neck stump like he did to his own adopted son Ganesha because he was paranoid that Ganesha was fucking his wife. Something like that.* Anyway, I'm way worse. I'm raising the hopes of thousands of women who think I'm viewing their profiles with honest romantic intentions, when really I'm just ruthlessly using them as stepping stones to get to number one on the Nerve Internet Most Popular Daters List. I am so fucking pathetic.

Click.

Click.

Click.

But wait. I just realized that Shiva would approve of this. "Half-full Schaeffer" has discovered a spiritual loophole. I'm actually helping these women to feel wanted. When they get back from working all day at the diner and shut the screen door on their trailer, they'll have a semicute, marginally famous New York bachelor having viewed them. So, in fact, as it turns out . . . I'm benevolent.

A single mother with a picture of three adorable father-wanting kids?

Click.

Recently widowed?

Click.

I'm a good person.

Click.

Click.

Click.

I've risen from thirty-ninth to sixth on the list. I can smell Namaste's pseudosoy stench, and I know he knows I'm coming for him. I go to bed, almost unable to sleep with excitement. I'm getting on average four hundred views a day now, and another thirty in the night between three A.M. and eleven. I check throughout the night, on the way back and forth from the kitchen, when I night eat. But today I got worried.

I haven't moved up at all. I was sixth last night and I'm still sixth this morning. I have to step my game up another level. *But how?! I'm raw from clicking.* Neck cramps, right forearm spasms. *What to do? Wait a minute. Oh my god. I . . . am . . . unparalleled! THE GAY MEN! How could I not have come up with it sooner?! No, I just can't. I mean that's really cruel. The women are somehow okay. I'm heterosexual and in some convoluted karmic way might really want them, but the guys?* Truly perplexed, ship-wrecked in a conundrum I don't have time for, I ask the ultimate question. The question I ask when I really need to do the right thing.

God, what would you do?

Would you click on the gay men even if you weren't gay, to try to beat Namaste?

I had already systematically gone through every state in the nation and every country in Europe and the Eastern Bloc. The African contingent of available female Nerve girls wasn't very plentiful; only in the dozens on the entire continent, from what I can recall during my bleary-eyed perusal of that part of the Nerve globe a couple of nights ago, before moving on to Scandinavia. I really feel I've exhausted the entire portion of humans who possess vaginas. I'll give it one more day of girl clicking. If by tomorrow I haven't hit number five, it's game on for the gay boys. I can't stop now. This is Darwin. *Like Luke to Darth Vader, I bow down to you father, but alas, Namaste, I must destroy you.*

I made it. Number one. And I didn't even have to accept the gracious help unknowingly offered by the gay community. There's a warm comfort to finally being on top, yet also an anticlimactic sadness. A postpartum depression. It's been a long, hard road, but already it's yielding results. A hot advertising chick, "Amy75," has written, and "Filmmaker Chick" from L.A. has also made a move. And, as luck would have it, I'm going to L.A. for work soon, so Filmmaker Chick gets the first response. Her real name is Donna. My intention wasn't to climb to the top of the Nerve's Most Popular List to get more girls, it was simply to topple IM4U and Namaste. The plan all along was to retire at number one as soon as I got there. I have, but I'll still just go out with these two anyway.

Filmmaker Chick

"So, Donna, what kinds of films do you make?" I asked on the phone.

"Porn," she matter-of-factly replied. I laughed.

"Really? Excellent."

"I'm serious," She said as if she was so used to saying it, she didn't get annoyed anymore than she had to. I was trying to vamp until my stunned mind could figure out how I felt about this. I mean, she was supposed to be a possible wife, and she had a picture of herself hugging her sweet old Midwestern dad on her profile.

"Like, soft core, *Cinemax*, 'only-see-above-the-girls-eyes-as-her-head-bobs-giving-a-blow job-we-can't-see' kind of porn?"

"No. Hard core." My brilliant mind quickly seized a very possible out. If I could tell my mom at the first introductory Thanksgiving dinner that Donna was a "director" of porn, I thought I could sell it.

"Interesting, so you direct, right? You're not actually in them."

"No, yeah, I'm a director. Not an actor."

"Hmm. Cool."

"Have you ever been on a porn set?"

"No, as a matter of fact I haven't. And I'm gonna be in L.A. for a work thing next week." So there it was. Our first date was going to be in Topanga Canyon, on the set of her new film *Doughnuts Aren't the Only Things with Sweet Holes*. Perrrrrfect.

The date was set for Friday night. I would fly on Friday afternoon, drop off my stuff at the hotel, and go straight there. As I packed Thursday night . . . now, by pack, obviously I mean bring enough things that can fit in the overhead and under my seat. I am king of the carry-on. No, really. Yeah, I know you think you are. But trust me, I am king. Like, bags hanging off me in ways you couldn't imagine bags could hang off a human being from limbs you didn't know existed. A spell I cast over even the most hardened, crusty, Barbara Stanwyckian stewardess so she's nondairy creamer in my hands. I behead between six and eighteen passengers with my swinging eighty-pound satchels as I skillfully sashay down the aisle, selfishly stealing every inch of your overhead compartments along the way—I think I had a happy-ending massage girl in L.A. once named Sashay? Sasha? RAY! That's right. Ray. I'll tell you about her later. So anyway, as I was packing, the most heinous thought popped into my head, as they often do when I'm feeling happy. It's like, *Is that a hopefull thought? No, we can't have that. Better remind him who's in charge.* The evil thoughts.

You're gonna die on the plane! You won't live long enough to meet the wonderful girl God has intended for you. That's just the kind of hat pin God is. He teases you with the love of your life and then has you die in the plane crash on the way there.

Excellent.

That wasn't the thought this night, though. That's a standard fallback if there's nothing more frightening available. Along with the thought that I'm dying of AIDS from having kissed a girl. This was a much worse thought, though, but luckily my eternal optimism outweighs my eternal pessimism by just enough to keep me moving forward. I figured out a solution. I called my friend Dan in L.A. He could help.

"So Dan, long story short. I met this girl online."

"Okay . . . "

"She's in L.A. I'm flying there tomorrow for our first date; I have to be there anyway for some stuff . . . "

"Uh-huh . . . "

"She says she's a porno director but what if she's actually a snuff film director?"

"What?"

"A snuff film director. You know, where they film people getting murdered?"

"I thought CNN put those films out of business?"

"What?"

"You can watch it for free on cable now."

"I'm not kidding. Be serious. What if she lures nice, unsuspecting guys like me off an Internet dating Web site up to her 'porn set,' and then they grab you, tie you up, and film you being killed. You have to go with me."

Pause.

"Honey! Schaeffer wants me to go to a porn set with him to meet a girl he met online. Can I?" Voices, voices.

"Bonnie said I can go."

"You're not gonna ask her if she thinks it could be a snuff film?"

"No. I'm not."

We drove up Topanga Canyon. So the cops would know who my killers were, I left a note for my mother in my hotel room, telling her I loved her and that if I didn't return by Monday to call the police. I left the porn set address. My heart was racing.

"Dude. Relax. It's definitely not a snuff film."

"You're a nice Jewish TV producer who has pictures in your office of you hugging Uncle Miltie in Cantors and Magic at the Forum when you were twelve, and you live in Manhattan Beach with your beautiful wife and three animal rescue dogs. What the fuck do you know?"

"That's not a very nice thing to say."

"I brought a knife."

"What?!"

"It's down my pants. Don't take any left-hand turns too fast, or my left nut is history. Do you need both balls to have kids?"

"You're fucking crazy, Schaeffer."

"There it is! There it is!"

"Fuck!" Dan said, confirming it. A ranch-style house in the hills with movie lights outside. A couple of cargo vans and a lone panel truck in the driveway.

"Motherfucker!" I said with excitement as I shoved Dan back and forth.

"Stop!" I was getting him a little nervous now. We parked and walked up the hill toward the driveway.

"Where's your knife?"

"In my dick."

"Good call to bring it, Schaef. Just in case."

"Thank you." We cautiously made our way up the driveway, our senses ultraheightened, like the first time you broke into your father's pot stash while he was asleep four feet away. Our eyes darted like a bird's head at the slightest sound.

If a wanna-be-pretty-actor-boy tried to impress his fake blond counter chick by changing his facial pose while waiting for his chai latte in the Coffee Bean outside the Virgin Complex on Laurel and Sunset 5 miles away, I would have heard the air move around his sculptured cheekbones as he did it.

"It's fine. Look," I said, and all the adrenaline was suddenly drained as fast as strike three with the bases loaded in the ninth, down by one, two outs. No World Series for the Mets this year.

"Wow," Dan said as, through the window, we spotted a blond girl getting fucked over the back of a couch in the brightly lit living room. Somehow, the initial freakish intrigue of visiting a porn set for the first time had been completely squashed because, apparently, there was no chance anyone was going to be killed on film that day. I mean, unless he fucked her to death. That was the best we could hope for.

But wait, I might meet my wife in a few minutes. I was excited again. We walked in the front door and it was completely identical to every film set I had ever been on. Bored grips eating doughnuts in the corner waiting to light the next scene. PAs whispering into their walkie-talkies. A badly mauled craft service spread, and the only difference . . . two people fucking on the couch. I spotted my "date," the director, Donna. She smiled and beckoned me to the video monitor, where she watched what the cameraman was shooting.

Basically, a short, stout Italian-American guy was piston-pumping a blond English-English girl from behind.

"So, how's it going?" I whispered.

"Great," Donna whispered back.

"I'm Eric." I reached out my hand for a polite shake.

"Donna." She giggled and took my hand.

"This is cool," I said.

"I'm glad you came. We'll break in a minute and we can talk." I gave her the thumbs-up. She and Dan waved acknowledgment.

"Okay, Sally, sit on Bill reverse cowboy on the couch, please," Donna shouted to the two fuckers. Sally stopped her bad fake sex screams instantly, and Bill withdrew his stiffy from her with equal bizarre nonchalance. It was as if they could have been engaged in activities that had nothing to do with each other, in separate universes. They moved to the next position and started up again. Her screaming, him pumping. Man, they were good actors. They seemed so bad when you first saw them. But when you see the in-between moments when it's truly as if the other one doesn't exist, you realize how deeply in love they seem when they're fucking. I noticed something and leaned in, whispering in Donna's ear. "Pull back a little so you can see her feet."

"What?" She was confused.

"It's really sexy to see her feet while he's fucking her and your shot is cutting her off at the ankles."

"Oh, good. Duffy, widen out a little so you get her feet in the shot." Her command was reflected in the monitor as the cameraman widened out his shot so you could now see her feet in the frame. After my smile and the thumbs-up from Donna faded, a strange feeling came over me and I was sure my face looked like a baby's does when gas invades every nook of his little torso and he's about to explode but doesn't know why. Dan noticed.

"What's wrong?"

"I think I just became a porno director."

"Nice to meet you," Bill said as he quickly stroked his dick to keep it hard while we were "taking five" so the new guy, Pierre, a French pinch hitter who was replacing the real "actor" who hadn't shown up, could get himself hard in the corner in preparation for the upcoming three-way scene. Pierre was having a "problem" getting it up, and a slightly embarrassing pall had been cast over the set. Since Viagra had come on the scene, "fluffers" were no longer needed. I guess a weak fluffers union made that a quick and unmediated transition, and the fluffers had to pick up other jobs. Back at Wendy's pushing burgers? Teaching nursery school? Maybe some made the jump to actual porn actresses and performed their craft in front of the camera instead of behind the scenes? Another mystery for another book, I suppose.

Being the gentleman he was, Bill knew it would be gauche to extend his off hand for a handshake under these circumstances; a friendly nod of the head wouldn't be thought of as rude.

"Hey. I'm Eric and this is my friend, Dan."

"Nice to meet you. I'm from Jersey, Donna tells me you're from New York?" *Donna must like me. She's been a-talkin'.*

I smiled at Donna confidentially.

Donna smiled back at me coyly.

Bill continued jerking off at us vigorously.

"Yeah, just out for some work stuff . . . and a blind date." I grinned toward Donna.

"Stop!" She hit me.

"Sweet. Well, nice to meet you guys. Donna, I gotta pick up my kids from the Lakers game, and I'm getting a little raw."

"I know, I'm sorry. Pierre, you just about ready?" He nodded, he was good to go. I interjected quickly. I needed an update of how the date was going. "Do you think I'm less cute, as cute, or cuter than my pictures?" Donna was taken aback slightly more than I thought she'd be by a question I thought was kind of sweet. To be honest, she actually looked a little nauseous.

"What?!" I, of course, hit it harder. When in doubt, lay it on thicker. Might as well go down with guns blazing.

"Are you more, less, or equally as excited by how the first date is going than you thought you'd be?" I said flirtatiously, as if she was enjoying this line of questioning as much as I was and not, instead, about to vomit on the spot. I waited. She was speechless. Finally, hoping it was all a bad dream or that maybe she had misheard me, she managed, "Do . . . I . . . what?" This was Donna the porn director, not

April the emotional recluse. Donna had to just be playing tough. I wouldn't let a little thing like that dissuade me. I continued the assault.

"I really like you and I have a butterfly-in-the-stomach-like vibe. Do you?" She stared blankly at me for three seconds or so and then finally said, "I'm sorry. Can we talk about this later? I just have to get this shot now."

"Of course. Do your thing." It had been a little bumpy, that first "check-in" but I had faith it would turn around when she wasn't under the bone-crushing pressure of pornographic filmmaking and could just let the Schaeffer love wave gently wash over her in a more relaxed fashion. It can be an acquired taste for some not used to its unusual flavor bouquet.

"Excellent. Okay, everyone. We start with Bill getting a blow job from Sally while Pierre fucks her in the ass, and then after a couple of minutes we move to the ATM. Let's go!" Everyone fell in with the precision of a gold-medal Olympic synchronized swim team—necessary, I guess, as Pierre was only working with a demibone, and who knew how long that would even last.

The action began. Confused, I glanced at Dan. It was clear that he was having a commensurate lack of success in unriddling my new girlfriend's instructions. I mouthed to Dan, "What's an ATM?" He shrugged back. We pondered. "Reverse cowboy" had been easy enough to decode earlier in the filming and, while not the brightest crayon in the box, I at least used to be able to tackle Monday's *New York Times* crossword puzzle back in college, and even now on a good Sunday if on a plane and attempting to impress a lovely lady with a furrowed brow, I can get a couple other than the sports and movie ones, but this ATM thing was a real stumper.

"After the Mount?"

"Add the Man?"

"Ask the Maid?"

Dan's face lit up like it hadn't since he was voted "kid with the best bar mitzvah of 1981."

"Ass to Mouth!" He whispered and we quietly high-fived. *How fucking inside are we, man!* Pierre stopped his backdoor action and swapped places with Bill to complete the ATM, and that "was a wrap!"

As the crew broke down the location, which basically consisted of throwing away the used condoms, I declared once again how much I liked Donna and how I thought we were cute together. She said I seemed too "insecure" for her and didn't think us "a good match," but "good luck and thanks for coming to meet me." Dan and I made a hasty exit, walking back down the hill to his car. "I'm too insecure?" I was livid.

"You do like to 'check in' a little early in a relationship for some. I mean I'm not saying it's bad, just not everyone is as open as you are and wants to talk about how things are going twenty minutes into a first date."

"I'm too insecure!"

"Well, she—"

"Fuck her. Porn bitch!"

"Come on. Be nice."

Although a little ego-bruised, I was actually relieved since, even with my elite level of self-delusional rationalizing skills at full employ, I was finding it hard to imagine how I was going to convince myself that she could be my wife.

Donna was my first ever Nerve date. Not to be defeated by one bad encounter right out of the box, I soldiered onto the next girl waiting in the cue to date Mr. Popular! *Okay, just how much of a loser are you going to make yourself out to be here?! Really! Even joking! Jeez.* Whatever. I wrote Amy75 and told her I was back in town and interested in meeting up. She was excited. With high hopes, I took her to dinner.

To this day, as with Brooke in second grade, I still use the lure of a fine dessert as my premier wooing tactic, but only with women I really really like. With women I feel won't make a second date, a piece of pie at the restaurant is plenty. But with a woman I think could be my wife, which are few and far between, my homemade "vegan–banana–chocolate–chocolate chip–peanut butter brownies" must be made as the after-amazing-first-date dinner dessert. (Yeah, you don't even understand how good these things are, so wipe that they-have-to-suck-if-they're-vegan smirk off your face until you try them. They don't taste "just like" real brownies. They taste *better* than real brownies.) And the last girl who got them before April was Amy. That's how well the dinner went . . . or at least how well I was able to rationalize how completely pedestrian it was, in desperate hopes some miracle transformation of her entire personality would occur in my apartment allowing me a chance of actually liking her.

"You just want to get me over to your house," Amy said with a streetwise mug.

"Please, if I wanted to get you over to my house, all I would have to say is, 'Let's go to my house and watch *Sex and the City* reruns' or something stupid like that. I wouldn't have offered to make you the best dessert in the history of desserts," I said with enough earnestness that Amy took a step toward the street from the sidewalk, her disapproving look evolving into a sly smile, my indication that I could raise my hand and yell, "TAXI!"

Amy and I got in the cab and went to my apartment, and I made her my famous brownies. She tried to be polite, and I think she wanted to continue hanging out, but I could tell she hated them, so after she tried them I checked out and heard nothing she said. She launched into a story about her latest ad campaign for Bumble and Bumble, but all I heard was my own silent internal question, "Should I jerk off or watch DVR'd *American Idol* after I give her ten more minutes and she leaves?" She was history. Not just because she didn't like my brownies. They are a metaphor. A barometer.

Even though I sent her away, I still felt like the one rejected. Unfortunately though, unlike after being rejected by Brooke in first grade, there was no chubby Chinese girl named Louise nearby to soothe me. I would try to convince Louise that she was my first choice all along. She knew it wasn't the truth, but would still, after enough arm-twisting to make me cry, grant me a make-out session in the auditorium. No such luck now. I mean unless I wanted to pay for an Asian dominatrix, but I wasn't in the mood this night. Hey, maybe that's why they're so sexy to me now. Hmmm. Interesting. Anyway, alone again. A late game from the coast would keep me company. Along with the entire tray of brownies that thank God Amy didn't want any of.

The great truth of all addicts who yearn for more and handle sadness with self-abuse: The real fun happens when the girl goes home and you can binge in peace. No talking. You can just eat and watch the game. The game is always there for you and always makes sense. A clock. A beginning. An end. Easy rules you can understand and that don't change midgame. Whoever gets the most points wins. Nothing can go wrong. The one rest for my obsessive mind. A moment to reenergize so I can start planning and worrying and figuring again on the pillow before trying to go to sleep. But for now, some comfort. It used to help if I played my guitar, but I stopped when I was ten after my mean guitar teacher told me I was "an idiot" for messing up chords.

I've had three third dates in the last seven years since my ex-fiancée Liza and I broke up. Maybe April will be the fourth.

will you marry me?

"So, we met before you know," April said with a churlish smile as we were about to leave the upper level of Riverside Park and head for West End Avenue to get her a cab.

"No way. I would have remembered."

"It was at the premiere party for *Fall*. We talked for two hours."

"We did not talk for two hours. I definitely would have remembered that. Did you like the movie?"

"Not my favorite. I love *If Lucy Fell*, though. My sister and I still quote it."

"No wonder I repressed you if you hated my movie."

"I have to like all of your movies?"

"Pretty much, yeah. I mean, if you don't like my movies, you're not going to like me."

"Oh, man, are you another forty-four-year-old nonabsorbing narcissist who just likes to hear himself talk?"

"That's a type?"

"Oh, yeah."

"And you go out with a lot of them?"

"I seem to be lately."

"I've been asking you tons of questions about yourself."

"Not so much."

"That's bullshit. I know you went to Spence. I know you have a sister who works in advertising and that you are a huge fancy successful writer and live in Tribeca. I know about your parents on Fifth Avenue where you grew up. Many things. And you're so full of shit. You're saying you don't care if I like your books?"

"I don't even care if you read them."

"I don't believe you."

"You like me. Who cares if you like my books."

"So you could love me even if you hated my movies?"

"Sure."

"Not me. If you're a sucky writer, we're done."

"Okay."

"Do you suck?"

"You'll just have to find that out for yourself."

"If I weren't such a nonabsorbing narcissistic forty-four-year-old who's only talking so I can bounce off of you, I would tell you what happened to me on this running path, but instead I'll just get you a cab so you won't be late for your dinner."

"And a pouter on top of it?"

"I'm not pouting. I'm just being conscientious of your time. Have you had any fun at all?"

"Oh, shut up. I'm smitten." That's actually not what she said. I would have been in love with her if she had. What she really said was, "I'm here, aren't I?" And I wanted to throat-punch her. I hate that. Just answer the fucking question. She sensed my displeasure.

"You like to do play-by-play, don't you," she said, my vitriol building.

"No, I'm just not a secretive withholder." I had to summon all of my acting ability to choke out a sincere "I'm-just-joking-and-not-really-hating-you" smile.

"It's not called withholding if I've only known you for three hours. It's called not being a psychopath."

"With everything in the world that you're not allowed to know, I just like to know what I can know. So yes, if I don't get a read on something, I check in."

"And the fact that I've gone on a three-hour walk with you on our first date isn't any indication that I'm having fun? I need to say the words?"

"I prefer it. Yes."

"Well, you'll just have to let it unfold. It'll be good for you." I knew then that any serious relationship with this girl was out of the question.

Well, I actually knew it in the first three minutes when, after the first harmless blue joke I made upon picking her up outside her writing partner's building on Eighty-fifth and West End she replied snidely, "No wonder you're still single at forty-four." Shit, she's thirty-two, which is seventy in man years, so she's no one to talk, but I let it go. Maybe she was nervous or had her period.

But by now, after the fifth time in three hours that my stomach alarm had gone off telling me to run for the hills, I despised her. She made me nauseous. I literally wanted to vomit. But not being a quitter and wanting to champion that little spark of sweetness I did see in her, the sweetness that came out in between her radical projections and revolting judgments, I figured I could will myself in the other direction if I tried hard enough. *Like Lenny Bruce said, "Guys'll fuck mud."* So I turned to her and said, "I really like you." She smiled. "You do?" Her cheeks got red and she looked at me like she wanted me to kiss her. *Maybe I don't loathe her.*

"Yes. You're sweet," *under that devil personality that makes it impossible for me to be around you, you self-centered, spoiled little cunt! Telling me I'm a fucking nonabsorbing narcissist!? If I hear one more pretentious fucking Upper East Side pontification about an Op-Ed piece in the* Times *come out of your machine-gun mouth, I'm gonna stab you in the eyes with the quills from an Australian pine.*

"You see those spiny, pointy bunches on those trees? They're there so the koala bears can't climb up the trunk of the trees and eat the leaves and kill the trees. They're called Australian pines. I'd been running on this path for twenty years, and I never noticed them until I was arrested and put on a chain gang in the park a few years ago."

"What are you talking about?" She said, finally with real interest, probably because a criminal record would eliminate me from the running as a long-term boyfriend.

"Oh, sorry, I forgot. That would require another story about me, which I wouldn't want to risk at this point. And you're gonna be late. Let's get you a cab."

"No, I wanna hear. Tell me. Pleeeeeeeeeease." She was begging a little, with a sexy smile. There was hope. But if she was going to play games, as much as I don't like to and almost never do, I figured just this once I'd give her a taste of her own medicine.

"I'll tell you another time. I wouldn't want you to be late for your dinner." But no games with you my faithful new friends. This is the story I didn't tell April.

The Wood Chip Story

I was so devastated by the breakup with my ex-fiancée Liza that for months I wandered around crying. It was epidemic. Uncontrollable. Since it was rampant and I couldn't let it stop me from doing things, I just continued on with my life as usual, as if it wasn't happening. I would walk down the street, sobbing. Push the shopping cart down the aisle at Whole Foods, tears streaming down my face. Ride the exercise bike at the gym, weeping. I was lucky no one called the cops on me.

It was the only time in my life I seriously contemplated suicide. I thought of just walking in front of a bus. I don't know why I thought that would be the best way to kill myself. Maybe because my first word was "bus" and subconsciously I thought it would be poetic to end my life the way it began. I had to go to God for help. Ironically, Liza had tried to get me into yoga, telling me that I, of all people, would love it. It was spiritual and physical and lyrical. I was a dancer in college along with being a writer and actor, and she thought I would take to it. I thought it was going to be old ladies stretching, and thought it would be dumb. I somehow stumbled into a class one day at my gym, and my life forever changed. God has come to me like that. In circuitous ways when I need him most and expect him least.

For the addict, 1 + 1 does not make 2. Red means go; and green means go faster. There's only one way to recover as an alcoholic–drug addict–sex addict–compulsive overeater: have an earthquake upheaval shift in thinking. A spiritual awakening. I wasn't raised to know about God but could always sense, though I didn't have a name for it, a presence near and undeniable. It was my presence that was often suspect. When I talk about God and the Devil, I just mean Light and Dark. Good and Bad. Right and Wrong. The primary terms being the best way to describe it, the latter two I tend to shy away from. As I get older, adjectives like "good" and "bad" hold less and less meaning for me, except in cases we all agree are undebatable. Pedophilia, rape, and murder are Wrong and Bad. But getting fired from a job you really love may not be as Bad as you think it is, if your office was on the hundredth floor on the World Trade Center and your last day was September 10.

My lessons are usually more obscure.

For instance, to stay thin, I mean healthy, I run in Riverside Park, the real New Yorkers' Park. I love Central Park, but in the way I love Times Square. They're postcards, not prayers. In the '60s and '70s they were more magical, but now they're not. Now they're Toronto. So I run in Riverside Park on my running path. Suddenly, one day in the middle of my run, Seal on the Walkman, (yes, it was 1990) a HUGE WOOD CHIP PILE appeared directly in the middle of the path. I mean, this thing was literally ten feet high and fifty feet around. And isn't that just like New York City to put it directly in the middle of my path. So I ran around it. Day after day. Week after month. Summer, it had rain on it. Fall, it had frost on it. Winter, it was covered in snow. I mean, the thing was not going away. When would they spread it out already?! I went off to drive my cab. I was six years out of college and would spend my days feverishly writing screenplays in an attempt to achieve my dream of making movies, and my nights driving a cab so I could pay my bills. I was working seventy-hour weeks. I did that for eight years before I made my first film, My Life's in Turnaround, with Donny.

When driving the cab in the early '90s, I had long dirty-blond hair that went past my shoulders (it was that three-year stretch when long hair on guys was back in style again. It was such a lovely call back to my high school hippie days, I had to sign up), so from certain angles I looked like a semicute girl, and driving a cab elevated me from semi- to supercute. At least in the eyes of the cop who, after stopping me for one of the few red lights in history I actually didn't go through, displeased upon clearly seeing my face, yelled back to his partner in the squad car, "Yo, Jeff! It's a fucking *guy?!*" So then he was really pissed, and I had no chance of getting out of my third red light that year, which was going to be, like, 450 bucks. A week's salary at that time.

"Hack license and registration." I gave him the stuff and he went back to his car. *I am so fucked! I can not afford this. Wait! I have a plan! I've seen it on TV!* I got out and soldiered up to the police car.

"Hey, so, can't we just take care of this right here?" They looked at each other for a moment, only slightly taken aback.

"Be more specific," the cop said.

"I don't know, can I take you guys to Sizzler or some shit?"

"Be more specific," he said again.

"I don't know. How 'bout fifty bucks?" He turned to his partner to see if he should close the deal. His partner looked down, thought for a second, and then looked up at me from across the front seat.

"Our sergeant takes care of all that. You wanna follow us to the precinct?" There were two possibilities. Either they were telling the truth and the sergeant *was* in charge of all the "dirty money" that came into the precinct, or they thought I was dumb enough to follow them there so they could arrest me. It couldn't possibly be that one.

"Okay. I'll follow you."

"You will?!" The cop said with a surprised glee that at the moment I didn't quite catch because all my brain could focus on was that I was getting out of a $450 ticket. So I pulled up outside the Twenty-third Precinct on Eighty-second Street between Columbus and Amsterdam. Now, mind you, I was eight years sober from drugs and alcohol at that point, deeply ensconced in a new spiritual way of life that was all about honesty and doing the right thing. And what I was doing seemed about as right a thing to do as any I could imagine at the time. Certainly more right than paying 450 bucks when I could pay fifty.

I was escorted into the station and told to wait. "What about my cab? It's double parked," I asked, not wanting to get another ticket while in the cop station bribing them out of the first one.

"Don't worry about it. We'll keep an eye on it." They were such nice policemen, taking such good care of me. Maybe we could all go out for a bite, a legal one, just as pals. It would be nice to have some buddies in blue. They would give me one of those "citizens for cops" honorary badges or whatever, which I would flash when pulled over and declare, "I got some friends on the job." Very *Law and Order*. Cool.

Once inside, my new friends disappeared into the back, telling me they'd return momentarily and we'd do the deal. I sat in a plastic chair like the ones we had in high school. The pale blue bucket seat ones. The desk sergeant, another seemingly amiable chap, asked me if I had the time. I told him I didn't have a watch.

"Okay. Thanks anyway," he replied with a polite smile.

An hour went by. I was getting restless and a little scared. *Why is it taking so long?*

"Do you have the time?" The desk sergeant asked again. It was the third time in the previous hour he had asked. Was he mentally retarded? "No, I do not have a watch," I said, trying not to be curt to the "challenged" man.

"Okay. Thanks anyway," and he went about his paperwork again. Another hour went by. It was now three A.M. I tried calling a spiritual advisor friend of mine, as something in my stomach told me this might not be kosher and that maybe I should just pay the ticket. He wasn't home. Or maybe he was sleeping. Right, three A.M. I knew that because suddenly I noticed there was a clock on the wall above the pay phone in the waiting room. *A clock on the wall above the pay phone in the waiting room?*

"Do you have the time?" The desk sergeant asked again. *Okay, what the fuck was up with this?!*

"Yeah, it's three A.M."

"I thought you weren't wearing a watch?"

"There's a clock on the wall right there? Are you new here?"

"Oh, right. I forgot about that. Sorry. Thanks." He seemed sincere. "Sorry. I'm an idiot," he said. He was sweet. *Come on Eric, be nice. You're just frustrated having to wait so long and jumpy because of the circumstances. No need to take it out on the nice mongoloid desk sergeant.*

"I'm sorry. I'm just tired," I said.

"No problem. I understand."

Two more hours went by. "Listen, you know what? I'll just pay the ticket. It's been five hours now. I could have made a couple hundred bucks to offset it at this point."

"Just a few more minutes. I promise," the desk sergeant said earnestly. "We just have to wait for one uncool cop's shift to end. If you leave now *we'll* get in trouble cuz Sarge already knows about it." Well, I didn't want to get the poor cops in trouble. "Okay. I'll wait."

A couple of minutes later, the two original cops came out and ushered me back behind the desk into the inner sanctum of the police station where their *female* sergeant waited. My apprehension was mitigated just a tad by the presence of a woman.

"Tell her what you told us."

"I said, could I just give them fifty bucks instead of getting a ticket."

"Okay," she said, looking for the money. I took it out, my heart racing, and put it on the desk. Then, thinking quickly, juuuuuuuuuuu-uuuust in case something wasn't on the up and up, I put a nearby napkin over it, so like, I hadn't really taken any money out . . . and put it anywhere for any cops to have . . . as a bribe and shit. I'm street like that, yo. Word.

"YOU'RE UNDER ARREST FOR FELONY BRIBERY!" I probably had guns and knives, crossbows and bazookas taped to my body with homemade *Taxi Driver* curtain rod contraptions enabling them to fly out and shoot evil-doers if I blinked my eyelids with sufficient force to initiate them, so thank God "for all our safety" the cops immobilized me with catlike kav magraw CIA ballet moves, pulling my leather jacket down over my shoulders and handcuffing me.

"So, you just give me a ticket right, and then I go home?" They all laughed.

"Felony bribery, my friend. You're in the system now." Not only had they scored the *Serpico* lottery bust of the century straight out of the academy, but they also got paid double time to do it, since I had followed them to the precinct and was willing to wait the five hours until their shift ended before they arrested me. Fucking Einstein.

Hands shackled behind my back, I was returned to the desk sergeant. They put all my personal belongings, the cash I had made before the arrest and my house keys, in a manila envelope for safekeeping, adding, "The Tombs can get a little rough. They'll take this shit off you the minute you get there. Better we keep it for you." And then, the pièce de résistance of this enchanting evening:

"Do you know what time it is?" the desk sergeant asked, as if he hadn't asked me seventeen times in the previous five hours. A pristine, mirrorlike lake of a first query. My brain lumbered, trying to deconstruct this verbal whodunit. And then, the sick, sly smile that leaked out of his hitherto championship poker face in consort with my involuntary knee-jerk reaction to look at my wrist even though I couldn't at that moment due to my restraints, and hadn't worn a watch in a decade anyway, guided me to the answer.

When you're handcuffed, you can't look at your wrists, so even if you were wearing a watch, you wouldn't be able to see it. Dastardly!

As I was led away to the holding cell, I looked back at this master of the con. He was smiling a demented smile and nodding his head in slow motion. A denouement he would not be around to witness and couldn't control, the only movement left to complete his perverse opera. Had he been speaking in the secret tongues of cop to try to warn me of the trap that lay in wait? Or, knowing I was a newbie and would never get it, just foreplaying me as a titillation, helping him build to his barbaric orgasm. Unfortunately, I can't imagine that fucked look on his face as they led me away belied anything other than the latter.

I made a phone call so my mom and, more important, Helen knew I was headed for the Tombs. I love my mom but being a little spacey at her best, let alone at four A.M., I felt Helen, my rebel–activist–lesbian–priest–best friend, would be the best person to handle the case.

I wept for a moment, feeling that at least since someone knew I was in "the system," I wouldn't turn into a bad Tom Selleck movie of the week. But my tears of comfort quickly evaporated upon seeing DIE WITEY written in thick red blood streaks on the holding cell wall. If the cozy Upper West Side station holding cell was this bad, what would the Tombs be like?! With the same quick thinking that had gotten me here, I decided it best to sully my youthful countenance to appear less attractive to the AIDS-infected anal rapists that awaited me. I wiped dirt from the floor all over my face and tucked my hair under my hood.

Now I knew what every woman in New York felt like, preparing for her morning subway commute.

We rode downtown in the cop's squad car as the sun rose. The dawn held no promise of a new day that morning. It felt like my death was imminent.

"Yo, Malcolm X, you dropped your thing there," I said to the wild-eyed crack addict whose homemade eye-gouging coat-hanger prison shank had accidentally been liberated from its hiding place, his ass, during our strip search.

Somehow Malcolm had a lucid enough moment to grasp that what I was telling him might to be the single most important thing he ever heard in his life. "Oh, thanks." And without the "bulls" seeing, he picked the weapon up off the floor and tucked it back in its sheath; the nonexistent flesh that would exist as a butt on anyone other than a bony, no-assed, crackhead. He winked at me. I had a friend.

It had been ten hours now, and I was no longer scared I would be killed and then necrophilia-group-raped since, besides Malcolm, who now just bounced and hummed loudly in the corner of the fifteen-by-fifteen holding cell that was home to ten of us, I had two other protectors: angry, incestuous, steroidal gay muscle brothers with blood-stains on their shirts. I had befriended them by giving them my quarter daily Spam, Velveeta, mustard, and sugar packet sandwiches. And so the fear gave way to boredom. Waiting and more waiting. Slowly, all of my peeps were being "processed" and leaving our dank tuberculosis den for the warm environs of the courtroom upstairs. I started to get a little concerned when even new criminals who were brought in to replace those who left were being processed before me.

It had been twenty hours. The gay brothers and even Malcolm had gone. Oh, but wait, Mustafa, the guard I had fallen in Patty Hearst captor love with, was coming. *He would take me up to the courtroom with him, I just knew he would,* I thought in a voice sounding eerily like Dorothy talking to Toto.

"Mustafa, is my case up now?" Now, for some reason, not only was I thinking in a voice like a diva in a '40s movie, I was actually speaking with a Garlandesque lilt as well.

"No. And if it's not called in the next round, you're going to Rikers for the weekend." I was a statue. I had lain with my mother and been turned to salt or whatever the fuck that Bible thing is, instantly crystallized with a pervasive fear I had hitherto never imagined could exist. There are truly no words to describe what "You're going to Rikers for the weekend" means to a nice, white, middle-class, honorary-goy Jew from the Upper West Side.

It's the place where you will be skinned alive and your insides eaten while you watch until your last breath is ended by your head being severed with a jagged chunk of glass, and then, while you are still just barely conscious, six giant penises will fuck the eyes out of your free-floating skull and mash your brain out of your ears. On your best day. And I was headed there in an hour if my name wasn't called. I was taught in my various addiction recovery groups and by my many spiritual teachers never to pray specifically for myself. I hadn't ever before. This time, I did.

"Dear God. Get me the fuck out of here before I have to go to Rikers and I SWEAR I will NEVER EEEEEEEEEEEEEEEEEEEEEEEVER do ANYTHING bad again." I fell asleep. I was awakened by Mustafa.

"Howard, Sanchez, Borden, and Schaeffer."

"Schaeffer?!" I screamed.

"Yeah," Mustafa confirmed.

Going from the holding cell to the courtroom was like being dried off by your mom after your bath and put into your flannel footies. It was the best feeling in the world. She and Helen were there. I started crying. I wasn't going to Rikers. I heard the judge say something about, if I never wanted to come here again they would reduce the charges to a misdemeanor of obstructing justice and I would get off with a two-hundred-dollar fine and twenty hours of community service, but I could never run for public office. Either that, or I could go to trial and take my chances.

As much as it pained me not to follow in Alec Baldwin's footsteps and give up my amazing upcoming political rise to power, I took the deal and left in the arms of my family and friends. Let me tell you, my non-white-trash white and middle and upper-class black friends, there is nothing like twenty hours in jail at twenty-nine years old and eight years sober to make you appreciate your life, and what plain old ordinary Constitutional freedom means a whoooooole new light. If your definition of happiness is to be breathing and not in jail, you have an excellent chance of jumping for joy everyday.

The next day, the chain gang and I showed up for our community service, helping the Parks Department. Amazingly, it was in my beloved Riverside Park. I approached the foreman and asked what he wanted me to do. He gave me a wheelbarrow and a pitchfork, and said, "You see that big wood chip pile over there on that running path? Spread it out."

Tears welled in my eyes as they always do when God graces me with the antidote for my doubt. His radical and clear visit. His love.

I guess the moral of the story was, "If you want something done, stop crying about it and do it yourself."

On the last day of my sentence, while finishing spreading the wood chip pile, I noticed a group of fifty people heading toward me and my fellow inmates. It turned out to be a troop of hot young Esprit models volunteering for the Parks Department. I thought, so this was the real reason God put me through this elaborate journey to end up in the park that day. To meet my wife! I saddled up to the prettiest one, "What are you in for? Murder? Me, too." She didn't get it and went off to rake another area of the park. I was asked not to fraternize with the models and to stay with the chain gang. Stuffy prison guards. Stuffy Esprit models. It's not like I had an orange jumpsuit on, or anything. What, she had never broken the law? Most girls like bad boys. I guess I was just a little too bad for her. But at least I was free. There are no do-overs when you're arrested. Your mother can't save you. I had never wanted my mother as much as I wanted her when I was in jail for those twenty hours.

My Mother

"IIIIIIII once had a girl, or should I say, she once had me." I would shut myself in the bathroom with my guitar to be alone and play songs until Mom got home from work. Al Green and Jungle Boogie were just around the corner. It was 1971. I was nine and still wanted to be the Beatles.

"She told me she worked in the morning and started to laugh . . . "

"Eric. Get out of the bathroom now! Unlock this door!" My mother yelled angrily. I didn't know why she was so angry but she usually was. Because the door would stick I didn't have to lock it. Even throwing all of her slight, five foot two frame against it still wouldn't make it budge if I shut it real tight.

"Open this door right now, or you'll be grounded!"

"Fine." I pulled the door open on the third yank.

"I'm going to play football." I went to my room and slammed that door.

It was dark outside when my mom got home at six in the winter. I loved that. I always have. The darker the better. I love the night.

Under the streetlight below I could see the kids playing in the small park that separated Upper Riverside Drive from Lower Riverside Drive on 102nd Street. The big lower level park was west of that, next to the Hudson, but that was too far away. The small park was a perfect football field size, anyway. Or baseball field size if it was summer. The old wooden windows rattled in the hard wind off the river. The radiator clanked as the heat came on. I would wrap my arms in Ace bandages so I looked meaner, tougher. Old Raiders Otis Sistrunk, Kenny Stabler, Fred Biletnikoff, and Marv Hubbard were my heroes. I put on my shoulder pads and my Raiders helmet. I was ready.

"If you leave this house, you're grounded."

"I'm going to play football!"

"We're having dinner soon, it's too late."

"Fuck you." I bolted out of the house and raced down the thirteen flights of stairs so she couldn't catch me waiting for the elevator.

"Slow down, Harric, you not supposed to run in the lobby," Julio admonished. He tried to bar the front door instead of performing the more conventional doorman duty of opening it.

"See you later." I swung the door open, raced out of the building, through the courtyard, across Riverside Drive, and hopped the fence to the park where my friends were already in midgame. I excitedly ran up. This was my favorite part of my life.

"Can I get on a team?" I said and then suddenly tripped on a frozen footprint and fell. Everyone laughed. I got up, embarrassed beyond belief. Not really the steely tough entrance I was looking for. But what was to come would make that pratfall and subsequent public ridicule seem like nirvana next to the Armageddon that was moments away.

"LOOK! He's got SHIT ON HIS HELMET!" A kid screamed with a kind of wild-eyed euphoric dementia I have to this day never again witnessed on any other human's face. The menacing group of kids circled around me like we were in some bizarre Fellini movie, jeering and pointing at the kid with the dreaded fresh pre-pooper-scooper-law dog shit on his head. While I have had many, many public humiliations in my life, including the New York Times saying I'm the worst filmmaker in the world, which doesn't feel too nice, this moment was the second worst only to the first day of seventh grade a few years later.

It was the first day of basketball practice on the first day in a new school and the girl I liked, Rachael Moody, and all her friends looked on as I tried to impress. Suddenly, I felt a breeze. A draft. I was playing well in spite of the strange chill that invaded the gym that warmish September day. Rachael and her friends giggled and pointed at me. She must like me a lot! I felt a pumped-up sense of pride that I had previously never experienced. In the grandest moment on the biggest stage, I was killing 'em! I was king. The coach blew his whistle, stopping practice, came over, and put his arm around me.

"Go fix yourself," he said quietly out of the side of his mouth.

"What do you mean?" I was completely confused. As nonchalantly as could a man who has to deliver the catastrophic news to a young boy that his left testicle might be hanging out of his gym shorts in front of everyone, Coach motioned with his eyes toward my groin.

I looked down.

My left testicle was indeed hanging out of my gym shorts.

I left the gym. I still have recurring dreams of being humiliatingly exposed in public.

With my friends' jeers echoing in my shit-smeared Raider helmet, I retraced my recent steps to Riverside Drive, hopped the fence, and walked back through the courtyard and into the building past Julio, after stopping at the deli on Broadway to buy a Rheingold, of course.

"Herric, come here. I have something to show you."

"Not today, Julio."

I rode the elevator back up to my floor. I went into the communal trash room by the service elevator at the end of the hallway and threw my beloved Raider helmet away.

"What are you doing with that beer?" My mother asked, amazingly catching not only the detail that her nine-year-old son had entered the apartment but also that he was carrying a beer.

"Men drink beer on Sunday and watch football." I stalked to my room. That answer seemed to satisfy her. She went back to whatever it was she was doing that didn't include me. But before she did, "No TV and no football for a week."

"Why?"

"I told you not to go out. You're grounded."

Underage drinking apparently wasn't the crime, playing football was.

"Fuck you! I hate you!"

"Don't you talk to me that way!" She jumped up and raced after me. I slammed the door to my room and quickly barricaded it with my bed, my mini-pool table, which was still pretty big, about half the size of a real one; my dresser, Battleship game, hockey set with the little tin men you make move with long iron rods; and every other game I could find. There was no way she could get in. I curled up on the floor with a pillow and started crying. I had my small, black Panasonic transistor radio under the pillow, and turned it on to drown out my mom yelling at me. Soon she would stop and I would hear her primal screams while she beat her bed with a tennis racket to get out her anger. Then, offering to reconcile an hour later, I would get the option of either also beating my bed with a tennis racket or playing tug-of-war with a towel. Both options made me want to vomit. Instead, I chose Marv Albert and the Knicks. I loved Marv Albert. He spoke to me with more concern than my father did. And way more often. During basketball season from October to June, I could count on Marv and the Knicks to be there for me. And if I need to summon tears for a scene in a movie now, all I need to do is remember the NBA finals in 1970.

It was the last game of the playoffs. The Knicks against the hated Lakers. Willis Reed nearly had his hip broken by Wilt Chamberlain in game five and was told by the doctors that he couldn't play. It was up to my and every other New Yorker's hero, Walt "Clyde" Frazier, to win the championship, which was tied at three games—all. Clyde wore big fur coats, mutton chops, a café au lait complexion, and a medium-size Afro. He was cool personified, and had a Puma sneaker named after him—the first basketball player to do that: "Clydes." He would have help from Dave DeBusshere, Bill Bradley, Dick Barnett, and Cazzie Russell, who was going to play for Willis. It would be tough, even at home in Madison Square Garden. The Knicks were facing a dynasty Laker team: Jerry West, Elgin Baylor, Wilt. Without Willis, no one gave us a chance. But, wait.

"There seems to be some commotion going on . . . " Marv reported, and I could hear the crowd swell with a buzzing excitement in the background, which made no sense because the game was still a while away from starting and the teams were just warming up.

"I think Willis Reed is coming out of the tunnel? Yes. Here comes Willis! And the crowd is going wild!"

Against doctor's orders, on one leg, Willis Reed hobbled out of the dark underbelly of the Garden like a gladiator appearing from some dank recess to save his city. The Lakers knew, in that moment, it was over. Willis jumped center against Wilt to start the game. He hit the first two baskets for the Knicks and didn't score again. He didn't need to. The Knicks, led by thirty-six points from Clyde, made it a blowout by halftime and were the champions in 1970.

The Garden holds nineteen thousand people. A million claimed to have been at the game. Although I only got to hear it on my transistor radio, I felt like I was there, too. And that was enough to hold me until I got to play Clyde myself, one on one on the Garden floor, seven years ago, a year after my girlfriend Liza left me on my knee with a ring in my hand.

Liza

I had an hour to get my bets in. Ordinarily, since it was only eleven, I would have had two hours, but it was that magical coalescent time of year when the universe smiles on the sports fan, overlapping football and basketball and the Knicks were playing one of their famous Sunday noon games; infamous now, in my mind, since it made Liza break up with me. She didn't end it because she got fed up with the "never-allowed-to-see-me-on-Sundays-and-can-only-talk-for-a-quick-second-in-between-the-last-game-and-the-first-sports-center-around-midnight" rule, no, for something far worse. The gambling addiction she thought I had. At least, that was the catalyst.

Before I get into that, let me just clear up why Sundays are out. The headline is, because it's my day. My day to just lie on the couch and go Neanderthal. I wake up at eleven so there won't be any chance of being bored until the Knicks or football starts. I turn on the pregame shows and finish up solidifying my picks for the day. I already started the process the previous Monday, allowing the various betting possibilities to percolate. The Jets, −5 at Oakland. The Giants, +3 at New England. Maybe a two-team six-point teaser. Maybe a parlay? No, too scary. I'm fond of six-team six-point teasers known as sucker's bets. They're just more fun because you have action on a bunch of games, and the pay-outs are bigger than a straight bet because you get better odds, but you have to combine many games' outcomes to win the bet. If one of your teams loses, even if all the others win, you lose the bet. So, I watch the pregame shows for two hours, finding out any last-minute injuries that might impact the games, and peruse my prepicks just to see if I still have the same vibe I had on Tuesday or Wednesday. Around twelve, I order my scrambled tofu and oatmeal waffles with stewed apples and cinnamon, toast, and extra miso spread. That's brunch. Okay, so maybe a little met-rosexual thrown in with the Neanderthal, but if you haven't figured that out by now, I don't really know what to say. (Not that I look like I've been made over by *Queer Eye for the Straight Guy*, but food wise . . .) I also order a kale-walnut salad with carrots and currants, no dressing, so that if I'm winning money and feeling good, I'll have enough self-esteem to make a big salad with that as the staple, adding my own cucumbers, apples, and homemade hummus balsamic vinaigrette, garnished with sunflower seeds. But if I've lost and feel like shit, the kale-walnut salad stays in the fridge and I order a bacon cheeseburger deluxe as comfort food.

Feeling secure with my picks, I call them in to my guy who acts as a middleman for an offshore gaming site, so I don't have to use the Internet. He's not technically a bookie; I get paid from Costa Rica so it's legal, well, as legal as anyone's decided offshore Internet sports gambling is. It's a little sketchy.

Once, in my infinite paranoia brought on by that twenty hours spent in jail for felony bribery, I Googled the legality of computer gambling. I found that the Wire Act was as far as Congress ever really got, using it in the early '90s to try to prosecute a guy who ran an offshore gambling site, and it wasn't very successful.

But with my "Schaeffer's Law" theory, which makes Murphy seem downright lucky, I needed some further investigation. My friend Donny tried to convince me that even if they could prosecute, they would never go after small recreational gamblers like me but only the purveyors of the sites. Even so, I didn't want to be the first one, you know, they made an example of. I couldn't find out online just what the law was. It seemed very ambiguous. None of my lawyer friends knew, either. So after calling Information to get the number, I picked up the phone and dialed it. A mean-sounding woman picked up. "District attorney of New York," she said coldly.

Suddenly, I thought, *What are you doing, you idiot! They can trace the call!* I hung up fast, knowing from TV that it hadn't nearly been long enough for the trace to hold. Or had it? It was a long time since I saw *Colombo* and, with technology what it was . . . well, they didn't know why I was calling, so they probably wouldn't investigate. At worst they would note my file. I went to the pay phone on the corner of Seventy-ninth and Amsterdam. Though I lived on 110th and Broadway, I figured they could triangulate the signal or something if I used a pay phone in my neighborhood, so I hopped a quick cab far enough away that I felt safe from the authorities' espionage capabilities.

"District attorney's office," the same awful woman said. I disguised my voice just in case, making it higher pitched and a bit effeminate, my racing heart and butterfly stomach probably making it even higher. I sounded like the eunuch I was.

"Hi, is it illegal to gamble on sports on the Internet?" I was sure SWAT teams would simultaneously drop out of the sky and emerge from the manholes and have me prone on the cold, hard cement in a five-point restraint instantly! But so far, so good.

"Excuse me?" She was incredulous.

"Is it illegal to gamble on sports on the Internet?"

"I can't give you that information."

"Why not?" *Is it illegal just to ask the question? God, I'm such a fucking pussy.*

"Because we don't supply that kind of information."

"But you're the highest court in the land, or whatever. If you don't know the laws, who does?" I was proud of my gumption. *Maybe I'm not such a pussy after all.*

"I don't know, sir. Maybe a lawyer can help you." And she hung up. *Wow. Now what? Fuck it.*

I decided to just continue living dangerously, taking my chances with my middleman. He lets me make unsecured bets. I don't have to leave money in some bank account with the offshore site as collateral for losses, which removes wire transfers, credit card charges; you know, a paper trail. No money ever exchanges hands between us on American soil. That I settle up, via check, with the offshore people. I'm willing to pay taxes on winnings, which I have to do if paid by check, rather than risk IRS problems. I'm the only gambler who won't accept cash. Hey, you spend twenty hours in the Tombs and tell me I'm crazy.

So, on the day that was the beginning of the end for Liza and me, I called in my bets and ate my scrambled tofu. It was noon. Time for the Knicks game. Along with playing the game that day, the Knicks were holding a Knicks for Kids charity auction.

Throughout the game, they were auctioning off different items. Whoever was the highest bidder when the final buzzer sounded was the winner. Autographed balls and courtside seats were big draws, but I was after the grand prize. A one-on-one game against Walt Clyde Frazier on the Madison Square Garden Court. I mean . . . get . . . outta here! Walt was my childhood hero.

In a frenzied flurry of phone calls, bidding against unseen opponents, I was last in at halftime at $16,500. I was so excited. I mean SO EXCITED. I was so excited my heart was flooded with love and I wanted to share it with my girlfriend. Oh my god! It was Sunday. Football was about to start in three minutes and I wanted to leave, get in a cab, go to my girlfriend's house twenty blocks away and share the excitement with her?! I would miss the first half at least, and I didn't care. This was serious. I had been praying for this kind of sign for two years. *Should I marry her or not?* If I was willing to give up the first half of football to share something with her, I must have gotten my answer! My heart raced even more; maybe I would ask her to marry me right there on the spot! I ran downstairs, out of my building, and hailed a cab. I rushed out of the cab, up the five flights of her walk–up, and found her leaning in her half-opened doorjamb, looking more beautiful than she ever had, a quizzical smile on her face. "What's going on?" she asked.

I was about to drop to my knees but I just had to tell her about the game with Clyde first. "I'm one half away from winning a one on one game on the Garden floor with Walt Frazier."

"Who?" She asked apologetically. It was okay. Even her sports ignorance couldn't knock one knot of wind out of my sails this day.

"He's one of the fifty greatest basketball players of all time. He was the guard for the Knicks in the seventies when they won their championships, and he was my childhood idol."

"How do you get to play him?" She was getting excited now.

"I'm in a charity auction war with other people watching the Knick game. It's halftime now, I'm leading. Whoever has the highest bid when the final buzzer goes off, wins!"

"Wow! That's so exciting! How much have you bid?"

"Sixteen-five."

"What?" She didn't understand.

"It's at sixteen-five right now."

"I don't get it." She was so cute. Naive, from Seattle.

"Sixteen thousand five hundred, honey." Her face slowly dropped.

"What's wrong?" I asked, my stomach seizing, sensing what was coming. Red blotches started forming on her face and neck, which meant tears weren't far off, and I wanted to punch her in the face. She started crying.

"If we have kids, would you just gamble away thousands of dollars on a basketball game?" She was gone.

"It isn't a 'basketball game,' it's playing my childhood idol on the floor of Madison Square Garden, and the money goes to a kids' charity. And if we had kids and I made a million dollars like I made this year, yeah, I would spend it on whatever I want. Would I take food out of our kids' mouths? Of course not. If I only made twenty thousand dollars, like I made last year, would I spend sixteen thousand on this? Of course not." She was gone.

"My grandfather was a gambling addict and I just can't handle this." Though I tried to be sympathetic and understanding, knowing that her reaction was triggered by a bad memory from her past, it just seemed like she was always defeatist and down and it was like a torrential downpour on my parade. I left and went home. We broke up a couple of months later on the day I proposed to her.

It was the Tuesday before the millennium. I had wanted to do it on New Year's Eve but I couldn't wait. I had gotten the ring. A simple elegant antique thing from the Hasidim on Forty-sixth Street in the Diamond District on Monday, and it was burning a hole in my pocket. Once I had decided she was the one, I didn't want to wait another second. Fuck the drama of asking at midnight on the most exciting night in the last thousand years; a rainy Tuesday at 9:47 P.M. a week before was the perfect moment. I loved her so.

When I first saw her down a hallway in the office building where she worked in Seattle (I was there screening *Fall* at the Seattle Film Festival, which she was working for along with her advertising job) I thought to myself, *That's the woman I'm going to marry.* I had never said anything like that to myself before.

I walked down the hall and asked her to lunch. She turned bright red and, without saying a word, retreated into her office.

"Is that a yes?"

"Sure."

We went to lunch and had a second date while I was in town. She told me she didn't want me to pursue her, but before my plane landed in New York the following night, I had a message on my machine from her, thanking me for the dates and saying she hoped we saw each other again. Classic Scorpio push-pull secretive game-playing. She was my first Scorpio, so at that point I didn't realize how insidious and pervasive a character trait it was. I just thought that she was being twenty-six years old, so I forgave it. I bought her a plane ticket and anonymously left its locator number in a classified ad in the "I Saw You" section of a Seattle newspaper and told her to look for a surprise there. She met me in L.A. for the premiere of *Fall* and we flew to Vegas the next night for fun. It was very exciting.

Our first kiss was on the fake Brooklyn Bridge at New York New York in Las Vegas, on our third date. It was perfectly kitschy. I loved it, except that the kiss itself had zero chemistry, which concerned me. It was a foreshadowing of our lack of chemistry in many areas including sexually, which I was afraid of, but I fell in love with her nonetheless. I told her that night that there was something I had thought the first time I saw her that I would reveal to her at some point in the future.

So three days before the millennium, I rushed into her house, giddy with excitement and fear. On the second floor of her building I stopped, got quiet, and prayed, just wanting a confirmation. "Dear God, should I ask Liza to marry me right now?" *Be still and know that I am God.* I waited for the answer.

"Yes." That's what I heard. Loud and clear.

"Yes."

I resumed racing up the stairs. She was waiting for me in her doorway as usual, a quizzical look on her face. She had been home in Seattle for a week and it was her first night back, but still I seemed more enthusiastic to see her than usual, having called to say that I had to come over right away.

"What's up with you?" I was jittery and giggle-laughing uncontrollably in a manic way, unable to catch my breath. She had never seen me like this.

"Eric? What's going on?" She was worried, which had always been part of the problem. When in doubt, worry. But I soldiered on, undaunted. I leaned in and whispered in her ear. "Do you love me?"

"Of course."

"More than ever?"

"Yes, honey. More than ever."

"Do you remember in Las Vegas on our third date when I told you there was something I thought when I first saw you in Seattle that I would one day tell you?"

"Yeah?"

"You know what it was?"

"What's going on? You're kind of freaking me out."

"When I first saw you I thought to myself, 'that's the woman I'm going to marry.'"

She pulled away so she could see my face. I had tears running down both cheeks.

"Awwww, honey, that's so sweet." She still didn't get it. Trying not to start sobbing uncontrollably, I got down on one knee. She gasped.

"What are you doing?!" She covered her mouth with her hand, smiled this weird nervous smile, started muttering, "No, no, no, no, no," and hit both knees so she was eye-level with me.

I choked out the words, trying to breathe in between and not cry.

"Will . . . you . . . marry . . . me?"

"Really?" Not the response I was looking for but I went with it.
"Yeah."

She just looked at me with this scared smile frozen on her face. Five seconds went by, which when waiting for an answer to that question, is a fuck of a long time.

"You have to say yes or no."

"Ummmmm . . . Yes?" Again, if ever you don't want a question mark at the end of a yes, it would be then, but I let it slide, thinking she was just completely freaked out. I took out the black box and opened it up. She was losing it. I went to put the ring on her finger. Suddenly she pulled her hand away in the strangest, sudden, knee-jerk way. It was one of the weirdest things I'd ever seen. Then she relaxed and let me slide the ring on her finger. She called her mother, which seemed to put even more doubt in her mind and we had to have a "talk." She explained she didn't want to stay in New York. She wanted to move home and didn't want to "carry baby carriages up subway steps," which apparently we would have to do since I was a degenerate gambling loser who frittered away money on kids' charities. She said she wanted to think about it and that's what the engagement period was for.

"No, an engagement means you're betrothed to your beloved and you're planning what color to make the bridesmaids' dresses. It's not to decide if you're going to get married. That's what dating is for. If you say you need time to decide, then we're not engaged yet and you need to take the ring off." She did and quickly handed it back to me.

"Well, my parents were engaged and unengaged three times before they got married."

"Yeah, not a goal I aspire to match." I left and never saw her again. After two years of Liza repeatedly asking when I would be ready to get married, I had finally asked and she said no. Well, yes and then no.

I had been engaged for an hour. The closest I've ever come.

Three months later, I was flipping through the channels and landed on my old pal Conan's show. Hey, no hard feelings. I had been on his show for each of my two first films. When my publicist called in to get me booked to promote my third film, *Fall*, I was amazed to find out that due to my previous appearance promoting If *Lucy Fell*, one I thought went swimmingly, I had been banned for life. Apparently, I had been "abrasive and confrontative."

On the appearance in question, Chris Rock was on before me. Though I loved him and knew he was going to try and bogart my segment, a move I would have made were I on first, I couldn't allow it to happen. He jumped in on Conan's first question to me. I turned to him, armed.

"Excuse me, Mr. Already Famous, you wanna give someone else a chance?" The crowd ooh'd as if I was now one up in a playground dissing contest. I was so straight with my delivery, Chris actually thought I was pissed.

"Sorry, man," he said apologetically.

"I'm just kidding. I love you and that's a snappy suit." He did look sharp.

"You give him a hard time coming on my show dressed like that?" Conan barked at me. I was doing my "shabby chic" look with a rumpled linen shirt and beat-up black leather jacket.

"Uh, it's Agnes B? A famous French designer? Ever hear of her?"

"Oh, be quiet. Just fill it up and check the oil." Everyone laughed. I thought it was a witty comeback and was having fun. We finished the interview without further incident and I left thinking everything was fine, not knowing I had been so "abrasive and confrontative" as to acquire a lifetime ban.

That all happened in 1996. Two years before I ever met Liza. At some point during our relationship I told her the Conan story. Being in advertising and not in show business, she had never met him, and although she liked his show, she sided with me out of allegiance.

The exact moment I clicked onto Conan's show that night, three months after Liza had left me, he was doing a sketch. He was having some random NewYork advertising company come up with an ad for a bed store in Houston or something like that. They panned the room of ad executives and THERE WAS LIZA. I couldn't believe it. I was stunned and confused and had a really bad feeling. After not seeing her since I had been rejected on one knee with tears in my eyes and a ring in my hand, there she was on the *Conan O'Brien Show*. And then, a week later, I bumped into her in Times Square. She didn't want to talk. She said it was "inappropriate to have a personal conversation in the middle of the street." This was coming from a woman who was taught it was inappropriate to hold hands in public. I, on the other hand, am a bit of a freak so, yeah, we were ill suited in that and many areas; and though I meant my proposal profoundly, in retrospect I'm grateful she said no.

I told her that sometimes you have to have conversations in places you don't think it's "appropriate to have them in."

"I quit my job," she said with an apologetic smile.

"So when are you moving back to Seattle?"

"I'm not. I got a new one here." I was speechless.

"I thought you said you hated New York."

"Does it really matter where I live?"

"When your reason for not wanting to marry me after saying you wanted to for two years was because you wanted to move away so you wouldn't have to carry baby carriages up subway steps? Yeah, it matters."

"I don't want to have this discussion here." She started to walk away.

"And what the fuck were you doing on the *Conan O'Brien Show*?!"

She disappeared into a sea of people.

Three months later I read on Page Six that she and Conan were engaged. I guess they met when he randomly picked her advertising agency to do the skit. Or she had been fucking him before, having an affair on me. I never suspected that but she was a secretive person, so who knows.

"Happy Thanksgiving," I said out loud even though it was July and I was alone in a Motel 6 in Hyde Park at my first yoga retreat ever.

That's what I say now when I really want to say something else. One year during a Thanksgiving Day football telecast, Chris Collingsworth, ex-player turned commentator, witnessed a player making a bonehead mistake.

"It's Thanksgiving, my friends. I'm not gonna say anything bad about anyone today. All I'm gonna say is Happy Thanksgiving." It's worked well for me in all seasons.

That day, after Liza cried about me being a gambler, I went home and eventually won the auction at $26,500 and got to play Clyde. It was out of control. I was pump-faking the man who invented the pump fake, or at least made it cool. I was hitting fadeaways from the left baseline on the playground of my dreams. I beat him eleven to nine. Fair and square. He missed a lot of shots, but I hit two threes. NBA threes. From behind the arc on the Madison Square Garden floor. On a rainy Monday afternoon with a janitor, a couple of Knicks PR guys, and a photographer watching. The Garden was filled to capacity in my mind, and the crowd roared as loudly as they did when Willis came out that night thirty years ago. A "dream come true" doesn't begin to tell the story. No words could. On my bench were three people. My mom, who videotaped it. Helen (my lesbian–priest–best friend who got me out of jail that night), who thought it was the coolest thing in the world. And my publicist Liza, who bore the same name as my ex, so I guess she was represented after all. I kept the towel Clyde tossed me to dry off with after the contest, and have a bus stop–size poster of him on my living room wall, smiling, backing me down in the post, trash talking as he goes.

Normally, when there isn't a Knicks game on during Sunday football, eating and phone calls with Donny take me up to kick off at one. Then it's watching, napping, Nerve whoring, jerking off, napping, maybe a dominatrix or a special massage girl, and the four o'clock games. They end at sevenish. I take a walk down Broadway to clear my head, and then it's the Sunday night NBC game at eight. After that is *SportsCenter* and the highlights of all the games. I have satellite so I see parts of all of them live, but the Sunday ritual would be incomplete without the highlight show. Oh yeah, and before *SportsCenter* there's time for the girlfriend check-in call. If I have a girlfriend. I haven't gotten into the whole sports of it all with April but I hope she's cool with my Sundays-on-the-couch thing. It's kinda of a dealbreaker if she's not. Until kids come along of course, then I'm totally down with all hell breaking loose and having no time for myself.

demi moore

"Fine. Don't tell me your running path story. I'm not going to beg." April was a little annoyed. To once again endear myself to her and to distract her mind from thinking me obnoxious, I threw a softball right down the middle, into her and every girl's wheelhouse . . . unabashed desire for her.

"Come to Vermont with me for the weekend."

"I can't. I have a dinner party I'm throwing in five minutes."

"You're famous. You don't have to be there."

"I'm hardly famous, but it's my family and friends. I set it up."

"That's exactly why you don't have to and in fact shouldn't be there. Come on, I'll go to Whole Foods and get a bunch of amazing organic supplies while you go downtown and pick up your dogs, and I'll pick you up in an hour. By midnight we'll be eating putanesca in front of the fire with a movie on my couch in Vermont. You'll have your entire own wing. You can go off and do whatever you want, go for walks, go to town, go to the auction in Wilmington they have every Saturday morning. You don't have to feel obligated at all to hang out with me." She smiled. I could see her mind racing, trying to figure out how she could make it work with all the plans she'd have to cancel. It made me really hot for her. I went in for the kill.

"The outlet stores in Manchester? Outlet *shoe* stores in Manchester?"

"And I'd have my own wing?"

"Absolutely." She paused. The moment of truth. The entire park vanished. The purple and pink sunset back-lit her beautiful long red hair, delicate alabaster face, and soft red lips. I could marry this girl if she said yes.

"I can't. It sounds amazing and I always wish I could be the person who says yes to an offer like this but I just can't."

"I totally understand." I really did but my heart still sank a little. When would I meet a girl who *would* just say yes. To it all.

"And I kind of feel like it would be a setup. You know? I've only known you three hours and we'd get up there and . . . "

"It would be like 'Vegas, baby'?"

"What do you mean?"

"You know, in *Swingers*? The excitement of the impulsive trip to Vegas at midnight, and then three hours later in the middle of the desert when it's one in the morning, you have another two hours ahead of you and the novelty is so gone? 'Vegas, baby.'"

"Kind of. It's a setup. It could only end badly."

"Or really, really well."

"Or really, really badly. Why risk it?"

"Why not? What's the alternative?"

"A normal second date. I know you think that's really boring."

"No. It's perfect. We'll have a normal second date." I was being as sincere as I could be while being so disinterested in that plan that it was hard to move my mouth to get the words out.

We approached the thirty-foot stone wall at 104th Street that, like a fortress, protects Lower Riverside Park from the rest of the city. We started climbing the uneven, cracked, black granite staircase that used to smell much more like piss before the East Siders, her people, started taking over my neighborhood, the real Upper West Side. Above Ninety-sixth Street. No Lincoln Center bullshit. Closer to Harlem than Zabar's. Okay, I'll give you anything north of Gray's Papaya on Seventy-second Street.

"I love these stairs. I've been climbing them for nearly half a century. I don't know why I've recently started using that term. I probably should keep it at bay for as long as I can, I mean, I'm only forty-four but it somehow feels very impactful. 'Half a century.' I guess when it serves my point. Anyway, I liked them better when they smelled more like piss."

"I'm really sorry I can't go to Vermont. Thanks for the invitation. I could go in two weeks on the Fourth of July?"

She thought I was moving too fast by asking her how many times she thought of kissing me on the first date, but she was throwing out a long holiday weekend in two weeks when we could go away together? My stomach clutched a little with fear. Somehow, the impulsivity of going away for a weekend with a girl you just met three hours ago seems fun and light and romantic but in two weeks, you've had five dates, slept together, and know the person enough that feelings are starting to grow. It would be way too intimate to go away together then, especially on a holiday. Three weeks *maybe*, but not two.

The window is now, or in a month.

I forced a smile through my mild nausea. "That would be great. You don't already have plans?"

"No." How could she not have plans already? You could tell inside of three minutes of meeting her that this girl had planned every second of every day of her life for the next century to avoid any chance of being alone with nothing to do but be with herself. It was her biggest fear. It would mortify her. She told me she meditated for twenty minutes, three times a week. I guess "meditation" was her cute euphemism for "planning sessions." I mean, she had plans to plan. Hey, no judgment. At certain times of my life, I have been her. Sometimes I still am.

We were at the top of the stairs, about to hit Lower Riverside Drive where, although sparse, a cab might be found.

"We're all gonna be dead really soon. *Really* soon. You already know what you get from a weekend of dinner parties and drinks and brunches. Come to Vermont right now. Just say yes. If it's a disaster, you take the car and drive home and I take a cab to Bennington and rent myself another one. Who cares? Come on. Scrabble. Food. Kissing. Valtrex. TV. Fires. Alone time. Hikes. Shopping. Kissing. Food. My amazing vegan chocolate–chocolate chip–banana–brownie cake . . ."

"I can't." She could but wouldn't, which I hated.

"Taxi!" *Get her the fuck out of here.*

"Don't end our first date making me feeling like I disappointed you." *You and every other unromantic girl you're the leader of, are and has, since I was fucking eleven.*

"No. Of course not. I totally understand." *How do you survive being you?*

"Can I call you while you're there?" *No.*

"Sure." *Why?*

"Thank you for the walk. I had fun." *Of course you did. You talked about yourself the whole time, yet deluded yourself into thinking I did so you could be the sanctimonious victim of yet another "forty-four-year-old nonabsorbing narcissist." A perfect date.*

"Me, too." *Fucking torture. But I am forty-four and alone. Maybe I'm being a baby.* "So we're on for a normal second date next week?" I opened the cab door.

"Yes, please."

"Great. Call me over the weekend." I slammed the door with a smile and a happy wave. I hated her. I grabbed another cab and picked up my rental car at Hertz on Seventy-seventh Street and Amsterdam. Realizing I might change my mind and end up liking her, I decided I better hook her just in case, so I'd have the option.

I bought a Green and Black's organic chocolate bar, wrote a cute note about how sweet she was, and pulled up outside the restaurant on Seventy-sixth and Columbus where she was hosting her dinner party. I double-parked outside, left the flashers on, and stormed in, confidently marching up to her table. Her face lit up when she saw me coming.

"Pardon me for interrupting," I said to her three guests. I handed her the chocolate bar and note and, without saying another word but flashing a piercing look, turned and left. Three paces later, I threw a smile back at the table. They were all wowed by my romantic gesture. She had probably just been in the middle of telling them about our walk-in-the-park date, when I appeared.

"Thank you. Have fun in Vermont. I'm sorry I can't go," she yelled after me. Yeah, she definitely had just been talking about it. I was in. I felt half warm and fuzzy and half defective and corrupt. Deep down, I wanted so badly to like her and have her like me. I was so lonely. But I was scared she wasn't the one and scared I was an asshole for trying. I jumped in the car and hit the West Side Highway at Seventy-ninth Street heading north. I blasted a Patty Griffin CD to inspire the gods to make it love. My father has been married three times. Magnificent women, all of them, but I only want one wife in this lifetime. And I hope it will be April.

My Father

As soon as I hit Springfield, Massachusetts, and the radio stations start playing Blue Oyster Cult and Lynyrd Skynyrd, I start wanting to drink, drive, and fuck. That's all we ever did in Vermont when I was in high school. I moved there to live with my dad when I was thirteen, after a bad summer. I had gotten busted for writing graffiti, but that wasn't the worst of it. Not by a long shot.

We all wrote graffiti on the subway trains when we were thirteen. I was "Devil 1." My best friend, Latrell, was "Joker110." We would steal Pilot markers from Golden's art supply on Broadway, and Kyron spray paint from AJO hardware on Amsterdam, and make "pieces" with our names on the big concrete wall in Riverside Park. It was like the green monster at Fenway in Boston, a fifty-foot-tall barrier keeping long fly balls from being hit out of the ballpark never to be seen again or, in our case, keeping us from having to retrieve them from the upper level of the park. The baseball fields were on the lower level of the park by the Hudson River and West Side Highway. The wall was our canvas, along with "tagging" the trains, which we rode for hours. They were our playgrounds when we weren't playing ball.

"Taki 183," "Moses 147," and "Stayhigh 149" were the original kings of the trains. Like art students studying the *Mona Lisa*, we copied their names in notebooks, seeing if we could re-create perfect forgeries, then we would branch out, practicing our own names in our own styles. One day Latrell told me that Taki was a crazy murdering psychopath and had once blown up a subway car with dynamite and wanted my base-ball glove or he would kill me and my mother.

"But I don't know Taki. I've never even met him," I told Latrell, terrified.

"Well, he knows you and he wants it by Friday." I gave Latrell my baseball glove to give to Taki.

"Don't tell anyone about this or he's gonna kill you." I swore secrecy.

For the next three months, while I lived in the most paralyzing fear of my life, certain my mother and I would be murdered, Taki, through Latrell, took everything that was precious to me. My transistor radio, my games, my allowance every week, and my basketball cards. Clyde included. My mother finally noticed something was wrong when my small pool table was the only thing left in my once very cluttered room. I confessed everything, and she had a black FBI agent friend of hers interrogate Latrell under a single stark white GE in the kitchen the next time he came over for my allowance.

It turned out that while Taki did exist, he wasn't a homicidal extortionist and knew nothing of me. Latrell had made the whole thing up and had been extorting me himself all along, which made it clear why he always had my stuff after I gave it to him to give to Taki.

"I haven't seen him yet to give it to him" he would say as we played baseball, wearing my glove while I used my bare hands or a borrowed one. I had been cuckolded in front of the entire neighborhood, who all knew what was happening. I was mortified. I couldn't ever face them again. I told my mother I wanted to live with my father in Vermont.

As Latrell and my friends looked on, my dad, his best friend, Ron, and my mom packed what little was left of my things into a U-Haul trailer as I, sick to my stomach, watched from my apartment window until it was dark and the kids left. Only then would I come down and get in the car. I finished my beer and dropped some acid. Oh yeah, I had started taking hard drugs that summer. I was thirteen.

The car was loaded and my dad waited to take me to prison in Ver-mont, but it was still better than the hell I had been enduring in New

York. I don't remember if my mother hugged me good-bye or cried or just stood stoically in the doorway and watched me leave as she had when I would run away in the night when I was six. I always did and still do miss my mother terribly when I'm away from her. And I'm always scared for some reason that, God forbid, I'll never see her again. I didn't turn back to wave. I wanted to cry but didn't.

My crazy academic father was going to "discipline me into being a proper young man." He was equal parts knee-jerk-liberal-hippie-college-professor and closet-conservative-Republican. He occasionally used drugs and had an excellent array stored in a blue Twinings tea tin on his dresser. Windowpane, Panama Red, cocaine, and hash. He smoked pot once in a while, mainly on weekends. The other drugs were gifts from friends he just banked. Every morning I stole something from the tin. I shaved the corners off each side of each Windowpane with an X-acto knife so they would get smaller but never completely disappear lest he remembered he had four of them. By the end of the first fall semester of eighth grade, all four still remained but were microscopic versions of their once much larger selves. One summer I stole some of the white powder, the cocaine, thinking it was hash. Since my father studied pot for the government (and did a big report called the Jamaica Study, in 1971), he was very technical about it and explained to me that the way they made hash was to let the marijuana leaves dry and then shake the dried resin, a white powder, from the leaves and that was then formed into hash, so I assumed hash was a white powder. Wendy Shine and I smoked some at a David Bowie concert at Radio City Music Hall in 1975, the Diamond Dogs tour. We got so fucked up from this stuff, Wendy asked to see the tinfoil I had got the "hash" from. When she saw the white powder she exclaimed, "That's not hash, that's ACID!" So we thought we had smoked acid. We hadn't, it was coke I later realized, but whatever. It did the trick and Bowie, my hero, was amazing. Bowie was the ultimate cool reject. The in-outcast. I had always felt like an alien, too. So he was my champion. And I needed one. Badly.

Breakfasts in Vermont with my dad were the most depressing things in the universe. It was always freezing in the house in the morning because my father only allowed us to heat the entire house with one big Ashley wood-burning stove that was in the living room, and that fire was dead by the time we woke up. It was pitch-black and my depressed dad was always vacant, caught up in his mind contemplating something morose. The only thing that got me through it was the comfort of knowing that after my morning granola and forced NPR listening (which I fucking hated. To this day, the theme music to *All Things Considered* makes me want to slash my wrists), I would get to drop the killer Windowpane acid I stole from his drug tin on the way to school. It helped me deal with getting beaten up every day by the rednecks. By "beaten up" I really mean threatened, which to me had the same, if not *more*, pain associated with it than actual punches to my face, because of the memories it dragged up of the fear of impending violence I endured during the Taki ordeal. But they *would* also punch me hard in the arm, every kid drilling me as I passed him in the hallways between classes. Football practice was the worst, and gym class. They cornered me in the locker room and took turns hitting me in the arm. I found that if I cried they would leave me alone. They just laughed at me, which was fine, so that became the ritual. They hit me in the arm. I cried. They laughed, but stopped hitting.

For the first month of eighth grade, it was a daily occurrence. They only stopped when they realized I was an excellent basketball player . . . and had good drugs. After complaining to my father every day after school for weeks, he finally complained to the school. I met with the principal and the meanest kid, Brad Johnson, who beat on me every day and said he was going to kill me. We sat in front of Mr. Scudero and, with tears in my eyes, I said, "I just want people to like me." I guess without the other kids around Brad could show his soft side, because he seemed strangely sympathetic in that moment. When we left the principal's office and were waiting for our hall passes to go back to class he said, "So, you're from New York?" I said, "Yeah. You want some acid?"

"Sure." And I had a friend. They called me Al from that point on. Apparently the last murdered transplant that moved there from New York was called Al, so that was going to be my name, too.

It also didn't hurt that my first girlfriend, who took my virginity, was the daughter of the basketball team's head coach. Mary Boudrau, five foot two, huge breasts, drove a VW bug, and was nineteen. I was fourteen. Nice.

I had started a rock band, Distorted Visions. My father vetoed my first choice of names, Genocide. I was the lead singer, modeling my style after my rock heroes who I saw on frequent trips back to New York, where I got drugs to sell in Vermont. Led Zeppelin, Lynyrd Skynyrd, Jethro Tull, the J Geils Band, the Rolling Stones, Black Sabbath, Bowie, and of course, my father was my biggest hero. He had a great voice and a huge hi-fi system, back when speakers had to be big to be good (his were four feet tall). He would belt out "You and I" from *Talking Book* along with Stevie, and send chills down my spine. He lit up and in those moments was magic.

He was a dad.

Like when I was eight years old and would climb on his strong back, and together we'd dive onto my Flexible Flyer in Riverside Park and, with complete abandon and snow blowing up into our faces, blinding us, fly perilously down Dead Man's Hill on 116th Street, laughing our guts out. We'd jump ship at the bottom before slamming into the black iron fence that overlooked the lower level and the West Side Highway twenty feet below. He and his second wife, Jane, a gorgeous, fun, hip hippie of a stepmom, lived on 115th Street and Broadway above the Take-Home-E market across from Columbia. He was getting his master's in anthropology, with Margaret Mead. After he completed his dissertation, he and Jane moved to Vermont to start a commune, Johnson's Pastures. Before the move to live with him full-time in eighth grade, I spent every other weekend and a month in the summers with them. I cherished my time with my father and missed him so when we weren't together, which was most of the time.

He was an amazingly charismatic singer/composer/musician/song-and-dance man in the New York theater in the late '50s, when he was twenty-one, just starting out and doing very well. He was a dancer on *The Perry Como Show* and was moving up quickly in the musical theater world. His father, my grandfather, who I never knew, left him a brownstone on Thirty-third and Lexington. My father sold it for a hundred grand in 1961 and used the money to produce a play and a movie. They both bombed, but he met my mother on the movie and cast her as the lead. I wonder why I have always had this fantasy that the girl I cast opposite me in my films as the leading lady will end up as my wife. Interesting. Honestly, it took twenty years of therapy for me to see that parallel. Don't be so quick to judge; you lads still can't even admit you fantasize about having your girlfriend butt-fuck you with a strap-on once in a while, and you gals, upon occasion, imagine having your boyfriend play rape with you; tying you up and cumming on your face.

So, Distorted Visions' first performance ever was at the rec hall in Brattleboro in the fall of 1978. I was fourteen, had hair halfway down my back, and wore a purple mirrored dashiki and leather knee-high six-inch platform boots. I burned off my right eyebrow during the performance, nearly engulfing myself in flames igniting our cheap pyrotechnics show while wasted on three hits of gnarly green blotter acid and a bottle of Gilbey's Gin. I forgot the third verse to "Stairway to Heaven," but rebounded by nailing a raucous rendition of "Freebird."

My drug and alcohol addiction really blossomed in Vermont in eighth grade. After the morning-acid-with-shredded-wheat breakfast, I dealt pot to kids in Wilson's Woods before the first period. We'd smoke a couple joints to help kick off the acid trip, and maybe down a few Molsons. Lunch was a horse tranquilizer. It softened the acid trip comedown and kept the afternoon interesting. That shit would slam you. You felt like your face was flattened by a freight train in the loveliest of ways. A couple more joints and a six-pack of Genesee (the champagne of rural America) after school before basketball practice, to wake up, and then bong hits in my room throughout the night, stealing gin from the liquor cabinet periodically, unbeknownst to my depressed dad who graded his college students' schoolwork in his study. At least that's what I thought he was doing. It wasn't until my little sister Ani's college graduation from Sarah Lawrence fifteen years later that I found out what he was really doing every night in his room.

It was the spring of 1993. He stopped the car near the stage where Ani and the rest of the graduating class sat awaiting commencement. (Ani was the product of my dad and Jane, who I felt was my only ally while living under my father's iron rule in Vermont. She was kind and more like a friend than an authority figure.) Me, my dad, and three women were in the car: his third wife, Nancy, a wonderful loving woman who looked like a beautiful bluebird and was always smiling; their daughter, my little twelve-year-old sister, Tess (As I was in college when she was born, unfortunately I haven't been able to get to know her nearly as much as I would like to. Hopefully, as adults we'll forge a closer relationship), the sweetest child on earth; and my girlfriend, Wendy. They all got out first. I started to follow but my dad gently grabbed my arm. "Wait," he said to me and then shouted to the girls, "We're gonna park the car. We'll be up in a second."

Something was up. He was acting strangely, which scared me, but whatever he was going to say would still be more palatable than his usual fatalistic diatribe about how he had ruined his and all of our lives and what a bad father he was and how I should do everything differently than he had lest I end up like him, old, broke, and lonely. I just couldn't take another of those. In reality, he had an amazing life; his three kids, though all from different moms—all had turned out pretty damn well. He had a roof over his head and enough money to survive, and Nancy loved him to death, but he never saw it that way. That would be too optimistic. I braced myself.

"What I'm about to tell you is very important because it may affect you dramatically."

I was definitely worried now. This wasn't how the speech usually began, so my suspicions had been confirmed. This was a new catastrophe.

"I have spent the last forty years suicidally depressed. I would sit crying for four hours every night, thinking of killing myself. I just was diagnosed as a manic-depressive and have started taking medication and it's saving my life. I feel like a completely different person. I never knew that I had a disease, and that's why I felt the way I did." Tears welled in my eyes. I was so happy for him. I never knew it was that bad for him. Like every boy in the world, I felt my dad was a god, both a good and an evil one.

He was talented and funny and gorgeous and judgmental and selfish and loved me. And he was very sick, and until then hadn't had any treatment. My heart broke for him yet he still could press my buttons easily and, at that point, I was still unable to fully forgive him.

I *have* completely forgiven him now, though. I only have deep love for him, and a sadness that he can't find more joy in his life.

It was a long road to completely forgive him, which culminated the year after Ani's graduation and the admission of his diagnosis to me. Wendy and I had gone to Kitchener, a suburban town outside Toronto, to visit him and Nancy. I said something that was important to me and he did his patented condescending laugh, which I have always hated. I asked him why he always did that. Laughed like that. He said it was my "perception," and not what he had done. He always met honest emotion with intellectualism, to avoid feeling anything. The discussion ended with my sobbing in the kitchen, telling him that I felt he never loved me and that I was never good enough for him.

"You're right. And you never will be good enough." Somehow hearing him confirm it was comforting.

"And you know why? Because I feel that I'm the most worthless piece of shit in the universe, so how could anyone be good enough for me?" He held back tears and a lifetime of self-hating rage. I hugged him and cried like a baby in his arms. I felt embarrassed but it had to happen at some point, or I would never be able to be close with anyone in my life.

Until you've stood in your parents' kitchen at thirty-five and had whatever version of that scene is for you, you'll never stop hating yourself and therefore hating the world. I forgave him unconditionally that night.

Wendy and I left the next morning on our "find the great American winter" road trip because I was sick of the weak New York City winters and wanted to bask in some serious frigid cold that year. I wanted to go to that little semicircle on the map the weather guy always pointed to that was at the top of the country in the middle. It was always the coldest. Montana, Minnesota? Wherever, just freezing.

I've always loved the winter and the freezing cold. I don't like to *be* cold, I like to be all bundled up and warm but out in the cold. Of course that year, 1994, was the coldest on record in New York. It was subthirty, like, twenty days in a row, and snowed, like, ten feet. I would watch the local news in a Motel 6 in Bismarck, where it was a balmy twenty that, with their dry air, feels like an East Coast fifty, as they reported the "deep freeze" in New York, and lament the Schaeffer curse of bad luck. My dad was good enough to pound that belief into me. This was the classic manifestation of it.

You drive to the North Pole to find winter but, in a freak occurrence never before witnessed in the history of time, it's hot there and arctic in your hometown. (Or maybe it's because of YOU! Because you use SIX TOWELS at the gym every time you go, you selfish fake tan freak?! You may not care that you're killing your own mother but I sure as shit care that you're killing mine. Not to mention ALL THE OTHER PEOPLE ON THE PLANET?! Global warming? Ever hear of it?! You can't use 6 towels anymore, dude. Two at the most, okay? Get in the fucking game!)

At least I was with Wendy and not alone trying to find midwestern truck stop whores for company, like some scene out of *Fargo*. I loved Wendy. She was one of my three great Aquarian girlfriends.

* * *

I've had six great loves in my adult life since college, not that I really consider anyone under, oh, let's say, thirty-five an adult. It's amazing to me that we let the child minds vote and drink and have jobs. They should be in adult training until at least thirty, sequestered from real adults during that completely heinous midtwenties section when they think, because they don't live in a dorm and have stopped referring to time in semesters, they actually know something and have the skills to negotiate real life.

And then there's that astrological deal, the Saturn return, when all the twenty-nine-year-old girls go nuts. That should be the rebirthing into adulthood, just after they recover from that at thirty. Then, they might have a shot. Anyway, going by today's recognized standards of adulthood, starting after college, I've had six big loves. Every second one, though, was clandestine, and while they certainly counted in my heart, they didn't in the real world. If the criterion for a "real girl-friend" is being able to introduce her to your mother as your "girl-friend," I've had three of those.

I've often wondered about that "good one, bad one" pattern. I think, when I do the breaking up with someone, I believe on a profound level it means I'm evil and should be punished, so I shack up with some unavailable woman who has no choice but to hurt me even worse than I hurt whoever I broke up with. Grace was my first girlfriend after college, also my first sober girlfriend. She was heavenly.

Grace

Grace was the first of my three great Aquarian girlfriends, and a "good one." I met her through some mutual friends. She was beautiful in that Upper-East-Side-tall-Irish-long-reddish-hair-blue-blood kind of way. She smelled great, Chanel No. 19, and looked like her mother, who was one of the most gorgeous movie stars of all time. I was four years sober, twenty five years old, driving a cab and writing screenplays on spec, trying to make my big break. She was two years sober, twenty-eight, and working in fashion, trying to figure out if she wanted to be an actress.

A group of us stood around on a street corner deciding where to eat. I ambled over to her and dove in. No toe in the water bullshit. The icier the ocean, the bigger the swan dive I make. Life's short.

I decided long ago that the pain of taking the risk and getting your heart broken—in any phase of life, work, love, friendship—while profound and annihilating, is still far easier to live with than the pain of staring up at your ceiling in the middle of the night, not having had the guts to try.

"Hey, Grace."

"Hey." She looked right at me. I loved that about her.

"Are you single?"

"Yeah, why? You want my number?" Her directness gave me butterflies.

"Yes." She handed me a piece of paper with her number on it. She already had it in her hand.

"You were prepared for my wooing? Or are you so deluged with suitors you have them printed up and keep them at the ready for easy access and economy of time?" She laughed.

"No. It wasn't intended for you. It was for Ellen. She wants me to help her with something."

"You wanna go on a date?"

"Absolutely. When?"

"Tomorrow night."

"It's my birthday."

"Oh, okay, well, how about . . . "

"No. I want our first date to be on my birthday." I fell for her then and there. You know how few women I've met in my life who stand rock solid, look you in the eye, and say yes? Even when they want to? They're all so fucking afraid. I'm not saying it's only women. Of course, men are terrified as well. Myself included. But if courage is action in the face of fear, not the absence of fear, I wish more women had the courage to risk the hell that is rejection for the chance of the utopia that is real union.

Grace and I had a wonderful, loving, sexy, tumultuous one-year relationship. We broke up when she was, see, I told you, twenty-nine. When women go crazy in their Saturn return. She got mad that I gave her a See-and-Say Barnyard Animal pull-string toy and a Mets uniform for her twenty-ninth birthday presents. I was going to give her a fancier and more romantic gift privately, but those were the ones she opened in front of all her friends at her big party. We had a fight after the gathering and broke up that night.

But it was a wonderful and crucial relationship for me. It was the relationship in which the insanely scary and treacherous challenge of navigating sex and intimacy first really reared its ugly head and, to both our credit, neither of us backed down from the fight.

Like a gentleman, I waited until our second date, for a first kiss. (Chivalry had nothing to do with it, to be honest. We both agreed to try some self-help book's plan of waiting five dates to have sex, so we figured we should slow the whole process down and not even kiss on the first date. It was the sexiest thing I had ever done, wanting to kiss her so badly but resisting the urge.) I finally kissed her and we started making out like high school kids though, unlike in high school, I threw in a little dirty talk as well. It was a lot of dirty talk, actually, which she seemed to like, so much so that with only the aid of my voice and some dry-humping . . . she came. It was very hot. As was our sex life during the "falling in love" phase that lasted the following six months. Then, she surprised me Christmas morning by wearing a black garter-belt-and-stockings outfit under her bathrobe and wanted to fuck me under the tree among the presents. I wanted to vomit, which wasn't quite the reaction she was looking for. She was incredibly sexy, mind you, and upon recalling it at this writing I will admit I'm conjuring up a demibone, but at the moment it really happened, it made my stomach turn. I thought she had crossed a line, and I wasn't even raised in any religion, certainly not Catholic. I just felt like Christmas morning was supposed to be filled with innocence and mothers, not porn sex.

"Porn sex?!" She was really pissed.

"Yeah. It's Christmas morning."

"So what? When your hot, young, girlfriend shows up in this outfit and wants to fuck your brains out, you do it! Christmas fucking morning or not! What's wrong with you? Do you know how many men's fantasy you're living right now?!"

We went to therapy. She didn't like my response to her Bunny costume on Christmas morning, and I hadn't liked her response to my response to her question the week before.

"Honey?" She had asked in that benign way, which lets you know you're about to have a really unpleasant conversation.

"Yeah?" I'd said, buying time to desperately ransack my mind for the possible things I had done wrong recently.

"Do you think about me when you jerk off?" Now, 99 percent of the men reading this think it's a no-brainer. Where's the dilemma? Thanks, honey, you lobbed a softball. You just lie. No harm, no foul. It's only in your head, for Christ's sake . . . But I don't believe in that. I'm into full disclosure. Tell the truth always, no matter the consequences. I mean, if you meet a girl for a blind date and you're just absolutely not attracted to her, and after the date she asks if you want to get together again and you don't and you politely decline and she presses you for reasons, do you say, "I'm not attracted to you?" Maybe not, maybe some minor bullshit vamping, "I like you but I just don't think we would make a good match." Which isn't a lie, just not the whole truth. I'm not advocating indiscriminant cruelty cloaked in the honor of complete honesty at the expense of someone's feelings, but certainly as close to the absolute truth as one can come without unnecessarily hurting her.

I would rather be told the brutal truth, no matter how much it hurts, than some line of bullshit designed to "protect" my feelings. I wouldn't like her for doing it, but at least I'd have respect for the girl killing me.

"No. I don't think about you when I jerk off," I said very matter-of-factly, as if I were saying I didn't like Brussels sprouts. Grace, of course, took that to mean I would have zero sexual interest in her for eternity and only wanted to fuck every other living creature on the face of the earth.

"Never?" She was grasping at straws and knew it.

"Honey. You're my reality. I don't want you as my fantasy. Reality's way better. I think about other girls when I jerk off as a fantasy so I don't need or want to go actually fuck them in real life, and that way I get to keep you as my reality."

Our therapist suggested I felt claustrophobic in the relationship and that, conversely, Grace felt I would abandon her. The fix?

Have Grace suck my dick while I looked at *Penthouse*.

I could fantasize about other women but have Grace with me in reality.

I don't think that was the exact remedy the shrink suggested, but something along those lines. *Grace* actually came up with the *Penthouse*/fellatio idea, and it worked like a charm. Just the fact that Grace was hot for it made me so much more into her. It definitely drew us closer. She wasn't afraid I would leave her, and I wasn't afraid she was trying to mind-control-suck-my-soul-away.

Unfortunately, though, we were both still too crazy. She was turning twenty-nine and entering her Saturn return. And even though I was four years free from active drug and alcohol addiction, I was still only twenty-five, a stunted child trying to find out who I was and learn the skills to properly relate to the world. So sadly, it ended.

Grace and I are wonderful friends to this day. She lives in L.A. with a loving husband and two great kids. Our bond is one that is deep and unlike any other in my life. Grace always got me like few have ever gotten me, and loved me for me, without needing me to change in any way. . . . And I her. It was just bad timing. And as unfortunate as the timing was between Grace and me, it was even worse with Wendy. She was another "good" one but Demi Moore, a clandestine one, was in between. Number two of the Aquarian trilogy.

Demi Moore

We're calling her Demi Moore. It wasn't really Demi Moore, though it *was* one of the Brat Pack. For sake of honesty and full disclosure, and to stay on point in this discourse of how and why I'm still single at forty-four, Demi's important to discuss, but I'm not into a kiss-and-tell thing—that's not the value in the story. That's why we're calling her Demi. Ah, fuck it. It's a much better story if you know who the real girl was, and I'll just leave out the more intimate details. I think that's the way to go. The joy of knowing the real identity without the intimate details is a far greater joy than knowing the intimate details but not knowing who the real girl was. And to be honest, I really just wanted to get the "We'll call her Demi Moore" joke in there because I thought it was funny.

Kind of like how when you wear an uncomfortable outfit that's too tight or too hot because it looks great? Once your date has seen it, it's like, "Okay, you've seen my great jacket. But I'm fucking sweating like Albert Brooks, so can I take it off now, please?"

I had been driving the cab for seven years in New York while writing twenty screenplays. I was twenty-nine and had been hacking since I got out of Bard. I drove for forty hours a week, and wrote for forty. I figured screenwriting was the most direct route to achieving my goal of becoming a filmmaker. As an actor and director, I needed someone to give me a job. As a writer, I could write myself a movie and then just find enough money to make it.

It was during the '80s spec script boom. A time when it seemed any script written by anyone would sell in a bidding war for a million dollars. I met a cute girl named Laura at a party; she got me my first writing job ever, a screenplay for a small production company she was working for. I got paid two grand, which seemed like a fortune to me, and it was for writing! I was a professional screenwriter! I was in the game!

I would drive my cab past film sets and just start crying, wanting so badly to be on one. But I didn't want to work my way up through the crew ranks. I only wanted to set foot on a film set when it was mine. So I drove and wrote. Laura introduced me to her brother, Boyd, who was a talent agent in L.A., and he signed me. I was over the moon.

What seemed like an eternity (but was really only three years) of writing twenty screenplays without even an agent to send them out was now over. I had a job *and* an agent. I knew I was about to become a star.

I wrote three more screenplays that Boyd sent out, but we got no bites. Then I wrote a romantic comedy called *Whatever Happened to Love at First Sight*. He sent it to Molly Ringwald's production company, and she liked it and wanted to meet me about it. I was sure it was fate. Two years earlier, six months out of college, I had been hanging out with Betty Buckley, whom I had met through mutual friends. She was sexy as hell, fiercely talented, successful, and had been Abby on *Eight is Enough*, which was totally hot being as I always had had sexy step-mom fantasies. Once during a snowstorm, walking up a barren Amsterdam Avenue, Betty broke into "Memory," which she made famous in *Cats*. It was enchanting. Her silky voice powerfully cutting through the dense white blizzard that engulfed us; the snow-rumpled rumble of taxi tires creeping over cobblestones her accompaniment.

Betty had a friend who was directing the next John Hughes movie called *Pretty in Pink*, starring Molly Ringwald. She got me an audition for the male lead, Ducky. It was my first big audition. Up to that point my claim to fame was playing the "Third Soldier" in the rain in an outdoor production of *Hamlet* in a courtyard theater in the back of a warehouse behind a police station on 54th Street. So when I say "first big audition," that kinda doesn't begin to do justice to meeting John Hughes, Howard Deutch, and Lauren Shular Donner.

It was epic.

I went in, thought I nailed it, but didn't hear back for a few weeks. When I finally did, they told me I didn't get the part. I was heartbroken. I had watched all of Molly's movies and was convinced I would get this role and we would fall in love. Forever, like Tracy and Hepburn. Or at least for a great three months, like Andrew McCarthy and Jami Gertz in *Less Than Zero.*

Six months later, I got a call from Betty. She said they were still having trouble finding a Ducky and wanted to see me again. I went in front of the same elite crew. I was much more low key this time, though, now in a phase of trying to always honor my "inner truth" and not put on fronts. Unfortunately, I didn't realize that Hollywood doesn't give a shit about how you really feel unless it's fabulous, and they certainly don't want to hear about your "inner truth" unless it'll make them money.

"So Eric, what have you been up to?" John Hughes asked, desperately wanting me to blow him away with my enthusiasm and charm and absolute Duckiness.

"Well, I've been kinda depressed lately. Lying around the house . . . driving the cab. I don't know, Uta Hagen kicked me out of acting class for not showing up . . . Whaaaaaat else . . . I'm excited about March Madness." If they had been casting *Uncle Vanya*, I would have launched my Broadway career right then. As it was, though, this was not the audition to grab me the lead in a huge bubblegum teen flick.

So *Pretty in Pink* went away and so did my chance, I thought, of making Molly Mrs. Schaeffer. But the Great Spirit, as it usually does, had other plans.

In 1991, I flew to L.A. to meet Molly about a screenplay I had written entitled *What Ever Happened to Love at First Sight*. Other than a six-month stint in 1986 (one of the months back home in New York to see the Mets win the World Series, so really five,) I hadn't spent any time in L.A. I stayed at a cheap West Hollywood hotel but, trust me, I felt like I was in the Beverly Hilton. I just knew Molly and I were going to hit it off and make movies and babies together and I would become a huge star and live all of my dreams. This meeting was going to be the portal. I had to look my best, which meant I needed some color on my pasty East Coast face. But the meeting was tomorrow morning and it was already noon. I'd better get crackin'.

I bought some baby oil, having no time for a gradual evolution from white to tan. My lone shot was the next three hours of California sun. I was an accomplished tanner and had a foolproof system, cultivated during my previous three summers in Greece. When I had the time, I started with SPF 8 on my face and 4 on my body. You may think for an Irish-complected man such as myself, that's way too little protection, but my belief is that you have to get burned at some point so it's really all about damage control rather than trying not to get burned. The "trying not to get burned" theory just keeps you in SPF 35 eggshell white hell for the length of your vacay.

Aloe and Nivea. That's my secret and now gift to you. One of many. You may claim it. I'm here to help.

You let yourself get burned but not too burned. You use the 8 and the 4 to supply enough protection that the burn is of a nature such that slathering aloe first to treat the injury of the burn and then Nivea for moisturization will be sufficient to prevent you from peeling. Burning without any sunblock on is, for some reason, a different kind of burn. Even if it's the same level of burn, you peel no matter how much aloe and Nivea you put on it. Therefore, you must use sunblock, no matter how low the SPF.

On the second and third days, you'll still be too burned on the first area you tan-burned to expose it to the sun. Usually the face, chest, and stomach. So you cover those areas and start the process on your legs and back, the parts only the people who you have straight and gay bottom sex with will see. On the third day after your initial burn, the fourth day of the vacation, the burn on your face, chest, and stomach, having been liberally saturated with the aloe/Nivea treatment, are a reddish brown and ready for the sun again. The same routine is followed from that point on, progressively diminishing the SPF of the lotion you use until only baby oil is needed.

But again, I only had three hours, so I needed to go to defcon 5. The very slippery slope of trying to sense when just enough sun had been burned into my face to produce, after the three-hour incubation period, a searing red that would, throughout the night, evolve into a golden tan by the following morning.

I jumped into my rented Mustang convertible and headed for Malibu from my hotel. Thirty minutes later I was on the beach, my face baby-oiled. I genuflected, staring at the sun, my nose and lips carefully lubed with SPF 35. My nose, because it seems to get triple the sun the rest of my face does, which is surprising to me because, although it's big, I wouldn't think that by jutting out a little from the rest of my face and existing on a plane containing a slightly closer proximity to the sun, that much greater of an effect would occur. But it does. And my lips, because I get herpes sores on them if they're exposed to the sun sans extreme block.

Three hours later, it was five o'clock and, although it was February, the sun was still very hot. I felt my face was at the perfect point and I better err on the safe side. I headed back down the PCH to West Holly-wood. Aloe. Nivea. Room service in bed.

The greatest moment of my life was twelve hours away. It and I would be perfect.

Molly and her head of development, Sandra, were doubled over in the kind of hysterical laughter that is so sublime that, even if you don't partake, you feel happy for the people engaged in it because at some point in your life you experienced laughing that hard, at the funniest thing you ever heard, thought of, or saw.

Apparently, the sight of me was all three to these two women. It had to be because while I have been known to be fairly humorous upon occasion, I just don't think "Hi Molly, I'm Eric" was really all that funny.

My face was as red as a Cher dress when red was the new black, save the glaring white nose and ring around my mouth where I had applied the 35. The reason for the ring? When a man applies any sub-stance to his lips, not having done it ten times a day since he was two years old, like girls, he believes he hasn't fully gotten every bit of his lips covered unless the substance is smeared a good few inches *past* his lips, basically as high as his nose, as low as his chin, and cheek to cheek on either side.

"What happened to you?" Molly asked after the laughing fit subsided to the extent speaking was possible.

"I wanted to have a nice tan for our meeting. I have a system."

"I don't think it worked. Unless that's what you were going for, in which case, congratulations." Molly and Sandra began another round of belly laughter, tears flowing.

"I'm sorry. You just look . . . I don't even know like what."

"Thank you. Yeah. I'm pleased with the outcome as well. Thanks. So, nice to meet you. Thanks for taking the time." I extended my hand for a shake as I pretended to leave.

"No, no, please. We're sorry. This is Sandra. She's head of my development. We both loved your script."

It was a good script, but I'm convinced I got the meeting with Molly only because at one point in the screenplay the two romantic leads are having a fight and the guy says, "I'm not your John Cougar Mellencamp," and the girl replies, "And I'm not your Molly Ringwald." I realize based on that snippet it sounds like the script sucked, but it really didn't. It was the early '80s, so give me a break. Anyway, if you want to meet a famous actor, just reference them in your art. A line in a screenplay about them, a sculpture that even approaches their likeness, definitely a song. Forget the radio or an actual CD. A homemade demo left under their gate, humming it from the bus stop as they fill their car at the adjacent gas station. If you're anywhere close to on key, a song will get you laid by the most famous of the famous, for sure.

The meeting went great. Molly and I hit it off the way I thought we would, dreamed we would. As it was ending, that awkward moment happened when you want to ask someone out but their friends are there (in this case, my agent and her D-girl Sandra) and you feel embarrassed and you're not sure if she wants you to ask her out but you thought she was flirting with you but you don't want to risk being a fool in front of other people if you're wrong.

"I'll meet you at the car, Boyd." That got rid of one of them. Sandra either got the hint or wanted to appear professional or both.

"Nice to meet you, Eric. I hope we can find something to work on together. Good luck with the tan." She was off, and it was just me and Molly.

"I'll walk you out," she said and we left her bungalow. Just being on the Warner Brothers Studio lot was magic. Like you see in the movies. Rows of little terra-cotta bungalows partially hidden behind sharply manicured hedges. Blooming flowers lining shady stone walk-ways. Interns riding golf carts delivering water cooler tubs and manila-enveloped scripts to assistants who will sift through them, handing off whatever is important to movie stars you haven't jerked off to because you were saving yourself for this moment that you knew would happen.

I'm a clutch player, baby. I always have been. But this was the big leagues. And I didn't want to fuck up a chance to work with her if I was misreading her. I felt sure she wanted me to ask her out but I just couldn't be absolutely positive. We pawed at the ground with our feet and did anything to avoid eye contact as we stood outside her office. Boyd was at the car behind me twenty feet away like a father waiting for his fourteen-year-old after the movie. Except this time I was in the movie. And the movie was real.

"Well, it was really nice meeting you, Molly."

"You, too . . . Are you going back to New York tonight?" *Come on, now it's for sure! Ask her out. What do you need? For her to drop to her knees and unzip your fucking fly?!*

"No. I'm gonna stay out here a couple days." *Fucking pussy! Get to it!*

"Okay, well, I'll be eager to hear any ideas you come up with. I really like your writing." *Last chance, biggest pussy of all time.*

"Absolutely. It'd be awesome to do something with you." *What kind of ambiguous bullshit was that, fuckbaby?! You're pathetic. All fucking talk!*

"Molly? It's Stacy for you," Sandra yelled, sticking her head out of the office door.

"I'm sorry. I have to take that."

"Of course. Take care."

She turned. "You, too." And she was gone.

"I almost asked her out," I said to Boyd as we drove back over the hill to West Hollywood.

"Well for once I'm glad you didn't do something crazy like that. I think we can make a blind script deal with them, and that's way more important than a date with her."

"Not in my world. Love is way more important than a script deal. I mean, both would be the best scenario."

"Yeah, well just don't call her or do anything. I'll follow up when I get back to the office." He could see my mind racing. "DO NOT CALL HER!"

"I won't."

He dropped me off at my hotel.

"Hey. Don't be depressed. You did great. You might have just got your first script deal! Be happy. And put lotion on your face. And DO NOT CALL HER!"

"Thanks, Boyd." I got out and went into the lobby of my pathetic little hotel that suddenly didn't seem so much like the Beverly Hilton. I had wimped out massively. It was no consolation that I had showed "restraint" and wasn't "impulsive." Attributes of the boring. The unadventurous. Normal people. At twenty-eight, after driving a cab ferociously for seven years, writing ferociously for seven years, working to manifest my dreams, to manifest a moment, *the* moment . . . I had . . . and I had choked.

"Excuse me, Mr. Schaeffer? You have a message." The man behind the desk held out a single pink slip of paper. I knew what it was but didn't even dare think it.

Blackout.

A spotlight on the pink slip of paper.

Everything in slow motion. Everything else in darkness except for my lobster red face and white nose and mouth illuminating the pink piece of paper.

"Thhhhhaaaaaannnnkkkkk yyyyooooouuuuuu." I took the piece or paper and then suddenly everything seemed hyperreal. Tunnel vision. Real time. Nothing slow about it.

From: Molly
To: Eric Schaeffer
Give me a call. 310-555-3478. Molly

It wasn't her office number. Her *home* number?!
YESSSSSSSSSSSSSSSSSSSSSSS!!!!!!!!!!!!!!! I kept it inside.

"Thank you," I said to the man behind the desk and immediately went into the lobby bathroom where I found a free stall, hit my knees, and started praying.

"Dear God, help me not pick up a drink or a drug, no matter what she says. Thank you." At that point I had been clean and dry for eight years but it was in the exciting moments, the dream come true moments, that I was most afraid I could drink. When feeling down and out the will to win carried me. "Fuck that. I'll be damned if I let this make me drink." But when spinning in the eye of the hurricane that is your wildest dreams coming true, the cunning and wily disease that is alcoholism and drug addiction can spot an opening when you least expect it. So I went in for some added protection in a bathroom stall. My makeshift church.

The phone was ringing, my heart about to burst out of my chest. I quickly took a deliberate deep breath away from the phone so she wouldn't hear it if she picked up.

"Hello?"

"Molly?"

"Yeah?"

"It's Eric."

"Hey. You got my message."

"Yeah. How's it going?"

"Great . . . So I was just wondering . . . are you doing anything tonight?"

"No."

"Do you wanna have dinner with me?"

"Uhhhh, lemme think . . . Yeah. I would like to have dinner with you."

Cool. Let me give you my address and you can pick me up."

"Great."

I got off the phone and was absolutely beside myself.

OH MY GOD, MOLLY RINGWALD JUST ASKED ME OUT! My whole career I've taken such shit for making choices that if given the chance, every man, woman, and child would make. Like going out with Molly. Casting a supermodel in a movie as a romantic lead opposite me? Wow, what a nut I am. I could have as easily been embraced as a home-town kid who made good, representing for all those who hadn't gotten the chance to live some of their dreams, but instead I've had to suffer vitriolic player hating from some instead. It's sad, but you know what. I'll take it if that's the price I have to pay for being in the game.

I ended up living with Molly in her Mulholland Drive house while I wrote *If Lucy Fell*, designed for her to star in. She never referred to me as her "boyfriend" and I slept downstairs on a foldout in the den, though there was a lot of time spent together in other areas of her sprawling home. Because of who I was at that time in my life and the self-esteem I didn't have, I signed up for my keeping. I felt the secretive nature of our "friendship" was deeply opposed to the kind of relationship I wanted, and how she treated me was deeply opposed to how I wanted to be treated when in a relationship, but I was the only one at fault, I was a grown man with ample ability to change my circumstance if I had wanted to. But I was willing to take the scraps. I figured Molly scraps were better than nothing. That was a philosophy that I have unfortunately practiced on more than one occasion since with other women, and has taken me a long time to abandon. It has been completely eradicated now.

No one wanted to do *Lucy*, so Molly went off to do *Betsy's Wedding*, and I went back to New York. Not having taken over Hollywood, I had no choice but to get back in the cab, a place I had triumphantly slammed the door on a few months earlier declaring, "I will never be in you again!" Luckily, my hack license hadn't expired so, once again, I was "shaping up" at three o'clock with the Pakistanis at the Forty-sixth Street garage.

Molly and I had tea a month later at Café Lalo on Eighty-third Street, and she reported she was in love with someone she had met on her movie so whatever she and I had been doing was now officially over. I was heartbroken. I was deeply in love with her still.

My crushing demotion was complete; from Molly's hot tub in the Hollywood hills in May to the sauna that was a 1991 Ford LTD in August in New York.

The only vestige of that relationship's existence, acting as a living monument, a reminder never to go back to one of that kind again, is a Pavlovian condition grooved forever into my neuro pathways, obtained while living with Molly.

I'm badly allergic to cats. As a child, I suffered through weekly being-pulled-screaming-as-I-held-on-to-the-coatrack-for-dear-life,-my-little-body-being-stretched-horizontally-to-the-ground-by-two-nurses,-unwilling-to-let-go-until-a-third-pried—my-tiny-fingers-from-the-steel-pole episodes at the doctor's office for years, there to get shots for my condition. The promise of an ice-cream sundae afterward was the only thing that even had a chance of getting me out of my barricaded room in the first place. Molly had three long-haired ones.

She also thought my cat allergies were psychosomatic and that I should just "get over it." They weren't. I couldn't breathe for the entire time I lived with her. I would sit outside for hours in the middle of the night in order to breathe, my throat seizing up, my eyes puffy and itchy, sneezing constantly. But I was extremely attracted to Molly, so I stayed . . . and sneezed. Was attracted and sneezed. Attracted and sneezed. Kissing and sneezing. Making love and sneezing.

To this day, fifteen years later, as God is my witness, whenever I feel a rush of randiness with a girl, *any girl*, whether engaged in the act or even if I just think about something sexy that might happen with her, I sneeze. Over time its decreased in frequency but there's still at least always one good ACHOO per tryst!

April had the earmarks of another Molly. Whether those untenable qualities fully materialized and whether I had changed enough to be able to walk away quicker if they did, remained to be seen. And maybe I was wrong. While the spots looked similar, they might actually turn out to be the colorings of a different cat. Either way, for now, I was willing to investigate further, and pray it was the latter.

girls are the new boys

"Where are you?" I yelled into my Blackberry. I know. Sorry. Forgive me. The only saving grace is that when I do go trendy, I do it so late in the cycle; it's cute because I'm so far behind.

"I'm on the right side, by the bar," she yelled into the phone.

"I was just there and didn't see you. Meet me at the top of the stairs where the entrance to the roof is, okay?"

"Okay."

I couldn't differentiate between the party noise coming from the party all around me and the same party noise coming through her phone onto my phone. The disorientation made me even more annoyed than I already was to be at this packed Fifth Avenue rooftop "event" filled with drunken, smoking, twenty-somethings whose dream was to be in a Jay McInerney novel.

There were actually three parties occurring simultaneously on the Twenty-eighth Street rooftop, which did have a gorgeous view of the Empire State Building and the bright orange and purple sunset. The premiere party for the new season of *Queer Eye for the Straight Guy*, a summer solstice launch party thrown by Heather Von Socialite, and some investment bank party. There are few things on God's green earth I hate more than navigating wave upon wave of Stanford alumni and the wobbly, coke-whore "fashion biz" cigar-smoking trollops drafting in their wake, immune to the concern of spilling their whatever-tinis on me when they abruptly turn around to yell to their friends floating somewhere in the sea of children-in-adults'-bodies behind them, "Hey, dude! Shake Shack burgers!!! Ahhhhhh-yeeeeah boooooyyyy."

I had always wanted to try the renowned burgers myself, and

being in the neighborhood of Madison Square Park, which I rarely was, I thought this might be the night. But apparently not because in twenty minutes, anywhere Bradford and his friends had any chance of being was not a place I would ever be again, for the rest of my life.

I had agreed to meet April at this party for our second date as a good-faith display of my willingness to sometimes leave my house, as she was afraid I was a pathological shut-in. She learned about my need for personal time, "isolation" she called it, and many other personality traits during the multiple phone calls and e-mails we had had over the previous seventy-two hours, she from various locales during her mul- tievent weekend in the city, I from my couch in Vermont and by meeting her at this thing, I was killing two birds with one stone, not only proving I *could* be around large groups sometimes but also proving, by agreeing that our second date could include her sister and another friend, that I was interested in getting to know her close family and friends as well.

Like an unbelievably foul fart, Bradford's entourage finally cleared out through the front entranceway and was replaced by the sweet smell of April. She was standing by herself at the top of the stairs, looking for me. She looked so pretty and was put together perfectly. Perfectly in a good way. My heart instantly calmed. She had that effect on me . . . before she started talking.

Not that I didn't like her when she talked. I did. She had said many funny and interesting things since we had begun dating but she just had a different energy when she was talking. Her "on" energy, which was very different from her "at rest" energy. And then there was The Voice. Now, I will preface this by saying that affected voices are partic- ularly annoying to me, maybe not to you. That's not a button for you. For you, it's when your girlfriend continually asks you if you still love her, or compares you to her friend's boyfriend. See, that wouldn't bother me. (Okay, of course it would, but just not as much.) For me, it's voices. I've broken up with girls because they had no control over their voices. Or just flat-out refused to stop using them. April had one she used as a fallback anytime she was uncomfortable or trying to make a joke, so, a lot of the time. I was trying to be sympathetic and wait it out, hoping that after she felt more comfortable around me her use of The Voice would wane substantially. Think Julie Andrews meets Diane Keaton; starting out very high pitched, each word said in a very slow cadence and then falling down the mountain in key and register, increasing in speed along the way, ending at the bottom with the punch line.

"Aaaaaaaaaaaaaand theeeen he told me Iwas awhore and never-wantedtoseemeagain."

Her younger sister, Jacqueline, was sexy, tough, had ADD, a very recent very nice tit job, and a rapid-fire laugh she talked through. "He-HAHA-did-not-HAHA-say-that-to-you-HAHA-April!" Then to me, "So I hear you're a Mets fan." Then to Eleanor, their mutual friend April had met at Spence, "Should we get burgers at Shake Shack?"

"We could," April offered. Always the politician.

"Uh, I think the line is, like, two hours at this time. If you guys are up for it we could go to my friend Louie's place. Better Burger? It's on Nineteenth and Eighth, and has organic burgers and baked French fries?"

"Ooooooh, that sounds great." If Jacqueline was in then, like a parent with a fickle child, you wanted to seize the opportunity, lest you never find another acceptable one for eternity.

We piled into a cab and fifteen minutes later were crammed into a booth eating "healthy" burgers. April sat across from me on the outside of the booth; Jacqueline, on her left side; and their friend Eleanor, on my right. I felt strangely neglected by April who, while telling multiple stories, rarely, if ever, looked at me. Her audience was almost exclusively her sister and Eleanor, who seemed to show me the most interest out of the three. If you were an objective onlooker, you would have thought she was my date and not April. Again, I was trying to give April the benefit of the doubt. Maybe she was nervous, turning me out on such a grand stage in front of her best friend and sister. And on only our second date, no less. But still, I was getting annoyed. If she was going to ignore me *and* almost exclusively employ her Voice, I was going to get pissed. Then, out of nowhere, she looked me right in the eye and, in her normal voice—one that carried with it wisdom, maturity, and a sexy presence—said, "So, Jacqueline is concerned, but I told her that although you seem crazy, you're actually quite sensible and open. For instance. If you were married to a woman who was Jewish and you were Catholic. You wouldn't put down the other faith. You would raise the kids to understand and focus on the good parts of that faith, teaching them to appreciate it rather than despise it, along with espousing the best qualities of your Catholic faith, right?"

"Yes, I would. But you know I'm not Catholic."

"I do. That's not the point."

"And you're half-Jewish on both sides, so technically not Jewish."

"Right. Again, not the point. It was just an example. Let me finish . . . So, in the same spirit, if you were married to a Yankees fan, being a Mets fan, you would teach the children that the Yankees were good and allow them to choose who they were going to root for, for themselves. You wouldn't put the Yankees down, right?"

"Would I forbid my children from going to a Yankees game if they independently chose to be Yankees fans? Of course not. Just like I would support them in any career or sexual orientation they chose. And all their life choices, as long as they were loving to God and mankind. Now, having said that, I do think being children and having impressionable child minds; they need to be taught the cold, hard facts about the world they're living in to help facilitate them in making proper, informed decisions."

"Of course."

"Like rape, murder, and the Yankees are bad and wrong."

While April fought back a laugh, Jacki gasped for air, her frozen mind so shocked it momentarily lost power to signal her autonomic nervous system to inhale. Luckily, it quickly kicked back in and she found enough oxygen to fuel both a breath and a response. "Did he just equate the Yankees with rape and murder?"

"Listen. If after having all the information they still chose to be Yankees fans, then I wouldn't stop them. But I wouldn't be doing my job as a good parent if I didn't do everything in my power to dissuade them from joining the Cunt Empire. So in short, yes, I would require them to be Mets fans or I would disown them. Still love them, mind you, but not allow them in my home or life."

Jacki rose to leave. April stopped her.

"He's kidding."

"I don't think he is." Jacki stared at me for confirmation. April continued to try to diffuse the situation.

"I think we should be pleased. He's way more open than I thought he'd be. He said they could go to games and, if they chose to be Yankee fans, he'd let them be. That's all we asked for." Jacki sat back down and was on to seventeen other topics before her ass hit the seat. I suggested we go to my house for my special homemade vegan chocolate–chocolate-chip cookies for dessert. April and Jacki agreed but Eleanor was off to meet her boyfriend. My only ally was bailing. I would have to go it alone.

I put the cookies in the oven and returned to my living room. Jacki and April wrapped up their whispering. "What were you saying?"

"Oh, nothing." April said, lying. Unless "nothing" meant the full-frontal assault they launched into before the word "nothing" had left the air. Jacki was the stiff jab; April, the left hook of this powerful one-two Emily Post–Mike Tyson combination designed for a quick knockout.

J—"Why is your sofa ripped up?

A—"You don't have cats."

J—"Why do you have a huge terrace and not one stitch of patio furniture?"

A—"That's just weird."

J—"The apartment is nice but you have it decorated very frat-boy bachelor pad."

A—"And you're forty-four?"

J—"Why don't you work on Mondays?"

A—"Who are you not to work on Mondays just because you don't like to?"

J—"Why do you run in ninety-degree heat? It's not healthy."

A—"It's compulsive."

J—"Why do you only have one dish to make brownie mix in?"

A—"And why is it Tupperware?"

J—"Whywhywhywhywhywhywhy?"

A—"Whywhywhywhywhywhywhwhy?"

Unflappable, I paraphrased the inimitable words of Winston Churchill, responding calmly, "While I may have an old couch, ladies, you both are bitches. ABC Carpet will have a sale tomorrow and I can get a new sofa." I didn't say that. I did say this:

"Because there's no girl living here and I'm not gay." That shut them up long enough until, "The dessert's ready."

J—"He does make chocolate dessert, though."

A—"Yeah, but vegan."

"You'll never know the difference." And I headed for the kitchen.

"Thank you for the vegan brownies. They really were amazing," Jacki said as she stood waiting for the elevator in my hallway. April sexily listed into my side just enough to touch hips and let me know I should kiss her the minute her sister was gone.

"My pleasure."

"Brunch with Mom and Dad at Jane tomorrow at eleven?" April said, trying her damnedest to conceal her depression at the thought of it by feigning a happy face and like a Canadian McDonald's server, using an upwardly pitched inflection on "eleven" for forced, supersize enthusiasm.

"It'll be fun," Jacki said to her new fake tits as she admired and adjusted them. I wasn't sure if she was talking to them or her sister. "Oh my god! I forgot to tell you!" She was definitely talking to her sister now. She helped us recognize this by looking up at her. "I was in the elevator at work yesterday and I overheard this guy telling this girl about all the prices on the menu for à la carte domination! There's a dungeon on the ninth floor! Two hundred for 'golden showers,' whatever that is. A hundred and fifty for 'strap-on play.' I can only imagine . . . and five hundred for 'group rape scenes'!"

"Oh-HAHA-my-god-HAHA-can-HAHA-you-HAHA-imagine!"

"Where do you work? Thirty-third between Broadway and Fifth, or Twenty-eighth and Eighth?" I said straight-faced. I could feel April's eyes go wide and mouth fall agape like a dead trout. She stared at the side of my face, hoping against hope.

"Thirty-third, between Broadway and Fifth. How did you know?"

"It's the Nutcracker Suite." I turned to April, knowing at this point I needed to talk her off the ledge, or at least harness her to the building with those canvas straps the window washers wear. "I could tell you I know that because I've scouted it for a film or because Headmistress Hilda is one of my favorites . . . or both." I turned back to Jacki.

"And 'golden showers' is pissing on someone."

With a gag-laugh, hand over her mouth, Jacki disappeared into the elevator. I shut the door and faced April. She was about to pass out, slither out of the window-washer harness, and fall to her death seventeen floors below. The hair on the top of her head just below my chin smelled really good. I put my hands on her hips to hold her up and divert her to a happier land.

One of the upsides of dating repressed girls is that if you suddenly end a conversation that they find distasteful in the middle without any closure, not only will they not get angry, but in fact they'll be more than happy to act as if it never happened in the first place. I took advantage of that clause and, smiling at her, said, "You look really pretty." Everything was fine and forgotten . . . for the incubation period. It's only really a stay of execution. They always come back to it at some point. Without tipping her head up lest I think she was a girl angling for a kiss, she moved only her eyes to look at me. It would have been too obvious otherwise. As with all good repressed girls, everything she did had to happen out of sight and have a built-in plausible deniability. A hip-to-hip touch could easily be an accidental wobble, the product of tired legs from Pilates. That wasn't a batting-of-the-eyelashes-come-hither invitation, merely a polite smile from guest to host. For now her passive-aggressiveness made her all the more sexy to me and I figured my annoyance with all her judgments would make for some excellent making out, so I kissed her. She seemed eager. We kiss-shuffled as gracefully as possible over to the couch, where I pushed her down and boarded her. After about three or four kisses, "Is there a reason why the air-conditioning isn't on?"

"That's how interested in making out I'm making you? Thinking about the climate?"

"It's just really hot." I turned on the air-conditioning unit over her head and we resumed kissing. It wasn't instantly good kissing. It was passionate but we weren't in sync, which concerned me, but from what I knew and could sense about April, still waters might run deep, so I didn't think it would be a deal killer, kissing chemistry being the metaphor for all chemistry, sexual or otherwise. Not that I had great chemistry in every area with all the women I had great kissing chemistry with—sometimes yes, sometimes no. But the opposite was definitely true. If there was no kissing chemistry, there was no chance of anything long-term.

She stopped kissing again and looked at me as if we had been in the middle of a conversation and not heavily making out.

"Do you have any more of your brownies left?

"Yeah, but if I gave you any it would cut into my eating-disorder binging batch for after you leave."

"Oh."

"Sorry."

"No. That's fine."

"I'm kidding. I mean, I'm not, but I'll share."

"No, I didn't really want any more anyway."

"Just wanted to find another reason to stop kissing?"

"Can't we kiss and talk at the same time?"

"If we wanna not have fun, sure."

"Fine. We'll kiss."

"I don't want to twist your arm. If you're not into it."

"No. I am."

"How did you feel when I kissed you?"

"Oh now *you* wanna talk!"

"Just answer the one question."

"You can't just ask those kinds of questions to a person on a second date. You're much too forward, you know. Jeez. The first date you talk about where you went to college, the second date a little smootching, the third date maybe some sex and you go from there. You don't just ask someone how they feel about things."

"Okay. Sorry. Now I know." We started kissing again.

"Have you really been with a dominatrix?" I sat up abruptly. "You want Rice Dream on the cake?"

"Yes, please." We were done kissing and I was back on the stand.

Amber and the Persian

They say pot leads to heroin, and in my case it did, but then again drinking milk also led to heroin as did kissing my grandmother and saving abandoned puppies, if you want to get technical about it. I did a lot of things before I shot dope. I don't know that any necessarily were linked, cause and effect. But if pot did lead to heroin, you might draw the similar conclusion that whores led to dominatrices. They did come first.

I never even considered sleeping with a prostitute until I was thirty-three. Me and Jesus Christ. At least I was in good company. Except in my case, I was the only one who crucified myself for it. My Mary Magdalene was this kind of cute, plump coed from an escort agency that I called at three in the morning after a Friday night taping of *Too Something*, the sitcom Donny and I had on Fox in 1995. I was living in the gatehouse of this massive stone castle called Wolf's Lair that faced Madonna's house and overlooked the Hollywood sign and reservoir. An effete sixty-year-old gay couple, Mr. Fray and Mr. Elkington, lived in the main house, and I rented the small building that overlooked the drawbridge entrance to the mansion that Mr. Wolf had built in the early 1900s.

My house felt like the inside of Rock Hudson's yacht. Off windy hallways were little rooms with dark red cedar-paneled walls and deep green felt paintings of dogs playing poker. A strange homoerotic slate sculpture that sat on the dry bar pointed the way through sliding glass doors to a secret passageway. It was a dark, moss covered, stone stairway that ended at a thick oak door that opened onto the street next to the front gate and another single, nondescript door.

The tiki room.

It was amazing. Mr. Wolf had built the tiki room as a place to throw secret lurid parties for his friends and the chorus girls of the 1920s. It was replete with the original leopard-print ceilings, wicker furniture, lush red couches, and player piano. You could cut the spirits in that place with a knife. I once came home late after a show and heard the faint sound of a radio. Following it, fire poker in hand, I was led to the tiki room, where I hadn't been for days. I turned off the radio and returned upstairs. I didn't feel in danger; as with both of my ghostly encounters, they just felt like playful or curmudgeonly ghosts, out for mischief not harm. The second episode occurred just a few years ago, when I was locked out of my farmhouse in Vermont. I had locked the door when I left, leaving the chain off and deadbolts open, obviously. When I returned after a long day and night of filming, the door was still locked but the deadbolt had been thrown. I broke in through a window and confirmed it. The only way to lock the deadbolt is from the inside. Creepy. I just asked the ghosts nicely not to do that again. My half–American Indian cleaning lady surmised the ghosts were annoyed I had had a forty-person crew in and out of the house the previous week, filming, and wanted to lock them out. They were used to, at most, me, Liza, and maybe one other couple. It made sense to me.

* * *

The one time I was picked up by a girl who was watching the live taping of *Too Something* at the sound stage (an occurrence I had wrongly assumed, like a rock star having a bevy to choose from after every performance, would happen with regularity), I took her to the tiki room where, for the first and only time in my life, the condom broke and she got pregnant. The ghosts disapproving? After the orgies that must have gone down in that room, you might have thought they would cut me some slack. Donny was convinced the girl was somehow trying to get money.

"Come on. She shows up at our show, picks you up from the audience, and then gets pregnant?"

"She didn't give me the broken rubber, it was mine."

"I don't know . . . "

Even though deep down I didn't think this girl was anything other than sweet, well-intentioned, and the covictim of an awful accident, with my vividly paranoid mind I did have a few terrifying hours until I got her on the phone and discerned that we were like-minded in that the only option unfortunately was an abortion, which I took her to get a week later.

It scared me enough that I didn't seek anymore transient companionship from strangers and, as had been the case for quite some time, my first choice of finding a girlfriend wasn't happening, so I was profoundly lonely. It was surreal. I was making a lot of money on my own network TV show, living in a castle, driving a brand-new charcoal gray six-speed convertible Porsche (people said it was an image I might want to rethink. I didn't give a fuck about what "image" it gave me, I just cared that it cornered on rails at 85 mph, tight as a roller coaster, on Mulholland), playing basketball during breaks on the lot with George Clooney because the ER soundstage was next to ours, chatting with Jennifer Aniston on the way to the commissary because the *Friends* stage was on the way, and being treated like a king by everyone and their mother. Hundreds of fans would cheer me as they watched us tape the show and then, after the ritualistic feast at Kate Mantalini's on

Wilshire at two A.M., which consisted of a twenty-four-ounce porter-house, mashed potatoes, two eggs over easy, bacon, French fries, toast, and warm chocolate cake with ice cream, I would end up staring at the dark walls of my ship/home alone at four A.M. Shouldn't I be at a cool party with a hot girl on my arm? Shouldn't I at least have a hot girl with me in bed? A friend to watch TV with, some fucking thing?

Too Something hadn't aired yet, so it was even weirder. It was August and we were making episodes that wouldn't air until October; I felt even more in a vacuum. I felt different than I had my whole life, nei-ther like a regular person who worked for minimum wage, nor like a famous person. I was in no-man's-land, and Donny had a girlfriend he lived with so he couldn't hang. I never felt more alone than I did that summer. *There must be some solution.*

Brainstorm. Buy a companion!

I looked in the phone book. *Under massage?* I'm telling you, I'd never even contemplated this before, let alone tried it. *"E?" Exotic dancers? There can't be a prostitutes section? "P?" No. What are they called again . . . ? Oh, right. Escorts!* I looked under Escorts. I called an agency that advertised "College Girls" and asked for a tall, thin, white, nineteen-year-old American girl. They said they had just what I was looking for and that she would be over in twenty minutes. It was 4:10 A.M. I told them to have her there in thirty minutes at the most, because I needed her to be gone by five thirty so I could fall asleep by six before the predawn birds started chirping and I got an anxiety attack brought on by the flashback memories of my all-nighter cocaine days. I didn't give them the entire explanation but they assured me nonetheless that she would be there in twenty minutes. I went down to the tiki room and waited excitedly, my heart pounding. *What would she look like? Would she be hot? Would I save her from her whoring life, fall in love, and marry her like in Taxi Driver or Pretty Woman?* Fifteen minutes seemed like an hour. She would be there in five minutes. BUT WAIT! What if she was a cop?! What if I was going to get arrested?!

"I just have one question. What were you thinking?" Jay would ask again on my inaugural *Tonight Show* appearance if I went through with this. I got really scared. *What are the entrapment laws, again? I have to be naked the entire time? No, I can't be naked at any time. She has to be naked before I get naked? I have to be naked first and then if she gets naked I can't get arrested? No, wait! If I ask her, she has to tell the truth! Right! That's it! But wait, on* Cops *and* America's Most Wanted,* *the johns always ask the girl cops pretending to be streetwalkers if they're cops and the girl cops always say no and they arrest them anyway, so I think that rule is a myth.*

To add to my rapidly rising anxiety, minutes started ticking away past the twenty I had been promised it would take for the police force to arrive. It was thirty. Then forty. At forty-five, I called and they assured me she was on the way and would be there any moment. I thought of canceling her but my fear was trumped by my loneliness.

Another hour and three more calls later, at 5:50 A.M. there was a knock on the tiki room door. Even as crazy as I was, I felt certain I would be breaking no laws if I let her in. Tentatively, I crept toward the door. My cheek brushed against a fake straw palm frond. It scratched me and hurt. Suddenly, a thought flew into my head triggered by the violence visited upon me at the hands of the bogus tropical tree. *How could I have been so stupid not to consider this before now?!* I had been distracted by my anger at her tardiness and the fantasies of ending up in the L.A. equivalent of the Tombs, and hadn't been thinking clearly.

What if she is going to kill me? Rob me and kill me with her pimp or whatever? But she was in the phone book! Listed! Yeah, so was Son of Sam. Another knock. Should I pretend not to be home? Come on, you pussy! I mean at this point you at least have to get a blow job. Arrested, beaten, and robbed, whatever. The penis must ejaculate.

"Yeah. Hi. Are you alone?" I yelled at the door. There wasn't a peephole.

---

* *America's Most Wanted* was my first TV writing job ever. I got fired for embellishing. My boss asked, "Did he say, 'Look, if you snap her knuckles like a pig the ring just slides right off' while he was killing her?" "No, but he didn't *not* say it? He must have said something! He's a white-trash butcher turned killer in Joplin, Missouri, hired by his plumber–best friend to kill his cheating wife for three New York strip steaks and ten pounds of ground sirloin. He's a bad man. You're worried about a libel suit from death row?" I replied. I lasted one month.

"Did you call for a date?"

"Well. I called for a 'companion,' yeah. Are you alone?"

"Of course, sweetheart."

I slowly opened the door. She *was* alone. Neither tall, nor nineteen, nor hot, but alone.

"Hi, I'm Amber."

She brushed past me quickly. Her half bottle of hooker perfume choked me. After my eyes stopped watering I could see a black town car idling in the dirt parking area a hundred feet up the road.

"Who's that?"

"My driver, silly. I'm not gonna hitchhike home."

Satisfied, I shut the door.

"Did you just wanna take care of the payment now, then?" she asked like a checkout counter salesperson at Wal-Mart.

"Before?"

"Yes. Why don't we just take care of it now." She was using a more authoritative tone now, obviously having been trained for this sort of resistance.

"Okay." I reached into my pocket and summoning all my courage blurted out, "You're not a member of any law enforcement agency are you?"

"Of course not." She laughed. "Are you?"

"No."

"Good. Then we can have some fun."

She was cute enough. Plump, stuffed into a beige dress, big tits, and twenty-seven. A little wired on coke but at that point, as long as she neither arrested nor killed me, she was Michelle Pfeiffer. I gave her two hundred bucks in twenties. She counted it and put it in her purse.

"Can I see some ID please?" She asked matter-of-factly.

"Excuse me?" I was terrified. I hadn't planned for that question. *What could that possibly be about?*

"I just need to verify your identity. Driver's license?" *What, now she's renting me a car? How many fucking jobs does this prostitute have?*

"Uh . . . " *I'm famous, Miss Whore. I can't end up in the tabloids or be black-mailed for life by you and your toothless crackhead boyfriend-pimp from Bakersfield.* "I'm sorry. I don't have that."

"Do you have anything? Birth certificate? Military card?"

"Listen. I'm me. Dave. Just regular Dave. Everything's cool. I just paid you and now can't we just—"

"I have to call in. Can I use your phone?"

"Who do you have to call?"

"My agency, to tell them I'm here and everything's cool and ask them what to do since you refuse to show ID."

"I'm not really 'refusing' to show ID. I just don't really see why that's—"

"Can I just use your phone, please?"

"Sure."

She dialed. At this point, needless to say, my dick had receded to somewhere in China's night sky and could only be located by using the Hubble telescope. For its recession to be countermanded, causing an actual move toward erection, an act of God would have to occur including, in my humble opinion, nothing short of Cindy Crawford begging to do unimaginably dirty things to me for eternity as an appetizer, followed by a main course consisting of a second eternity spent with the remainder of the Victoria's Secret models past and present doing anything I commanded to each other and to me. I didn't think "Amber" was going to do the trick, but let's just get past the screening process alive and then worry about that.

"Hi. It's Amber, I'm here and everything is fine except he doesn't have any ID. Yeah. Yeah. Uh-huh. Uh-huh. Uh-huh. Okay. She wants to talk to you."

I took the phone. "Hello?"

"Hi, this is Jamie from the agency. Is everything all right?"

"Yeah, it's fine. I just don't really think it's necessary to show any ID. I'm fine. I'm Dave and I gave her the payment." "Dave" started sounding creepier to me the more I uttered it. Like a name only ever used by people lying about their real name because they were skeevy perverts and accidentally, out of nervousness, had come up with a name that actually made them sound even more depraved then they already felt. But the ship had sailed, so I had to go with it.

"And what's your last name, Dave?"

"Johnson. Dave Johnson. David actually," that helped a little. "David Johnson."

"Right, David Johnson. And why don't you have any ID, Mr. Johnson?"

"I don't know, and I don't really want to talk about all this; I just really want to . . . at this point, it's six the morning, she was supposed to be here two hours ago and . . . "

"Could I speak to Amber, please?"

I passed the phone back to Amber.

"Hi. Uh-huh. Uh-huh. Uh-huh."

I was about to pass out with fear, rage, exhaustion, kill her, kill myself . . . *What could they possibly be discussing?* I mean how many options in this situation could there be. Blow him or don't blow him.

"Okay. Great. Bye." She hung up.

"Everything okay?"

"Yeah. Can I have something to drink?" She sat on the red sofa where I had unwittingly impregnated the girl from the audience of my show, and put down her bag. She was getting comfy. Sweet.

"Uhhhh, I have water."

"No, honey. Vodka?"

"No, I don't really drink."

"Any alcohol at all?"

"No. I've been sober for eight years."

"No, I don't care about you. I meant for me."

"No. Sorry."

"Never mind, then."

She looked around, finally able to take in the tiki room in all its splendor. Her hands were folded on her lap and she seemed as asexual as you imagine your mother to be. I sat next to her. Maybe she just needed to warm up.

The hooker . . . Needed to warm up.

"So now what?" I asked. That was my ultracool icebreaker.

"What do you mean?" She seemed genuinely confused by my question.

"What do we do now?"

"Now we talk."

"For two hundred dollars we talk?"

"Yeah. What did you think was gonna happen?"

"I thought we would . . . " *Is this the point I get arrested? Can I even say the words legally?*

"I thought we would get . . . more . . . comfortable with . . . each other."

"No. We just talk."

Excellent. I'm so pathetic I can't even get whores I've paid to fuck me. I sent her away five seconds later and went upstairs to bed, my first foray into prostitution having cemented my standing as the biggest nerd in the world.

I may be uncool, but a quitter I am not. I would pick myself up off the tiki room floor and live to fight another day, and that day came a year later back in New York after my show got canceled and Donny and I stopped talking in the ugly fallout. I was again lonely and alone in my apartment, but armed with the first time under my belt, I got back on the whorse.

This time, being the seasoned prostitution veteran I was, I looked in the back of the *Village Voice*, believing I would find a higher class of hooker there than in the phone book. (For those of you not familiar with the *Village Voice*, that would be tantamount to having the misguided idea that you could get a better steak at Arby's than Peter Luger.) I ordered up a girl with the same specs as the last time. Tall. Thin. Nineteen. American. They, of course, had just the girl. And only thirty minutes past the twenty

I had been promised she arrived, a short, olive-complected thirty-three-year-old Persian woman. Again, she had big breasts and wore beige. The it color for that hooker season, apparently. I was beginning to get the idea now that they counted the size of the breasts toward the height of the prostitute and it all just evened out in the end, or, could it be that they sent over any girl knowing that you were a lonely, horny man, who after waiting for hours and just wanting to cum and go to sleep, would accept anyone? Basically lying to you? No, that couldn't be. I must be missing something. Maybe a lack of communication. I would just have to be a little more specific next time. Not leave anything like "tall" up for interpretation.

See, cumming is not at all what I'm really after, and, not being much different from the next guy, I believe it is not what most men are after. I want to buy a girlfriend for an hour. My fantasy is like in a western movie. The tough guy rolls into town and his beautiful, Farrah Fawcett–dirty blond-St. Paul–girl–looking lass has been waiting for him, leaning against the wooden beam on the balcony of the bar/brothel. She waves him in, smiling ear to ear, and bathes him while they laugh and eat and make love. Only some strange twist of fate has her working in a whorehouse, a drunk, soulless, shell of a woman, fucking countless, faceless men, and he killing harmless, honest ranchers on the open plains, stealing their wagon trains and raping their wives and children. In a parallel universe they'd be living on a small ranch together with eight kids and a couple of horses, in love, churning butter, and watching the sun set over the canyons, the subjects of a wildly successful TV drama starring Michael Landon 150 years later.

Love is what I'm after for my two hundred bucks an hour. The sex part is just what happens as the natural result of a great date. Talking, laughing, flirting, and then fucking.

So the Persian comes in and is much cooler and more relaxed than Amber from L.A. It was a little awkward, but that was just because I was still a tiny bit nervous. I asked her if she was a cop. She laughed, said no, and then asked me if I was. I paid her and she took off her blouse, revealing very nice and large breasts, again, of course, in a beige bra.

We ended up having sex, though with my AIDS paranoia that meant a fully covered blow job and then very fast and not very involved intercourse. I was kind of grossed out by the whole event, not really wanting her whore perfume on my bed or my condom-covered dick in her pussy for very long, so the strokes were quick and shallow, just enough to get me off quickly.

I took off the rubber and threw it in the toilet, keeping the door open and one eye on what she was doing. I really didn't have anything for her to take, but just having a strange criminal in my home was unnerving. I felt like a teenager who had just popped his cherry. Well, how I thought one would feel. I, of course, hadn't felt that way when I lost my virginity, but had gotten a second chance with Persia. I felt young and coy yet as if I had become a man. She got dressed and I asked if we could talk for a while, still having half an hour in the bank. She was fine with that. I confessed my strange first misfire in L.A. and she was sympathetic. I asked her about her life and what had brought her to this point. She was free flowing and forthcoming. She had a male whore boyfriend, and had come to New York for school years before. She felt very sexually open, liked the money, didn't mind the stigma and her man worked in the same profession, so it was all good. She left me with a kiss on the cheek and it was over.

In the past ten years, I've dabbled. I've met some lovely women, some really hot women, had some nice times, some boring times, and been robbed by "protectors" who appeared out of back rooms demanding full payment when I wanted to leave before the event because the women looked nothing like what were advertised. I later learned that there are plenty of web sites and newspapers where you can see a picture of the girls first, and even Web sites where guys post reviews of the girls so you can get a sense of their performance and photographic authenticity, the only problem being that it's hard to suspend disbelief of their chastity and devotion to you when you've read how they fucked forty-six other guys in the last two days. Kind of like how you don't want to look in the kitchen of your favorite restaurant.

But the bottom line is the real draw is the rush of who will show up at the door, and will she pretend to be my girlfriend, and will she be good at it. I once had a prostitute ask me what I wanted.

"For you to love me," I said.

She grimaced and said, "I don't do that. If you want love, get a girlfriend."

"For two hundred bucks you won't pretend, even for just an hour?"

"Not for all the money in the world and not for even five minutes, friend."

Ray

So, acutely aware that love is really what I'm after and that prostitutes are apparently not willing to provide any, even inauthentically for an hour, I stopped buying them a few years ago. But I've been single since Liza and I broke up in January 2000, and I can get very lonely. While I partake in one-night stands and booty calls occasionally, I have deep ambivalence about them, since a serious relationship is what I'm really interested in. The sexual companionship and female warmth is very nice but, as I've progressed in seeking a spiritual path, sex has actually gotten to be a way more intimate act than it once was, and doing it with someone I'm not in love with, or at least in a committed relationship with, ends up feeling, yes, you guessed it, kind of empty. And then there's my pesky "no sleepover rule." A lot of women have a hard time with that one. I just feel it's way too intimate to spend the night with someone if I'm not in a relationship with them. Yes, I think it's much more intimate than having sex so very very rarely do I allow it with a booty call girl and even though they know the rule ahead of time, they can get a little agitated when it's enforced at 3A.M. For the odd occasion when I feel comfortable enough to have a friend stay over, I have an extra pillow in the closet that makes an appearance. I have to carefully comb it for stray hairs as it would be inhospitable if a red-haired friend found a long black hair on it. I only sleep with one pillow myself and since the "friend pillow" is so rarely used, I can forget to inspect it. Luckily, I haven't been busted yet and all has been smooth, but as you can see, it's just easier all the way around if they take a quick cab ride home and we all sleep in our own comfy beds alone. But not everyone sees it like I do, though. One of my dear plutonic friends, Hilary, who was once one of my hottest booty call friends, was a teacher and would come over at 4 o'clock in the afternoon after school, the time of the day when I am at my absolute randiest. (I think it's because as a kid when I was first becoming sexual, it was always after school.) She got to the point where her rule was "no sex unless I can stay over." The two rules kind of conflicted, and I know you think you know which one triumphed, but you'd be wrong if you guessed hers. Although I loved having sex with her, it wasn't worth all the tension that came with having a girl sleep in my bed who wasn't my girlfriend.

But after months of celibacy, at a certain point I just gotta make sure the shit still works; I mean, it gets ridiculous. A person has to get laid once in a while, for fuck's sake. Still though, it feels a little sad that the object of my affection in those trysts isn't the girl of my dreams, so I don't do it that often and, inevitably, when the frequency increases, I end up feeling as though I'm expending energy that would be better spent elsewhere. Work, workouts, spiritual practices, evolving friendships, hanging with my mom, anything.

So, a few years ago, without even any booty calls to satiate me, I decided to dabble in phone sex but it was tough to find a girl who took pride in her work and gave me what I wanted instead of just trying to keep me on the phone to run up the bill.

"What do you look like, Ginger?"

"Well, I want to know what you look like first, Dave." *You know, Ginger, I already know what I look like and for five bucks a minute I don't give a fuck if you know or not, I mean, unless you'd like to pay me to get you off in which case I'd* be more than happy to spend all night telling you all about my big, thick, ten-inch cock but short of that if you could just shut the fuck up and tell me how big your tits are, I'd appreciate it! I would end up getting annoyed and then get a headache and the mood was ruined. It doesn't get much lower than rejecting your own sexual advances on yourself using the excuse of a headache to get out of having to have self-sex.

I found a loophole, which worked well for a while. I would fluff myself, manually of course (I'm not one out of the hundred guys statistically flexible enough to blow myself, and wonder if I would do it even if I could. Who am I kidding? A blow job whenever you wanted one? Anyway, even with yoga I'm still not even close), and get a good hard-on working, and then make the call, so I could pop within a minute or two of getting on the phone with the gal and not waste thousands of dollars with the preliminaries. However, it backfired one day when, in my preorgasmic frenzy, trying to time it all perfectly, I accidentally dialed another very familiar similar 976 number, "Hey everyone, Howie Shine for Sports Line! The Knicks lost again 96–87 . . . " Not only was my boner gone in a flash, so was a hundred bucks, as I had the Knicks plus-six that night. The bitches couldn't even cover. That sense memory put a stop to the phone sex girls.

After the Persian girl, I mainly just looked at prostitutes' pictures and called inquiring as to their availability while jerking off, having no intention of employing them. The best of all worlds is a thirty-second phone call. I got the rush of wondering who might show up, cum, and all with no worries about diseases, robbery, or arrest. And I saved the two hundred bucks. But after a few years, the novelty wore off and I needed to be touched by a living woman. I had an occasional fling after the Liza breakup, it's not like I hadn't gotten laid at all, but had no second dates and no love. I was marooned on an island of celibacy until a friend told me about "rub and tugs." They sounded appealing for many reasons, not the least being they would help me not obsess on whether I got AIDS through the rubber from a prostitute's saliva, which of course is impossible. (But apparently "impossible" is not good enough for me, since I've been tested after every illicit blow job. Though only five or six times in twelve years, still immensely nerve-racking.)

I tried one and they were genius! I couldn't believe they existed! Where had I been?! It was the spring of 2000, three months post-Liza and I was back in L.A. acting on a midseason NBC show, First Years. I was also developing my own show at Fox.

I was living in the Oakwood Apartments, corporate housing for East Coast actors temporarily in L.A. for pilot season or the first year of a show, who don't want to commit to buying or renting a proper house for fear that their show might get canceled or that they might not land one in the first place. I liked the apartment feel of Oakwood. It reminded me of home, which was important because though I like many things about L.A., I inevitably feel my soul is slowly siphoned off when I'm there for more than a month.

I was in the Marina Del Rey Oakwood complex two blocks from the beach. I figured if you're going to be in LA, you should be near the water. I reunited with my old college friend Steve, whom I used to party with before we both got sober. He got clean a couple of years after I did, was living out there full time, working as a journalist, and turned me onto a Web site that advertised "Massage Girls" who provided happy endings. He vouched for their authenticity and manual prowess and, at seventy bucks for half an hour, one hundred for a full hour, they were less than half the price of prostitutes. Not that I was looking to buy a bargain girlfriend but, if it was a fun experience and some savings came along with it, what the hell.

I called Ray, a sexy, short, blond girl with big tits and an inviting smile. She advertised being twenty-seven, meaning thirty-three, which I liked. I wanted an adult. Someone I might actually be able to connect with, even if only for an hour.

Her apartment was only a couple of blocks from Oakwood, so I made an appointment for an hour later and drove over. I got there ten minutes early and sussed out the place. It was in a nice neighborhood and seemed benign. Having had a decent amount of whoring experience to draw from at that point, I wasn't nearly as scared as the first time with the "college girl" concubine in the castle. It was the standard two-call system. You call to set the appointment. They give you the general vicinity of where they live, you go there, call again, and they supply you with the exact address. They put you through the *Dirty Harry* runaround from phone booth to phone booth to prove your sincerity about keeping the appointment, if they don't already know you. They double-book in case you don't show, just like the dentist, doctor, and airlines, so the first time you usually have to wait a little until your "backup" is finished.

I went up to the front door, still a little cautious, and rang the buzzer. A different girl than the one in the picture answered. Although I didn't appreciate the dishonesty, she was hot so I didn't mind the bait and switch, which is usually the worst.

"Hi, I'm Beth. Ray's roommate. (The usual story. "Ray had to run out but I could see you if you want.") Come in. She's just getting ready for you."

Oh. It wasn't a bait and switch after all, and Beth was sweet, to boot. Maybe I would sign up for a little two-girl special. I sat down, deciding I would try Ray alone first just to check out the experience, and then would upgrade the next time if I wanted to.

It was a nice little Spanish-style villa in Venice, decorated kind of hip and funky as if two struggling actresses lived there, which, duh, probably did. The bedroom door opened and Ray, looking exactly like her picture, warmly greeted me with a smile and a hug, pressing her full body and big breasts firmly against me.

"Hi, Eric. I'm Ray. So, you're here for a half hour?"

"Yes." Already the vibe was *light years* better than any I'd had with a prostitute. Ray was direct, present, sweet, friendly, sexy, and seemed genuinely interested in me. I went into her bedroom, which was bordello-meets-mod. A red silk Chinese tiger tapestry hung behind her massage table, a big mirror on the wall to the left of it, strategically placed I was later to find out. I'm the perfect audience for movies and certain life experiences that feel like a movie. Complete suspension of disbelief. I never try to figure out the plot, I just roll with it, so I'm often surprised by things the normal person wouldn't be, for better and worse. I stripped and started to get on the table, but then reached back for my jeans, remembering I had to pay first.

"Sorry, I forgot the donation. Seventy, right?" *Donation* is the operative term used in the prostitution industry to protect them from any illegality. I assumed it was the same in massage. They usually prefer not to even discuss payment or physically take the money from you. They like you to just inconspicuously leave it on a chair or dresser.

"Oh, yeah. That's what I ask, but whatever you want is fine. We can take care of that later." *Whatever I wanted and later?* This was amazing. She was like a regular girl! What I always had wanted out of this kind of thing! I got on the table. She dropped her slinky blue silk teddy and had nothing on underneath.

"You wanna start on your stomach?"

"Perfect." I got on my stomach, my head turned to the left. I could feel the slightly cold dribble of oil as it landed on my back. It became a thick stream, followed quickly by her hands.

"Turn your head the other way."

Not knowing why but trusting her, I obeyed and, ahhhhhh. The mirror. There she was mounting me from behind, her shaved pussy grinding into my ass as she deeply rubbed my back. She smiled at me in the mirror.

"Does that feel good?"

Trick question? "Uhhhh. Yeah. That feels good."

"Good." She leaned over and started caressing her big, firm breast against my back as her hands crept down my sides to my hips. This was certainly a "full body-to-body massage" all right, and it was magic. And Ray loved catching glimpses of herself in the mirror doing it to me, which was cute. She massaged my whole backside from head to toe. She was skilled and had great hands. It was a real massage.

I had been hard from the moment she poured the oil on my back. After she finished with my feet, she started teasing my ass. I was about to come at this point from anticipation, like when I was sixteen and blew a wad in my underwear before Rachael Goldstein from Great Neck, whom I had met at an Allman Brothers concert at the Beacon Theatre, even got to my belly button. She had been systematically kissing my chest, heading south, and I stopped her abruptly before she could unbutton my jeans and find a mess instead of a hard cock waiting to be sucked and said, "I really like you and I think we should stop now. I don't want to go too fast and ruin it." She thought I was the most noble teenager she had ever met.

Being slightly more practiced now in the skills of the cum control, I paced myself, though Ray was making it awfully hard. She slowly moved her hand between my thighs from behind and reached under me, moving from my balls to my dick. The "reach around." Exceptional. Like you know how good it feels when the CMT masseuse is doing your head at the end of the massage and they reach their hands under your back and use your own body weight to dig deep into your neck and upper back? Imagine that but on your dick, and since it's also what you've been fantasizing would happen in every legit massage you've ever had, the fruition of the dream makes it unimaginably hot. And it's from behind, like it's forbidden and no one's allowed to know about it. Everything conspires to make it one of the sexiest things in the universe.

"You wanna flip over?" Oh, yeah. I was ready for "the flip." As the term suggests, the complete opposite vibe of the "reach around." Unabashed, unapologetic cock-stroking for all the world to see! I rolled over on my back and she dumped another heaping sploosh of oil on me, and started jerking me off. She was suddenly in another mode. No more teasing, just ferocious, resolved dick-jerking, which she was completely into and obviously getting turned on by. Then she mounted me and titty-fucked herself on me as I lay on my back until I came ridiculously hard. She lay on me out of breath and sweaty, gathering her wits. I really felt she had been moments away from slipping me into her and fucking the shit out of me and had summoned all of her professional strength not to do it. After a sly smile she said, "That was hot," and left me spent on the table as she went to the bathroom. She returned with a hot, wet towel, and geisha girl cleaned me up. It was heaven. She started talking to me as she wiped me off. But it wasn't obligatory small talk to mask the uncomfortable aftermath of anonymous whore sex, as with prostitutes. I once had a prostitute look me right in the face while she was giving me a hand job and, as if we were in a job interview in an office and not lying on my bed naked with her hand stroking my dick, say, "So, are you married? You have any kids?" It was creepy. But this was the opposite. Ray really seemed into me.

"Are you from New York?" She asked.

"How could you tell? I don't have an accent."

"Just you're whole attitude. I'm from the East Coast. Baltimore. What are you doing out here? Pilot season?"

"No, I'm actually doing eight episodes of a midseason replacement for NBC." Unlike with prostitutes, to whom I was afraid to give any personal information, I felt completely trusting of her.

"Cool. What's it called?"

"*First Years.* It's a legal drama. It's not mine, I'm just acting on it. I have my own show in development at Fox."

"Oh, really? Me, too. Who's your executive?" *Get the fuck out of here. Well, it is L.A.*

"Josh Gershstein?"

"Oh my god! Me, too! Isn't that funny?" *Yeah. Hysterical.*

"Totally. Is it about this?"

"Oh god, no."

"Does he know you do this? Do you do him?"

"No and no. I love doing this but I don't run around telling everyone. I do have a lot of clients in the entertainment industry and some of them have been really sweet and helped me in my writing career but there are still too many people who wouldn't understand, so I keep it on the down low. I'd appreciate it if you would, too."

"Oh, of course."

"I had a lot of fun, Eric. I hope you'll come back and see me again."

"Me, too, and I definitely will." She kissed me tenderly on the cheek. I put my jeans on and left her a hundred, thirty as a tip. She didn't count it, and I knew she would have been as nice if I hadn't tipped her at all.

It was a perfect experience. I finally found exactly what I had always been looking for in the rent-a-girlfriend trade but never hitherto gotten from prostitution, and it was 100 percent safe. As long as I remembered to check their hands for cuts, even my insane mind couldn't obsess that I could get AIDS from what they had done to me. I definitely planned to see Ray again, but I thought I might try a few other girls out as well.

The next day I was in the community laundry room at the Oakwood, folding my underwear, when my cell phone rang. It was a 323 number that I didn't recognize.

"Hello?"

"Eric?"

"Yeah?"

"Hey. It's Ray." *I knew I wasn't wrong and that she liked me!*

"Hey, Ray. How's it going?"

"Great. So, I was wondering if you wanted to have dinner with me tonight." Being asked out by two girls in ten years seemed pretty great to me. First Molly and now Ray. Women don't understand the global exhaustion men feel always having to be the pursuers. I'm telling you, for the average guy like me, I'm sure it's different for gorgeous model guys and famous or rich guys but guys like me, having a girl ask you out once a decade is the oasis you need to replenish your strength for the other nine years, eleven months, and twenty-nine days when you have to do EVERYTHING to even have a shot at a date. But, alas, I had to turn her down.

"I had an awesome time with you yesterday, Ray, and I think you're smart and funny and hot . . . but I just don't think I could handle going out with a girl who had your job."

"That's such a double standard."

"No, it's not at all. I love that the job exists. I love that you do it. I have absolutely no judgments against the job itself or the people who do the job. Thank God for it all, because clearly I like to indulge and, if you and it didn't exist, I couldn't. I just don't think I'm the kind of guy who could deal with having a girlfriend who did the job and I want a girlfriend, so if I go on a date and I like you and have fun I'm gonna want to see you again and have it progress, so I feel like why start if I know I can't ultimately live with it if we become boyfriend-girlfriend. Does that make sense?"

"No. I do massage. I'm not having sex with my clients. I'm not a prostitute. It's just massage. You couldn't have a serious relationship with a masseuse?"

"Okay, Ray, will all due respect, call it whatever you want but, to me, it's sex."

"No. Sex is intercourse. I don't even give oral sex or kiss or anything. I just do massage. I don't see the big deal."

"Ray. I can't have my girlfriend jack off ten guys' dicks in between her tits with her fingers up their asses and have them come on her face during the day and feel okay about that because it's called massage. Just the kind of hat pin I am. [Ironically, I got that expression from Molly, who used it. It seemed appropriate to break it out here with the only other girl in my life to ask me out. Although in my relationship with Molly the roles were kind of reversed. I was more the whore, sorry, "special masseuse" in that one.] I'm sorry. Maybe I'm square, but that's how I feel."

"Well, it's your loss."

"I have no doubt. I'm sorry."

"Me, too."

I hung up and finished folding my clothes. I pressed a warm stack of t-shirts into my face and took a big whiff. Solace. Familiar and safe.

I wanted a girlfriend for an hour or a girlfriend for a lifetime, but not both in the same girl.

I didn't get any more massage girls while finishing the show that month. When I returned to New York, still single and with no dates in sight, profound loneliness struck again. It was the awful anticlimax of having finished shooting the show (while you're working, it's always very exciting and filled with promise) along with waiting for it to air and the building stress of how it would do. A hideous combination. I needed some love.

I went on Craigslist and hunted for New York massage girls. I also perused Eros.com, where I found a place on Lexington and Fifty-seventh Street that had really sexy girls. I had a couple of good experiences there but then ended up accidentally sitting next to one of the women who did me, Natasha, while waiting for my dinner at my favorite vegan restaurant in the city, Caravan of Dreams, on Sixth Street and First Avenue. She sat right next to me but either didn't recognize me or pretended not to. I didn't want to possibly embarrass her and it was clear she was waiting for a date. I was fascinated to know who would show up so I just ate my salad and waited in silence. About ten minutes later a very yuppie-looking Wall Street man joined her. Although they kissed on the lips, their level of familiarity belied a third date at best. He was French like she was, he had her accent. She was in the film business and had told me postorgasm of the indie films she had worked on, but she didn't know who I was. Her ignorance was reflected in her tip. I'm just kidding. I worked for tips for eight years in the cab; someone has to really piss me off not to get 20 percent at least. Usually 30 percent plus. Especially if their job entails doing anything to my penis.

Again, the comingling of girlfriend for hire and real life felt a bit uncomfortable, so I stopped going to the Lexington joint and got a girl off Craigslist. A Suicide Girl named Roxy. She had tats head to toe and piercings in her nose, nipples, and clit. She was a sweet Scorpio with a mean streak (like all of them). I had no idea that she would create a monster of a sub in me. She wore an electric orange wig and was tiny, but packed a punch. She had a mischievous laugh and was always a little stoned, which I somehow didn't mind on her. She also had a nurturing, gentle, and very accomplished side. An artist, Roxy did "massage" to augment her salary. At first she was tender with me, but then sensing the sub in me, got a little rough one day, and jammed more than one finger in my ass as she brought me to orgasm. Unsuspectingly, I had been turned out. Though strictly heterosexual, ass play had always felt good, and dirty and wrong, so, really good. I was secure in my sexuality and therefore comfortable having prostate play administered by women. I had never been with a man nor even fantasized about being with one. I figured having a finger up my ass was purely physiological and made me cum harder, so what the hell. But then I had this dream that changed everything.

My First Gay Dream

In the late '80s when I was working on *America's Most Wanted*, in Washington, D.C., I had this amazing bizarre dream that both turned me on and freaked me out. In the dream, I was in an office building stairwell being raped by a faceless man, but I didn't seem to mind and he wasn't hurting me. He was fucking me missionary style. Slowly, I realized he wasn't fucking me in the ass, but in my pussy. I was me as a man but I had a vagina and could distinctly feel what it was like to be a woman being fucked. It was wild. Then, suddenly, I could see his face. *He* was *me*. So I was me as a man, fucking myself as me with a vagina. No breasts and not in drag or anything. Exactly the same as I am but just with a pussy instead of a penis. It was hot, but completely weirded me out. And in conjunction with this thing that had happened in the sauna at the gym the previous week in New York before I left, I was doubly freaked out.

It was the middle of the day, and the Paris Health Club on West End was almost empty. I had finished my workout and went for my sauna. Apparently, Tuesday afternoon was pickup time for the gay community since the only people there were gay men with invitational eyes. Never in any of my previous visits had I experienced such a concentration of gay men trying to get laid.

A couple of guys on the gym floor and another in the locker stalls made it clear they wanted to have sex with me by the way they glanced at me. As I usually do, I just turned away with a neutral expression, breaking what momentary eye contact there had been, attempting to neither hurt their feelings nor lead them on. Regardless of orientation, as long as someone's not annoying or aggressive, better to say "No thank you," than "Fuck off." I figure, be grateful someone thinks I'm cute. Girls? Listening?

So I went into the sauna and it was empty except for this one burly guy lying on his back, taking up the entire bench on one side. I only had one choice, to sit across from him, which I did. He rolled over on his side, facing me, propped his head up with his hand, elbow on the bench like he was watching TV on his couch, and started the per-formance. He stared directly at me with the slightest of grins and slowly began to stroke his dick. I didn't look but I knew what he was doing. *Should I just leave? Should I tell him that's inappropriate and ask him to stop?* It was very hot in this room and I felt myself becoming a bit aroused. *Am I getting turned by this guy jerking off or just wiggy from the heat? Don't look. Just ignore him.* I took a quick glance.

He had the largest dick I had ever seen, and it wasn't even fully erect yet.

I mean it was fucking monstrous. I looked away. I was gripped by the bench. The sauna door that was only a foot from me seemed a mil-lion miles away. I was frozen, unable to move, caught in the spell of the huge cock being rubbed for me . . . at me. At no time did I want to go over and deal with it in any way, but I also felt powerless to leave. A few more seconds went by. I took another quick glance.

Okay that's ridiculous. It was hard now and stupid big. I got up like a blushing schoolgirl and raced out of the hot box, went straight to my locker lest I bump into him in the shower area, got dressed, and left.

Was I gay? The guy was equal parts abhorrent and magnetic to me. Or was it just his huge dick? I mean, the phallus is a sexual phenomenon. I love mine. Mine turns me on both by itself and in conjunction with girls' bodies. But never with men, not as an adult at least. When I was six I used to butt fuck my little friends under the covers while we were playing "fort" and they would suck my dick and there was even one Italian kid from the ninth floor who liked me to pee on him in the stairwell . . . THE STAIRWELL! FROM THE DREAM?! Was it all coming together? Was my subconscious trying to reveal my closeted homosexuality to me at twenty-nine years of age? Or at least my bisexuality? Oh my god! Was this my Saturn return? I'm here and as it turns out I'm actually queer? I knew I loved women emotionally and physically, and only wanted to be with a woman for marriage and kids, but did I have a repressed proclivity for sucking dicks and being fucked in the ass as a sideshow? But wait, as a kid I was the top. In my dream and in the sauna, I was the bottom. Maybe I was a switch. I did go from being fucked by myself to fucking myself, so who the hell knows? It was all very confusing and alarming so I called my therapist, who I trusted implicitly. He was a very spiritual New Age kind of guy, a leader in the men's movement and very wise. He would definitely have the answer.

"William. I had this dream where I was being fucked like I had a pussy by myself with a dick and then I got kind of turned on by this guy jerking his huge dick off at me in the sauna. Am I gay?"

"No. You're angry at men."

"You've heard of this before."

"Yes."

"So I'm not gay. I'm angry at men."

"Yeah. Your father, mainly."

"So can I continue to fantasize and dream about men and still just be angry at my father but not be gay."

"Sure. Fantasies are just that. They're not real. Have you ever thought about killing anyone?"

"Of course. I have fantasies of driving my cab up onto the side-walk and just mowing down hundreds of people."

"But you don't do it."

"Right."

"So you're not a mass murderer."

"Right. Of course. Excellent. Thanks."

He was a genius, my shrink.

So I went on my merry way, satisfied that being bi in my imagi-nation didn't make me bi in real life. Not that I had any problem with it were I really to be bi in my real life, it's just that it would be very hard to ever do anything because of my AIDS paranoia. My sexual/romantic life is already confusing enough dealing only with women; if you threw in a whole other variable, it would just get too crazy. And in really giving it some thought, I realized that the things I find sexiest about a woman, I am disgusted by in a man. Kissing, hands, feet, hairlessness. It's just really the taboo, the subjugation, the domination and humiliation administered by the cock and the attitude of the mind behind the cock that was the real pull. (And, of course, the physical aspect, the male G-spot, the prostrate, being stim-ulated, making the orgasm volcanic, would be a nice throw in). If I could have all of that, but have it be a woman, that could be fun. An incident that had happened at a concert a couple of years back popped into my head.

In 1989, I went to my first of many Prince shows at Madison Square Garden. Prince was phenomenal and the vibe at that concert was very sexy. For the first and only time in my life, it was that night that I was picked up by a hot black model. We made out in the back of her limo after the show. It was all going swimmingly, so I went for second base. When I arrived at her breasts, I found padding. It didn't seem that odd; many girls wear padded bras. But suddenly, a single crystal-clear question flashed into my mind.

Was the slight scratchiness of her kiss not a mild skin condition covered by makeup but instead five o'clock shadow?

After some questioning, it turned out Danielle's given name was, in fact, Dan. He was a gay man in drag and, I'm telling you, he/she was smoking hot. Not cute. Hot. Naomi Campbell hot. And Dan liked me. "You don't want to keep going?" He asked, not so innocently.

"You're a very nice person, Danny-Danielle, but I'm just not sexually turned on by men. I mean, granted, I was just enjoying making out with you very much, but that's when I thought you were a woman."

"What if I were dressed up like this?"

"Dude, I would know." I politely ended the evening without further incident. I didn't even consider doing anything with Danny-Danielle then, but if it had happened during the "Am I gay?" phase in my life I might have taken him/her up on his/her offer of being my first. I don't know but, regardless, it had given me an idea.

Chicks with dicks.

I raced to the Internet and went on Eros. To my jubilation, there were dozens listed under "Shemale Escorts." And although some were nasty freaks (I mean children of God, God bless them, but just not sexy human beings) straight out of the basement of Show World before Giuliani turned it into the Laugh Factory, most of them were BABES! Exactly what my fantasy was. Hot chicks who had big, hard cocks. Donny, who shares some of my tastes, but definitely not this one, always offers that "They're guys with tits. Not chicks with dicks, it's a big fucking difference." I guess I just have greater suspension of disbelief powers than he, or I'm just gay and he's not. Whatever. Let's not split hairs.

But my excitement quickly gave way to the inevitable truth. That no matter how sexy these creatures were, in the end the fact was, they were gay male prostitutes.

I have gotten fifty AIDS tests in the last twenty years. I have only ever had sex with women, and 99 percent of the time it's been protected safe sex. Not even blow jobs were unprotected, unless with a girl who I've taken to my doctor to get tested and he's read me the results. Yeah, I'm crazy about this shit. Whether it's a psychological catchall bin for my other anxieties, I don't know, but I still get freaked out by even kissing girls and have to run to the CDC at four A.M. for counsel. My point is, after that first test in 1983 when I stopped shooting drugs, the only behavior that I've ever done that is indeed high risk, or any risk at all for that matter, there's never been a justifiable reason to get another one. I was negative, thank God, by the way.

But fucking a gay prostitute, and being the bottom, so, having a gay prostitute's dick in my ass, the number one way to get AIDS, whether it was shrink-wrapped in three condoms or not, just was never going to happen. I didn't want to go to a tranny club and meet one who wasn't a prostitute and cultivate enough of a relationship so that I trusted he/she was HIV negative, so my only option, like the end of my hetero whoring days, was to jerk off at their pictures while asking them questions on the phone as if I might have them over.

I used a high-pitched, "I'm an inexperienced college boy who's never done this before" voice, thinking that would buy me more time, but these professional she-men knew the game and were very businesslike and curt on the phone specifically to root out imposters like me. No freebies here.

Their voice was the most important thing. It was hard to find a tranny that really sounded feminine and not just like a slightly better version of my high-pitched-inexperienced-college-boy-on-steroids persona.

"This is Angel." Angel was Puerto Rican and drop-dead gorgeous. The Puerto Rican ones generally are the hottest, having the most feminine-looking faces. I could tell that her pictures weren't airbrushed, and there were enough of them that I trusted she really looked as she was portrayed. She was five foot eight, 36C-24-30, which was perfect. Even on girls, I tend to like boy bodies. Thin hips, broad shoulders. And of course she advertised nine inches, fully functional. Apparently, some girls can't get it up due to the hormones they take, but she claimed to be "hormone free" so that wouldn't be a problem. Lovely. She was also a top, which was what I was after. I liked her dick size since I'm average and, if I was going to fantasize about being dominated, I wouldn't feel too scared of anything less than eight. I already fucked myself in that dream; let me get something a little bigger. But every girl on the site seemed to be eight inches or bigger. Most were five foot eight and under, some as small as five three, so I knew they had to be lying. I've been in enough locker rooms and talked size with enough male friends in my life to know generally anything under five foot eight is gettin' you under six in the penile department. Anyway, she had a genuinely feminine voice that was hot. She sounded like an actual woman.

"Hello, Angel," I said with a fake quiver in my voice. "Um, I was looking at your ad on Eros?"

"You wanna come see me, baby?" Straight to the point.

"Um. I've never done this before?" Like a Glaswegian, I would end all declarative statements with an upward-sliding inflection as if they were questions instead of statements, for a maximum appearance of nervousness. She softened just a bit. "That's okay. Don't be scared." She was biting. *Slow-play her. Don't go too fast, you might lose her.*

"You're very beautiful."

"Thank you. So what do you like?" JACKPOT. *Free she-male phone sex!* I increased the speed of my masturbating not knowing when my dime would run out and she would bolt.

"Well, I . . . I guess I want to be on the bottom? Is that what it's called? Is that okay?"

"That's fine. Is that all you want to do?"

"No. I'd also like to have you . . . in . . . my . . . mouth?"

"We can do that. So you wanna come to me or you want me to come to you?" My time was about to be up. Maybe just one, two questions more at the most.

"Where are you?"

"Midtown."

"Are you cut or uncut?"

"Cut or uncut? You seem to know a lot of terms for someone doing this for your first time." *Busted! I better come quick. One last gasp.*

"Well, I've been reading up on it a little bit and looking on the Web site." *Almost there . . .*

"When you decide what you wanna do, you call me, okay. I don't have time for all your shenanigans." She hung up. I looked at her picture quickly, imagined her fucking me, and came. It was a little unsatisfying since I hadn't timed it right and she found me out before I climaxed. It would have been much better if she was still seducing me when I blew up, but hey, when you go for the gusto and try to get full on dirty talk out of them for free, that's the risk you take. Any novice could call them up, primed to shoot their load in seconds, and come on "what's the donation?" or some cursory first or second question. It takes someone with serious balls to live on the razor's edge and try to get them as far as "I'm uncut, baby, do you like that?" for the cum shot. That's how I roll, kids. You feelin' me? So even though this one didn't work out perfectly, it was still a nice session. Better than nothing.

As I lay back in my chair, postcoital, underwear around my ankles, toilet paper in my hand, I laughed to myself. "Shenanigans?" That was a strange word for her/him to use. It made me like her.

"Shenanigans."

She didn't want any part of all my . . . "shenanigans." It really made me laugh. Or was it nervousness and shame. *Would* I feel ashamed if I was bi? I never dreamt I would. I have many gay friends, my closest. Was I using my fear of AIDS as an excuse? Maybe I needed to do some more research. But how? If I wasn't going to try regular gay men and chicks with dicks were out . . . WAIT! I had an idea. Roxy was hot as hell. The tattooed happy-ending girl who finger-fucked my ass hard. Maybe there's something there. I went back to Eros and clicked on BD/SM.

Ohhhhh yeah. Now we're talking. Ridiculously hot chicks. Real biological chicks. I'm talking supermodel hot, and I'm not exaggerating. Five foot ten, six foot one in heels, dressed in black latex bodysuits, scowls on their gorgeous faces and eight-inch fake rubber hard-ons exploding out of their pussies. I got instantly hard again like an eighteen-year-old, and started running down their ads. This was it. I would have a dominatrix abusing my ass within the hour!

Mistress Domina XXX

There were all shapes and sizes of doms working independently and through dungeons. And there were many dungeons of varying quality. The bad ones looked like your third-grade haunted house at school. SpaghettiOs for brains. Fun then, but not for adult play. The good ones had their theme rooms done up very professionally with great care and attention to detail, as if decorated by a Broadway set designer. If I was going to pop my cherry in one of these joints, I damn well wanted it to feel like *Phantom of the Opera* and not *Waiting for Guffman!* The best dungeon was Pandora's Box. It was the most authentic looking and had the hottest-looking dominatrices. The medieval room, which looked like a torture chamber, had whips, chains, and scary-looking metal implements on the dark stone walls, an Iron Cross, and a table with ropes on big round pulleys on either side to stretch you. A hospital room for medical scenes; enemas, cutting, penis mutilation, piercing. And a classroom for teacher/student scenes.

My pick would have been the torture chamber. I like my dick just the way it is and did not want it butterflied in a surgical scene. I do enjoy a certain kind of pain, but no abuse to the cock or balls, please. I want to evolve my lineage one day, thank you. The classroom thing is fine but not terribly interesting to me. It's so wonderful and mysterious, human sexuality. What turns different people on and disgusts others. It's fascinating.

But no matter how clean they kept their establishment, this germophobe wasn't going anywhere anyone else had ever been. It totally grossed me out, so I opted for an "in-call" session as my first.

I scrolled down the "Independent Doms" and found a range of girls that ran the gamut from obese wearing a Renaissance mask and feather boa to drop-dead gorgeous. Mistress Domina XXX caught my eye. She looked like a young Charlotte Rampling. Deep, searing eyes and a soulful expression. Five foot eight, dirty-blond shoulder-length hair, and a slim frame. Her interests included:

Prolonged Teasing, CBT, and Denial
Foot, Leg, Boot, and Heel Worship
Corporal Punishment and Discipline
Humiliation both Verbal and Physical
Sensual to Severe Flogging, Caning, Paddling, and Spanking
Mental and Physical Bondage
Sensory Deprivation
Slut Training and Forced Feminization
Nipple Torment
Smoking Scenarios and Cigarette Torture
Elaborate Rope Bondage, Specializing in Japanese Bondage
Candle Wax and Ice Treatment
Breath Control, Mummification, and Asphyxiation
Enemas
Trampling
Electro Play
Knife Play, Needle Play, Branding, Piercing (Don't be afraid, I have
     trained under a professional body piercer and use only sterile
     techniques)
Golden Showers
Face Slapping
Spitting
Dildo Training
Sounds

She was my girl. I was like a kid in a candy store, reading her tawdry menu. I didn't know what half the things were, but they sounded fucking great.

"Yes, hi, I'll take the trampling to start, then have the electro play for the main course and, for dessert . . . ? Let . . . me . . . see . . . Ah, yes. The choking. Thank you." I dialed her number. I felt like I was back in seventh grade, after dinner, calling a girl whose number I got from her best friend.

"Hello?" She had the perfect voice for her face. Sultry and smart.

"Mistress Domina?" I felt a bit stupid calling her that, but had a feeling it was part of the game.

"Yes?" I was right. She seamlessly flowed into her alter ego with a subtle change in tone. She was the boss.

"I was looking at your ad on Eros?"

"Uh-huh?" She was perfect. Not "acting" the part, just seeming like a regular nice, cool, chick . . . who was deviant as fuck-all and would kick the living shit out of you for fun.

"I've never been with a dominatrix before." I wasn't jerking off to her. This was not my she-male–masturbate–while–talking–but–never–meet script. This was for real. I was going to have her over to my house.

"That's okay. What are you interested in?"

"Um . . . " I was scared to say it out loud. As if this woman hadn't heard everything in the book. But what if she laughed at me? Judged me. Cuckolded me. I took the leap.

"Strap-on play?"

"One of my specialties. What else." *Oh my god!*

"Breath play? Is that you strangling me?"

"Yes. I love that. What else."

"Um, just like, abuse me? Verbally? Like say mean things to me about how pathetic and—"

"I understand. Anything else?"

"Golden showers?"

"Okay. I think I have a clear understanding of what kind of session you want. Is there anything you specifically don't want to do?"

"Um . . . " I quickly perused the list.

"I don't want to be electrocuted."

"Okay."

"Or have my balls abused."

"Okay."

"Or have my penis mutilated in any way."

"Okay."

"And I don't want any smoking in my house."

"I don't smoke."

"Okay but you listed smoking as—"

"I understand. No problem. Anything else?"

"What are 'Sounds'?"

"Oh. Sounds are my absolute favorite. They're long, thin steel rods that are inserted into the flaccid penis at the tip of the head and slides down the shaft until stopping at the sphincter. They're divine."

"Yeah, no. I specifically don't want to do that, please, if that's okay. But everything else we talked about sounds great."

"Whatever you want. What time do you want to see me?"

I don't think I've ever felt such great anticipation. Everything was heightened. Hyperreal. Like the night before Christmas as a kid. Like at the seventh game of the 1986 World Series at Shea. Like when I met Molly for the first time. That pure joy. When you feel perfect. You love everyone and everyone loves you.

I worked out so I would have a glow and be as thin as possible, and then went to a spiritual meeting so I would be grounded and as present as I could be. Sitting in the pews of a beautiful church on the Upper East Side, I couldn't help but smile. I couldn't tell you what sect this church was, they're all the same to me, but from the little I do know, I had a feeling if I believed their doctrine, I wasn't supposed to be feeling giddy about what I was about to do in thirty minutes. But we were a non-secular group of people who just rented the church to hold our meetings, all gathered to help one another lead happier, more spiritual, empathic, and helpful lives. Few of them would judge me. And it's my belief that God doesn't judge me for exploring my sexuality as long as it isn't hurting anyone else, so I didn't really care if a few of them would have anyway. But still, it made me laugh to have the secret knowledge of what was about to transpire in my apartment, imagining the tidal wave of repentance I would be chastised to seek were this church filled with its normal congregation. And for a brief moment I adopted the sin/guilt paradigm of Catholicism, so I could get really turned on and understood the whole repressed Catholic schoolgirl/slut thing viscerally for the first time. It was divine. The one thing the concept of a punishing God is good for, I guess. The feeling you get when defying Him. The ultimate power. Playing God yourself.

I didn't hear a word that was being said in the church; my eyes were focused on the clock on my cell phone. 7:34 . . . 7:37 . . . 7:41. Fuck it. Eight o'clock was too far away and I wasn't listening anyway, so I left early. I jumped in a cab and flew up Madison. I was dressed in my favorite outfit, as if for a first date. We drove through the park, heading for the West Side. She would arrive at 8:30. I got home at 8:08. I lit some candles and put a Portishead disk in the CD player. I pressed "pause" so it wouldn't start playing until the doorman called up to announce her arrival. Portishead was what I played whenever any purely sexual event was occurring in my house, deviant or otherwise.

What Tom Waits was to shooting heroin, Portishead was to sex.

All of my credit cards were safely stashed in my *If Lucy Fell* lunch pail behind my computer, my little safe. I keep a couple of props from each movie as artwork. Some of it functional art. I put the two hundred bucks next to the TV, on the glass table that used to be my desk before I had an office. But then I thought the cash still might be a little out of sight, so I put it on the distressed Crate and Barrel wooden coffee table in front of the couch. No, too obvious. I put it on the speaker next to the tall, thin, black metal IKEA CD rack in the foyer and placed a rubber water bug on top as a cute aesthetic touch. I love this water bug. Helen gave it to me. She loves that I do crazy things like this, so she would love that the incredibly lifelike, disgusting rubber water bug was the marker on top of the dominatrix's money. Naaah, too cute. Mistress Domina XXX might think I'm an idiot. I took the water bug off the cash.

I straightened my outfit, smelled my armpits, and checked myself in the mirror. I was in good shape and smelled okay. I was concerned because that nervous sweat is always the smelliest sweat. But I was squeaky clean. Or was I? I had loofahed myself from head to toe, concentrating on the areas she would be dealing with so I would be immaculate, but I had run around a bit to the meeting and back. I still had six minutes, so I stripped, jumped in the shower, and gave myself a man whore's sponge bath. Underarms and ass, dick and balls. I redressed and sprayed a bit too much CK One on just in time for the short staccato rings from the phone that signify the doorman's alert. She was here.

"You can let her up, Jake," I said into the phone.

"Okay."

"Jake, wait. Is she alone?"

"Yeah, she's alone." Just making sure I wasn't going to get murdered. I trusted her implicitly, she sounded cool on the phone, but I always double-check. A few minutes (which seemed like hours) later, the doorbell rang. I pressed "play" on the CD player and Portishead abruptly blasted. I turned it down quickly, sure she was laughing on the other side of the door, mocking my virgin move of putting on the sexy music for her arrival. And clumsily at that. I looked through the peephole. Fuck, she looked hot, even through a blurry, fish-eye lens. I opened the door. She was stunning. A young Jacqueline Bisset in a fall palette. She was like a girl straight out of a Madison Avenue advertising firm that her grandfather owned; senior VP at twenty-eight, not because of nepotism or her Yale schooling but because of her innate brilliance.

"Hi."

"Get on your knees," she said in her dulcet, cold voice as she glided in and put her briefcase down. She had warm eyes but a brazen attitude, having delivered her first command before my front door was completely closed so the neighbors might hear. I was in love.

I got on my knees and hawked her every move like a scared cat. She casually took off her coat, taking in my apartment as she did, and laid it over the back of the chair in front of my computer. She returned to me, smiling sardonically, grabbed a handful of hair from the top of my head, and slowly craned my head backward so my face was uplifted, looking at hers.

"I should have made you open the door on your knees, you little faggot slut. Awwww, look at those pretty, big blue puppy-dog eyes of yours. Do all the girls say they love those pretty blue eyes?" I relaxed. She slapped me hard across the face. I hadn't been hit like that, I don't know, ever. I saw stars for a second, and my left ear rang. She chuckled. This was not playtime pretending. She was serious.

"Was that too hard?" She smacked me across the face again, on the other check this time, sending my head flying back the other way.

"Take off your clothes." She grabbed her briefcase and headed for the bathroom.

"Can I get up to take them off?" She smiled and paused, slightly breaking character.

"Yeah, you can get up to take them off." I seized the tiny crack in the fourth wall to lay some ground rules I had forgotten.

"I'm kind of a germaphobe; I don't know what . . . 'things' you're planning to use on me, but I don't want anything on or in me that's ever been touched by anyone else. And I have my own strap-on stuff."

"I sterilize everything after every session." Since her everyday personality wasn't all that different from her dominatrix's, she could talk business and stay in character, not ruining the mood.

"I'm sure you do, but that's not even good enough for me."

She walked back into the room and opened her bag, taking out each implement for my inspection.

"Rope?" It looked clean and white and I couldn't imagine any cooties being on it.

"Fine."

"Nipple clamps?" They were clean, shiny, steel clothespins.

"Fine."

"Ball gag?" A red rubber ball suspended between two black leather straps with buckles to fasten it to your head.

"Uhhhh . . . ." It had been in someone else's mouth. She knew what I was thinking.

"I boiled it."

"Okay." As squeamish as I was, at two hundred bucks an hour, I concluded that regardless of whatever stockbroker's or doctor's mouth it had been in, the boiling was disinfection enough. The real joke is that when I was an active drug addict, I used to give ten bucks to a homeless man who would cut his own mother's throat for a dollar, and ask him to go into an abandoned building to get me some white powder that I would trust was, in the best-case scenario, heroin, if not borax, and shoot it into my veins. But now I have to use the paper towel I dried my hands with in the restaurant bathroom on the handle of the door when exiting, lest I catch a flesh-eating bacteria.

"Get on your fucking knees, put your face on the floor, put your little pussy high in the air, and shut the fuck up until I tell you to talk or I'll fuck you dry, no lube, nothing. And trust me, you won't like that." She took her bag and went into the bathroom.

I know I've said it before, but I just need you to understand. This girl, and I'm not exaggerating, could have walked down a Victoria's Secret runway next to Elle and Claudia and no one would have blinked. She was that hot. I did what she told me to do.

I was getting more and more excited, anticipating I-knew-not-what as I tried to commandeer any clue I could from the sounds emanating from the bathroom. She wasn't using the toilet or the sink. Changing? Assembling Erector set–like torturous contraptions? I couldn't hear any metal clanking; it was actually pretty quiet. My face was right cheek down on the wood floor, my ass in the air. Amorphous childhood memories flashed from the smell of the smooth oak slats and the angle of my view. The floor had been my playground when I was a kid, much more than as an adult. I wasn't that close to it these days. A maid cleaned it; and the few times I fucked a girl on it my knees and back hurt, so the novelty wore off pretty fast and we relocated to a softer venue.

I heard the bathroom door open and the light switched off. My dominatrix was both ecologically conscious and polite. Maybe *she* could be my girlfriend. I mean, it was one thing to have a girlfriend who jacked off rich guys into her tits all day, quite another to have a girlfriend who gave rich guys the illusion of helplessness when really giving them complete power. One was not much different than being a prostitute, the other not much different than being our current president. (That last analogy doesn't really make sense so please don't reread it or think about it too hard. Just enjoy how well it landed the first time when it sounded good and allow us both a little poetic license. Thank you.)

From my vantage point I could see black stilettos and fishnets from the knee down, walking toward me very deliberately. Gone was the Madison Avenue advertising daytime uniform; corduroy and a crisp white button-down blouse. The nighttime one was a tad more risqué. Still Vassar waters apparently ran deep.

"What do I say if I want you to stop?"

"You can ask for mercy. I'll decide if you get it."

"So I say, 'mercy'?"

"Yes."

"But you might go further anyway?"

"Yes." I trusted her. I knew that she would stop if I really asked her to. She spread my ass cheeks wide apart.

"Oooooh, what a nice pink virgin pussy you have. I'm going to fuck that hard. Where's Mistress's cock that you bought for her?"

"In the bedroom." After I made the appointment with Domina XXX, before my run and trip to church, I stopped off at the only remaining porn shop on the Upper West Side on Seventy-fourth and Amsterdam. Luckily, the Giuliani-inspired community board hadn't been able to shut it down. Not that I frequent it; in fact, this was the first time I had ever been inside but, with the Toronto-ization of Manhattan nearly complete, I feel, on principle, we have to protect our last bits of remaining character by patronizing them.

Already the sex stores have been dramatically watered down. Like all porno shops, this one has to pretend to be selling something other then sex in 50 percent of the store. Candy, school supplies, whatever. The front window is surreal, dusty boxes of Twizzlers and shiny new Russian war encyclopedias on one side, leather wrist restraints and cock rings on the other.

I had the cab wait as I dashed into the joint, acutely aware of who was watching me enter, certain there were surveillance cameras running 24/7 from the apartment across the street, operated by I-don't-know-who. My mother. All girls who I would ever ask out. All good and decent people. Who knew I would feel such shame about going into a porn shop. I was well aware that most people who enjoyed them were just like me. Normal, sane, nice people. Did I have such harsh judgment against them? Is that why I felt judged? Of course. I've always had battling belief systems:

Good men get married, don't engage in deviant sex, don't gamble, and don't covet money.
Good men stay single, explore their sexuality anyway they want as long as it doesn't harm others, gamble, and covet money.

This battle is one of my biggest challenges: To try to reframe my definition of "manhood," embracing all parts of myself as human rather than "good" and "bad," instead of trying to extricate parts under the supposition that I will be a "good" man if and when I get rid of all the "bad" things. Some days it works and I applaud myself for living a life on the firing lines of adventure, self-exploration, and unconditional acceptance. Other days, I murder myself with self-hatred and shame. This moment, I wasn't really thinking about it too much, I just needed to buy a not-too-huge, high-end, rubber penis to get ass-raped with by a hot girl.

I felt judged by the macho Trinidadian counter clerk for rushing straight to the strap-on dildo section, but then realized that he'd seen it all and wasn't going to sell very much merchandise if he had an air of reproach. I don't think he owned the place; he probably made his money on commissions, like any salesperson at Bloomingdale's. He took one look at me and then went back to his *New York Post*. I bought a very lifelike seven-inch dildo and harness for a hundred bucks. The nice, unjudgmental clerk threw in the bottle of AstroGlide for free. "Oh those nutty eighteen-year-old-sisters I got back at the house," I half-heartedly mumbled in an attempt to influence his hypothesis about my intended use for this purchase. "I mean, *they're* sisters . . . the girls I'm having sex with. They're not *my* sisters. That's gross, I'm NOT into *that*!"

For the hidden cameras, wherever they may have been, I emphasized the point again, announcing it to every nook and cranny around and above me, right and left. "Definitely not into incest! That's against God and illegal and I do not do illegal or ungodly things."

At this point the clerk was more concerned that I was a crazy person than a pervert, and I saw him inconspicuously reach for a concealed bat under the counter in case the situation with the insane-ranting-man-talking-to-invisible-people-before-him escalated. It was time to leave the porn shop.

I raced back to the cab with my black plastic bag, the kind only used in porn shops or if you buy porn magazines from newsstands so there's no chance of anyone seeing the evil in your possession. The average person would be horrified to catch a glimpse of the filth hidden in the bag. Certainly, *they* don't participate in that kind of sin. I wonder who does contribute, then, to this multibillion-dollar industry. I only spent a hundred bucks that year. You? Wait, oh sorry, $103.99. There was that three-day membership to AnimalLove.com. It grossed me out, but I just had to see a horse dick in a woman one time. Crucify me if you will but, come on. You *have* to see that. For historical curiosity, if nothing else. I mean, Mary, Queen of Scots or whoever it was got killed fucking a horse, right? This shit has been going on a lot longer than Larry Flynt, okay. So get off your moral soapbox. You're going to throw the first stone? If you're really honest, you'll come up with enough dirt on yourself since last Monday, let alone in your entire lifetime, that if you begged at God's feet for eternity, you might, might, have a chance at heaven if he was in a really forgiving mood that day.

"Get up," Mistress Domina XXX commanded. She took the rope and, in a flash, skillfully had my wrists tied together and suspended heart-high on my chest. The same rope that bound my wrists was tied to my balls and penis, which were also bound together. If I tried to move my wrists anywhere, the rope would painfully tug on my dick and balls, but if I just left them where they were, everything just felt snugly bound but not painful in any way. I didn't know why but it felt good. Like being covered in sand at the beach when I was little, which always felt equal parts comforting and erotic.

The way she tied my balls and penis together tightly, though I wanted to I was unable to get an erection, which made it all the more enticing. "Come on." She pulled me by the section of rope between my neck and wrists, and led me to the bedroom.

"Lie on the bed." I obeyed, carefully falling back onto the mattress. I had put an old sheet on top of it in case of any liquid spills, so it wouldn't harm the million-count Frette sheets Elle had given me as an *If Lucy Fell* present years earlier. Now, for the first time, I could see Domina XXX's outfit in all its splendor. She had a sexy black and red bustier pushing up her perfect 36C breasts. She was closer to thirty-two than twenty-two, and they were real, so they were soft and had natural buoyancy to them rather than being hard and firm like water balloons. They were very womanly, as was she. She had very pretty black lace panties and a garter belt and then the fishnets and black stilettos.

"You look pathetic." She smirked and twisted both of my nipples really hard, until I had to let out a yelp.

"That's right. It hurts doesn't it?" She took two clamps and fastened them to my nipples. Then she held my head up and moved in, her beautiful red lips inching toward mine.

"Is Mistress being too mean? Do you want a little kiss?" Her lips parted, and she revealed her tongue just a little as she prepared to kiss me. I closed my eyes and opened my mouth, readying my tongue for hers. Suddenly she spat in my face. Most of it went onto my lips and into my mouth. She laughed again.

"You think I would put my beautiful lips on your disgusting mouth? Are you crazy?!" She slapped me again hard across the face. I reached out with my bound hands and gently touched her breast. I knew I would be in for it now.

"Don't EVER touch me, you piece of shit." She grabbed me around the throat with her left hand and skillfully squeezed hard, choking off my air supply as she repeatedly smacked me across the face with her right, in cadence with her admonishment.

"DON'T" SMACK!

"EVER" SMACK!

"TOUCH" SMACK!

"ME" SMACK!

"AGAIN!" SMACK!

I was struggling for air. Then, everything went quiet. Even the ringing in my ears faded from lack of oxygen. I could feel my face swelling. Red and white spots started dancing around Domina XXX's face. I was about to lose consciousness. Just before I did, she let me breathe and whispered softly in my ear, "Or I'll choke you to death." She gently kissed the corner of my mouth. Her lips were cool against the heat pounding from my reddened face. Soooo sexy.

She strapped on the dildo. I was getting more and more excited. She looked amazing. The perfect sex machine. A pussy, a cock, breasts, a gorgeous face, and lean body. Long legs, thin and strong.

"You like me, don't you," I said, trying to top from the bottom as she finished fastening the buckles securing her rod in place. She cracked a sly grin. She did.

"No. I don't. And you talk too much." She leaned forward and jammed her dick in my mouth forcefully, choking me again. I could feel it slide down my throat, which frightened me but seemed okay for the moment. I was deep-throating the thick rubber dildo like a porn star. Then I started to gag, and tears flooded my eyes as I struggled for air. She took her other hand and pinched my nose closed so now all my air was cut off. I bucked and twisted trying to kick her cock from my throat. Finally, when I was getting a little scared, she pulled it out and smacked my face with it. It was heavy and hard, and it hurt much more than I thought it would, but she knew exactly how much it would hurt. Dense rubber to my cheekbone. Like a hockey puck from a slap shot to the face. "What do you have to say now? You sucked that cock like a pro, you little faggot slut. Say 'I suck cock like a little faggot slut.'"

"I suck cock like a little faggot slut."

"You do, don't you. But I think you need to get fucked now. You can suck on it later if you're good." She took the red ball gag and shoved it in my mouth, fastening the straps around the back of my head to keep me from spitting it out.

"That's a pretty look for you." She got up on her knees. I widened my legs like a girl. As I had in the dream, when I became the stranger raping myself as a woman. She took two rubber gloves out of the box I had gotten at the CVS drugstore earlier. That was an interesting look I had gotten from the black, high school–age checkout girl from Harlem. All-purpose latex surgical gloves and a box of Trojans.

Domina XXX lubed up her right hand with AstroGlide.

"I'll be nice because you're being such a good boy."

She slid one finger in me. I had experienced that many times from girls who knew how to give good blow jobs. No big deal. She slid in a second.

"Look how loose your pussy is, you little slut." She slid in a third. That was getting a little tight. I rustled my hips to the side in sweet discomfort.

"Getting a little tighter? I don't know. Do you think you can take my whole cock?"

I nodded yes.

"Let's see." She moved in and hoisted my legs apart, spread eagle. I rested them on her shoulders. She slowly penetrated me with the head of the dildo. It hurt. It was a lot bigger than three fingers. She slowly pushed. I was afraid I was going to rip. She was strong, forceful, and deliberate. She had done this before and could sense my limits. The head popped in. A searing pain shot through me. I groaned through the gag.

"There you go," she said with a smile and didn't move for a moment, letting my body get used to the massive invasion. Slowly, she started fucking me. The pain gave way to a charming pleasure. Less a biological one, more mentally. I was completely under this incredible woman's control. I was her play toy. Her sex object. It was unbelievably hot to give over that much control, that much vulnerability to a stranger. I felt completely present. I was so *there* with her. It was thrilling. She fucked me harder, banging my head against the headboard, engulfing me with the full length of her strap on, and then she suddenly stopped, pulled out and stared at me, deliberating intensely with a mischievous look on her beautiful face. Then, resolved, apparently having received her answer, she left the room and went to rummage in her bag, which I could see on the chair in front of my computer in the living room.

She pulled out a shiny, silver, ten-inch-long steel rod, the width of a knitting needle. *Get . . . the . . . fuck . . . outta . . . here!*

A SOUND!!!

She returned to the bedroom, smiling. She didn't ask. She just did it. I wasn't scared at all, and I didn't want to be a pussy. If I was going to try this, I might as well try it all. I felt like I would be passing a limit most men wouldn't dare, if I let her stick a ten-inch steel dowel into my dick. *Take that, tough guy.*

"Just relax. Take a deep breath," she said, while she rubbed the rod down with that brown surgical disinfectant you see on hospital shows that sort of looks like rust-colored blood.

"It's Betadine. It's the most powerful disinfectant there is. I know what a clean-freak you are." I couldn't believe I was going to let her do this. That's what was so hot about it. The look on her face. She was so fucking into it.

Like a gorgeous mad scientist experimenting on a hunk of human flesh. I don't know. It was amazing. Having the balls to risk it. Some people jump out of airplanes. I was about to let Gwyneth fuck my cock with an iron pole.

She untied my penis and balls. Blood rushed through them. They started to regain their natural color, leaving behind the deep red they had become. She held my flaccid penis with her left hand and slowly guided the rod into its tip with her right hand.

I consciously inhaled and exhaled deeply and slowly, employing ujai breathing, a calming measured technique I learned in yoga.

I waited for the pain, watching intently. It was electric. I don't think I had ever watched anything with more concentration or interest in my life. Yes, actually, I'm *sure* I never had.

To my surprise, and utter joy . . . no pain was occurring so far.

I thought she would have to push the rod down but, all of a sudden, it just dropped by itself, like a ton of bricks, and all but two inches remained visible protruding up and out through the head of my penis. It felt strange and burned a little at the tip, I think from the Betadine, but there was no other pain at all. Certainly not the excruciating, unimaginable pain I had anticipated at the thought of the procedure.

IT WAS CRAZY!

Gravity, aided by some lubrication, had allowed my body to swallow eight inches of this metal rod . . . through my dick! I clinched my sphincter instinctively and it made the rod pop out a couple of inches. It scared me but didn't hurt. Okay, "Fun with Urethras and Steel Rods, this fall on ABC." Stupid Human Tricks? Yeah, check this out.

"It's resting on your sphincter. It's all the way in. That is so fucking hot," she said and quickly got up on her knees sliding her fake cock into me again. She carefully started rocking into me as she stripped the rubber glove off her left hand and jammed it into my mouth beside the red ball gag. She was pulling the side of my mouth open, her fingers in my mouth, her dildo in my ass, her sound in my cock.

"I'm fucking you in every hole you little slut, how hot is that?! I'm fucking you in every hole."

Beaten up, abused, and spent, I lay in the bathtub jerking off as she stood over me and pulled her panties to the side. She had the sexiest-looking shaved pussy I'd ever seen. I could taste it. She pissed on my dick while I masturbated. It's like the clouds parted and heaven was raining down on me. It felt warm and soft and gentle, and like the most lovely wrong denouement to the most lovely wrong opera. She concentrated her stream perfectly onto my hand and penis and balls. I hadn't been pissed on since I was six and the Italian kid from the ninth floor peed on my back in the stairwell. It was familiar somehow, even nearly forty years later.

I came hard and lay in the tub wonderfully exhausted, exhilarated, and calm. My own cum and her piss were her brand on my bruised and battered body.

Foreplay that doesn't kill you, makes you cum stronger.

As she washed her hands in the sink under the warm orange glow from the light over the fire exit door on the roof outside my bathroom window, there was a comfortable silence. I felt so present. So relaxed. So grateful I had given this to myself. I was so in my body, so out of my head.

Whether by sitting in front of an altar praying and meditating or being beaten and violated by a hot dirty-blonde . . . any way you can get there.

I looked up at her as she toweled off above me. I figured this was as good a time as any to make my move. "You wanna go to dinner?"

"I have a girlfriend."

"You don't like boys?"

"I like them fine."

"You like me."

"You keep saying I do."

"You keep smiling at me like you do."

"You were fun to play with." And with that and a sly smile, she left the bathroom.

She was back in her advertising uniform, waiting politely for me to open the front door, just like after a regular ol' first date. The only difference being I wasn't obligated to walk her downstairs and put her in a cab. I opened the front door.

"Here. As a parting gift." I handed her a VHS tape that was sitting on top of the speaker, home to all my movies.

"*If Lucy Fell?* What's this?"

"I made it. Watch it and let me know what you think." I leaned against the door jam as she walked into the hallway and pressed the elevator button.

"Okay. I will."

She pressed the elevator button and read the back jacket of the video box.

"I love Sarah Jessica Parker. I'll watch this." Just an ordinary girl. She smiled and disappeared into the elevator. I closed the door. She was gone.

I sat on the couch and turned on *SportsCenter*. Mistress Domina XXX had shown me more care, love, affection, consideration, kindness, respect, and unconditional acceptance than 99 percent of the people I had ever previously dealt with in any capacity or context.

So who and what was deviant? The previous hour, or the lifetime before it? *Why can't I find a girl like her? Minus the steel rods, maybe.* I laughed to myself and really felt proud for having pushed the boundaries of my fear . . . But then, as they are want to do, finding my serenity untenable, the voices of shame and self-hatred came flooding in, washing it away. *Wait a minute, what if you got AIDS from that steel rod?*

But you saw her disinfect it, and you can't get AIDS from a steel rod, anyway.

But what if it had some AIDS stuck to it that didn't get washed off with the disinfectant?

The air would have killed it anyway. It was in her purse for at least an hour before she came over, even if she had a client right before you.

Yeah, but it was in a plastic bag that could have incubated the AIDS and kept it alive! You idiot! You're a dead man!

I couldn't call my ex-booty-call friend Hilary, who had stopped being a teacher and was now in med school and usually was my first line of defense against my hypochondriacal obsessions, it was too late. She would be asleep.

So the CDC, who will barely talk to me anymore I've called so much, got the honor.

"CDC AIDS hotline," the Jamaican man said in a thick accent.

"Hi, yeah, is it possible to get HIV from . . . if a man had a steel rod inserted into . . . can you get HIV from an inanimate object if it's been doused in Betadine and in the air for a few seconds first?"

"What are you talking about, sir?"

"If someone had . . . if a man had a steel rod inserted into his penis, is there any risk of getting HIV."

"Why did you have a steel rod inserted in your penis?"

"Look, sir, I really don't need to discuss that. I just need some information . . . "

"Are you the guy that calls over and over all the time in the middle of the night?"

"Maybe I am and maybe I'm not, but your job is to answer whatever questions I have whenever and however often I need them answered." Were not my tax dollars subsidizing their jobs, I might not have been so indignant.

"Maybe a psychiatric hotline would help you more."

"Thank you for your counsel, but the only information I require from you tonight is if I can get . . . "

"No."

"No way?"

"No way."

"Even if the steel rod had old HIV semen or liquid on it from someone before it was stuck into mmm . . . y friend?"

"Your 'friend' is not at risk as long as it wasn't taken directly out of a warm body that was infected with HIV and somehow had semen or blood on it and then quickly was inserted into your 'friend' without being sterilized."

"Thank you for your help."

"You're welcome."

I hung up the phone feeling only mildly comforted. I would have the same exact conversation with my doctor as he withdrew blood from me for an HIV test in three days though, just so I wouldn't have to worry. And I, of course, get the PCR RNA test, which is 100 percent accurate seventy-two hours after your last possible exposure, unlike the ELISA test, which is conclusive only after three months. I'd go crazy if I had to wait that long. The only upside is the ELISA test results come back overnight once you've taken it, plus it's cheaper; the PCR RNA test takes a week to get back. But I'll take those six days of apprehension and pay a couple of hundred extra, over waiting the three months to even take the ELISA test and save a few bucks. But again, what began as a victory and source of pleasure, ended up a defeat and source of pain. I wish I could cut my head off sometimes. I'm so fucking sick of my mind when it does this to me. If I could just live with my heart, I'd be fine. That's another reason I don't understand why it's so hard to find a girl. Women are supposed to be the "heart people." I would think they would gravitate to me, as I'm nothing if not a heart person.

But Caroline says, "Girls are the new boys."

Maybe she's right. She would know. She's a new friend and my female counterpart. Finding it as hard to find a suitable man as I'm having finding a suitable girl, she moans she might just spend her remaining days working on a profile for her cat to post on a "cat play-date" Web site, or just sew her vagina shut. I feel her pain. But if girls really are the new boys, then conversely, boys must be the new girls. And if that's true, I have absolutely no problem honoring and celebrating my feminine side to whatever extent I must, within reason, because forever the optimist, I still have high hopes for April.

5

please have the fee be feces free

"So, you sure you want to hear?" I handed April a second helping of vegan brownies and vanilla Rice Dream.

"I don't know. Do I?" She started eating.

"Well, if you think my asking you how you feel when you kiss me is too forward for a second date, I think a disclosure of my experience in the world of sexual deviancy including but not limited to BD/SM, prostitution, and homoerotic fantasy might not be something you would want to hear tonight. No."

She agreed and changed the subject. "So you really don't like to read?"

"No. I hate it."

"But you're a writer."

"Right. Other people love to read and I love to write, so it's a perfect match."

"But you don't even read the *New York Times*?"

"Oh God, no! They're the devil. I boycott all media."

"How do you know what's happening in the world?"

"What have I missed in the last ten years by not reading the *New York Times* or watching the news, which would have made me choose to live my life differently for the better? Fucking evil spin created by corporations to forward their agendas to make more money at the expense of my happiness and serenity? Selling me fear and hate so I'll eat, drink, fuck, and buy more and more to avoid being in the present moment of terror, bewilderment, and hopelessness? You can have it. I'll go to yoga and watch football."

"But what do you talk about?"

"If all the people who talk about issues spent that time actually out in the world helping people—and I don't mean protesting but actually hands-on helping old ladies with their bags, giving away their money, smiling and being loving and caring, or even meditating on world peace—I guarantee you, the world would change overnight. What's talking about it going to do?"

"I do help people."

"Excellent." I could see her disappear. Shift. She had just made another decision about me, and again it wasn't good. They were stacking up.

"I just always thought I'd be with a man who was more informed than I am."

"I may be more informed than you are. Just not about things in the *New York Times*."

"I have a premiere party for a friend's play. I told everybody I'd be there by midnight. I know you don't like crowds, but you're welcome to join if you'd like?"

"Thanks, but I'll pass. You like to go out a lot, huh?"

"Yeah. Six nights a week at least. Not all parties. Plays, dinners with friends, art openings . . . I like to be social." I sighed to myself but nodded to her. I knew in my gut, as I had now more than once, that April and I weren't a match. But I wasn't yet willing to give in to that truth. I still believed I could make it happen.

"I'll take you down and get you a cab."

"That would be lovely."

The cab door was ajar and the driver was getting antsy to go. I thought maybe a better kiss might give us some hope and erase the fact that April and I were worlds apart in most every way, other than both being sweet souls clumsily trying to find love. So, I kissed her. Nothing had changed. Our mouths and tongues moved to different rhythms and we just couldn't connect. It was a metaphor for our lack of chemistry in every other area. I didn't know if she felt the same; I wasn't allowed to ask her questions like that, apparently, until a much later time.

The next date, if there was one, would be the third. By her system, we would be allowed to have sex, but not be allowed to talk about whether we liked it or not. She smiled and got in the cab with a polite, "I had a nice time. Thank you for the brownies. They were lovely." She was always polite and considerate on the surface, but viciously judgmental when it came to important things, seemingly wanting to hurt my feelings, as she had been hurt.

"Me, too. I'll call you later." She was very scarred and hadn't healed yet. But in the moments when her defenses were down and she was herself, the self she risked being so rarely and only for a few seconds at a time, she sparkled like a delicate snowstorm when it's really cold out. It's so rare to find that and it kept me staying, hoping that, by championing her, she would let more of that part of her out to play with me. And I was so tired of being alone.

I called her the next morning. "How are you doing?"

"I'm fine. A little tired. I got drunk last night and stayed out late." She sounded like she was over it.

"You sound weird," I said, anticipating a break-up speech.

"Yeah, well, I was out with my friends and talking and just felt so relaxed and nice, and I realized that your energy is very intense and gave me a knot in my stomach that only went away when I was around other people that weren't crazy."

My stomach went into a knot now.

"You think I'm 'crazy'?"

"You're kinda crazy. You're forty-four and you don't read. You don't have any patio furniture. You run in ninety-degree heat. You're compulsive, and I don't want a crazy compulsive person in my life. I want nice and calm energy around me . . . "

"Uh-huh." I was so enraged; I was just biding time so I wouldn't say something vicious that I'd regret.

"Jocelyn . . . " She always spoke of people I had never met and she had never mentioned before as if I should know who they were. It annoyed the shit out of me.

"Jocelyn is dating this married guy who's also sober and she said it's just really hard. He's very needy and wants all this attention from her and sucks her dry." That was the last straw.

"Okay, so, let me get clear on this. While you were out getting drunk last night, you were receiving counsel on how fucked up and needy sober people are from your drunk friend who is in an adulterous relationship with one particular sober guy who cheats on his wife?"

"It's not just that."

"Okay April, well, it was nice to meet you and good luck to you."

"You, too. I'm sorry it didn't work out."

"Yeah, me, too."

"Good luck with your book. I'm sure it'll be a smashing hit."

I hung up and threw the phone into the pillow. I was equal parts pissed and grateful that she had evidenced herself, once and for all, to be that fucked up. There was absolutely no way I could feel that there was some deficiency in me that was the undoing of our burgeoning relationship. Unfortunately, my tremendous low self-esteem and evil ego conspired to convince me otherwise, and I was prostrate on the couch in tears eight seconds later.

After a good cry, I called Lexi to give her the news.

"So, thanks for fixing me up with April but it's not gonna work out. We're just too different."

"I know. I'm sorry," Lexi sympathetically growled in her Julie Kavner voice.

"She called you?"

"She e-mailed me."

"What did she say?"

"She said . . . here, let me read it to you."

"No, don't. Okay. No . . . yeah, read it."

"Dear Lexi, thank you for fixing me up with Eric. Unfortunately we didn't make it seventy-two hours. Sad. Are we still going away next weekend to your house in Connecticut? I'm so looking forward."

"How could she be so glib and cold and uncaring?"

"I know. I'm sorry. But you didn't know each other that long."

"Yeah, but she came on really strong. I mean, she said that when we met ten years ago at one of my premiere parties, she had a feeling she was going to marry me."

"You met her ten years ago?"

"Apparently. I didn't really remember. She said we talked for two hours."

"And you didn't remember?"

"She looks twenty now, ten years ago she was twenty-two; she must have looked thirteen. I didn't want a little baby child, I was trying to pick up a sixteen-year-old model. It was a movie premiere. I didn't want to be grilled on the 'inspiration for my movie' by a sixth grader when I was focusing on landing a high school sophomore. I'm kidding . . . she was nineteen I think. Anyway, April said a lot of things to me about how into me she was, and then is just, like, 'We didn't make it seventy-two hours. Sad. Are we going to the Hamptons?' That's fucked up."

"I just think she's not ready. And you *are* a little crazy."

"No, I'm not. I'm honest and straightforward. Maybe that's crazy to shut-down, repressed people."

"She said you were in one of your tirades this morning?"

"What are you talking about? Where did she say that?"

"In the e-mail."

"Lexi, if you read me the e-mail, you have to read it all to me. What exactly did she say?"

"Let me see, where is it? Okay. Dear Lexi—"

"Don't paraphrase!"

"Okay. I won't. I'll read it word for word. 'Dear Lexi. Thank you for fixing me up with Eric. Unfortunately we didn't make it seventy-two hours. Sad. He was in one of his crazy tirades this morning and I just felt the downs outweighed the ups. Are you going to blah-blah-blah . . . '"

"Tirade? I didn't even raise my voice. She told me how she got drunk and talked with her adulterous friends about why sober people are crazy . . . You know what? Forget it."

"Really? That doesn't sound good."

"Whatever. Thanks for trying, Lexi, and thanks for listening."

"She wasn't for you. You're so sweet and funny. We'll find you someone else."

Three days went by. I wrote every day at my office at Spuyten Duyvil. It's a place that brings me profound joy. When I was a little boy, we'd cross the Riverdale Bridge at the northern tip of Manhattan Island and I'd look down at the Tudor buildings perched on the edge of the mountain that overlooks the Hudson and East rivers' divergence, the Palisade Cliffs to the west. It's a majestic vision that seems the gateway to the free world and makes you wonder what it must have looked like to the Dutch explorers when they first laid eyes on it in the 1500s when it was nothing but wilderness and Indians lived there. I vowed then to live in one of those buildings some day. I got off the West Side Highway a couple of years ago on my way to Vermont and checked one out up close for the first time. It was even more amazing in person. There was a Realtor's number on a gold placard that hung on the façade. I called and left a message telling them the story of my dream to live there. I figured, in such an amazing building, there would be a ten-year waiting list or it was a co-op. He called me back an hour later saying he had an apartment available right then. I took it sight unseen. It was incredible. Ten windows south and west, all on the water. Every time I go there it feels like a God-shot. A reminder that destiny is manifest. But that particular day I was miserable. Although I didn't like the way April treated me sometimes with her eviscerating judgment and pervasive condemnation of my character, whenever she looked at me she always blushed and couldn't help but smile and look down, revealing her deep fondness for me. And knowing she had that undeniable affection made me feel warm, and I missed it. It seemed stupid and way premature that we had broken up. *But come on Eric, are you just having revisionist thinking because you're lonely? Remember how bad it felt to be told you're a loser because you don't read and don't work on Mondays and run in the heat? Do you really want to sign up for another Liza? Even worse, a Liza who doesn't hide her hatred of you but freely enjoys assassinating you with it?*

Oh don't be dramatic. She's just young and a little emotionally stunted. Be the wiser one and call her.

Fuck her, she should call you.

You wanna to be right or you wanna be happy? You're fucking forty-four and still single, dude! You're going to die alone!

Yeah, but I don't want to settle. I would rather be alone than with someone who treats me like that!

Just give her another chance. Go with love. It's the only way. Go with love and you can't go wrong.

I called Lexi. "Lexi?"

"How are you feeling?"

"I think I wanna call her; have you talked to her?"

"Briefly, yesterday I think? *Sheldon! Sheldon put that down!*" I know that with friends who have kids you have to be tolerant, but when every second feels like life and death about a girl, I gotta be honest, I don't care if Sheldon gives himself a clay mask with Drāno, swallows the "pretend" candy (knitting needles), or plays airplane out the fucking window; I need an answer.

"*Sheldon . . . honey . . . Sheldon!* Eric, can I call you back?"

"Yeah, I'm thinking of calling her. Call her and test the waters for me but don't say anything. Okay?"

"Okay. I will." I hung up. More counsel needed to be had.

"Fredaliscious."

"Schaef! How come I haven't heard from you lately?"

"I've been dating April, remember?"

"Oh yeah? How's that going?"

"Well, remember how I told you she was really great and funny and smart but fucked up and repressed and judgmental and Emily Post–Noel Coward–Upper-East-Side–put-on a bit?"

"Yeah?"

"We broke up."

"Why?"

"She said sober people were soul-sucking, compulsive, crazy people and she wanted calm in her life."

"Okay . . ."

"And she said she wasn't interested. But I think she's just scared and making up stupid judgments about me so she can run away, and I'm thinking of calling her. . . . What do you think?"

"I think . . . Robert! *Robert, honey, you can't do that. Honey, he can't do that.* Sorry—Shaef, we're just driving to Diane's grandmother's in Philadelphia—"

"Hi, Eric!" Diane chimed in. Apparently I was on speaker.

"Hi, Diane."

"Don't bother with her. She sounds like a psycho."

"Thanks, Diane." Robert started crying loudly.

"*Robert, honey,*" Diane said.

"*Diane, don't take him out of the car seat, he'll only . . .*" Fred offered.

"*WAAAAAAAAAAAAAAAAAAAAAAAAAAAAAAAAAA*!!!!!!!" Robert declared.

"*Honey, I have to,*" Diane rebutted.

"Listen, just call me when you can, okay, Fred? Bye." *Who doesn't have a fucking baby? Donny. But he's heard this all before and doesn't give a shit. Fuck it. He's my last resort. And if I catch him when he's not in his own blinding depression he might actually help me.*

"I think you're full of shit. I don't think you really like her and you're just trying to convince yourself you do because you're lonely, which I totally identify with, don't get me wrong . . . " I lucked out. I had caught him in between his afternoon SuicideGirls.com wank and early evening tea. And he seemed to want to help me with some tough love. *Excellent.*

* * *

After falling out over the show in 1996 and not talking for a few years, I had written him a congratulatory note when he made his second movie, *The Suburbans*. That cracked the ice and we slowly resumed our friendship and now we're close again. He's a good friend.

"What are you talking about? Of course, I like her!"

"I think you like her fine. I just don't think you *like her* like her. But, you know, go back in for another round if that's what you need to really find out."

"I'd rather go back and risk your being right, than not go back in and risk your being wrong and it was just my stupid pride that kept me from the love of my life."

"Good point. Then call her."

"Maybe I should go to yoga first and I'll get the answer there."

Pause.

"You think, Donny?"

"Do . . . I . . . think . . . you . . . should . . . go . . . to . . . yoga . . . and . . . get . . . the . . . answer . . . there—rrrr . . . " he said, repeating my question very slowly pretending he was considering his response rather than what he was really doing, which was buying time to process it since he hadn't been listening but surfing the Net instead, disinterested in my latest dating problem. "Uhhhh . . . yeah. Absolutely. Go to yoga first."

I had lost him. He was booting up nineteen-year-old chicks from Portland with ink sleeves and perfect nubile 36B tits.

"Okay. Thanks. I'll obtain you later."

Halfway through lying on my back in *savasana*, the closing pose of most *vinyasa* practices, *corpse pose* in English translation, I realized I had to call her. It's interesting that the answer came to me there, as many do, while practicing lying on my deathbed. I had to go with love. If she said no, at least I wouldn't have to suffer not knowing if there might have been a chance.

I called from my cell phone from Thirteenth Street and Broadway, outside Jivamukti. I left a great message and followed it up with an equally cute text. She had once given me shit about asking her to give me her books instead of buying them myself, as if it were gauche to ask. I thought it was like the movie business. I have boxes of DVDs of all my movies in the closet expressly for that purpose. You know, to give away as gifts to girlfriends, family members, dominatrices . . . I would never want a friend to buy one. Apparently, books are different, because Lexi corroborated April's disgust at my request, saying she also hated when people asked her to give them copies of her books instead of buying them. April had given me all three anyway, saying it wasn't a big deal, but I knew it was another black mark against me on the growing list.

I typed into my Blackberry, "I left you a VM. Let's go for a walk in the park and make up. Come on, I'll buy your books. I'll have to, since I threw the ones you gave me away when we broke up."

I descended the stairs to the N,R,Q,W subway at Union Square, heading north to change to the 1,2,3 at Forty-second Street. There's no reception in transit, but when you transfer at Times Square, for a brief moment when you hang left past the shuttle and the Hispanic twins playing flamenco guitar, a signal will beam in any messages you got while previously underground.

The self-esteem light was flashing. I might have a life. (I just realized why I feel empowered by the sight of the flashing "Don't Walk" signal, and always triumphantly defy the electronic rebuff and soldier across the street in spite of it. Apparently, my Pavlovian response to *any* blinking red light is a release from self-hatred and patheticism and a rush of self-esteem. I should invent a portable pocket-size blinking red light that you can use to self-stimulate a positive response at any time so you're not at the mercy of traffic signals or your mother's phone message about a dish for a holiday dinner that's six months away, which leaves you more depressed than before because of the anticlimactic crash from the excitement of thinking it was from a possible girlfriend.) It was from April. "You can pick me up outside Clara's at five." Yes! It was curt but willing. Clara was her writing partner who lived only a couple of blocks from me.

It was 4:40. I had enough time to drop off my yoga mat and wet clothes at my house and be there on time.

I got to Clara's at 4:59. It was where I had picked April up for our first "walk in the park" date. I was five minutes late that day; she said ten but her phone was fast. Today, she ended up being seven minutes late by my Blackberry, twelve by her phone. Rude, no matter how you cut it. Clearly not a good start to a reconciliation date.

"Thanks for meeting me."

"I have a dinner on the Upper East Side in forty-five minutes. I'm walking through the park, if you want to walk along." *Wow, she is really being a cunt. Isn't she the one who broke up with me? Why is she being so rude? Fucking manipulation. I get broken up with, yet somehow I'm still the bad guy.* I let it go.

"Can we just sit on the bench where I used to cut math and get stoned in high school, please. Just for ten minutes. I'd rather be able to look at you in both eyes while we talk. Then we can walk. You'll still make it. And it'll be a calming sense memory, which will give us a maximum chance at reconciling."

She didn't even feign a smile at my joke. "Where's the bench?"

"Ninety-third in the park. I went to Columbia Prep for my last two years after bolting Vermont, remember?" *Anything nice about me? Anything redeeming? Prep school? I'm not a heathen, remember?* I hated her again. Now, you may ask, why, if it seemed Donny was right and I didn't really like her all along, was I so intent on getting her back? Childish ego? No. Again. I was single and forty-four at the time and had had three third dates in seven years since Liza and I had broken up. I was not going to dump someone who was smart and made me laugh and I found sexy just because I hated her after three days.

"Okay, we can sit." We headed toward the entrance to the park at Ninety-third Street. She was giving absolutely no quarter. Humor hadn't broken her, I hoped sweetness might.

"April, this is crazy. I don't want us to break up. I really missed you." I was telling the truth. She threw me a look like, "Yeah? And next I suppose you want me to believe that there isn't a copy of *Girls Gone*

Wild buried not so deep in your closet somewhere?" I was quickly running out of interest in trying to make up with this girl. I wasn't going to be a doormat.

"April. I'm here because I want to find a way for us to keep dating and not just chuck this thing because we're both scared or having trouble communicating. If you already know you don't want to try, then you should just tell me and I won't waste our time."

"I just think ninety-nine percent of men are useless. They're just not value adds." *Where have I heard that quote before? Hitler? No, that's right.* April had said it within the first five minutes of meeting her on our first date, but I had given it to her as her Mulligan. (For those of you who aren't familiar with the reference, you get a "do-over" for one bad shot per golf round you play, and it doesn't count against your score. This is in amateur golf, of course. The pros must count every swing. I give girls one fuck-up per date. A bad joke, a banal observation, a shallow comment, and I don't hold it against them.)

Interestingly enough April did have very similar astrological aspects to Hitler; my mother had found that out when she did her chart. I have Mom do the chart of any girl I have a second date with. Actually, at first it seemed April had similar aspects to Hitler but then I realized I had told Mom April's birthday was March 12 instead of the seventh. When she redid her chart with the proper date, it turned out April's aspects were in fact only similar to Mussolini's, not Hitler's, which was certainly a relief. Am I into next year yet with my one-bad-joke-a-month allotment? The first part is actually true. At first blush, my mom did do her chart with the wrong info and reported that I was dating Ms. Hitler; the correct data simply made her not an Italian dictator.

"You said that on our first date. Do you really honestly believe that men aren't 'value adds?'" I had a hard time even repeating her awful term, "Because I'm a man."

"Well, there are exceptions, but for the most part I just find that women dress so nice and say interesting things. Men are just stupid and dull," she said with a straight face. She wasn't joking. It was so outlandish, I couldn't really even get upset. It was just so obvious that she was not a candidate for me or any man who didn't want to be with a woman who hates our gender, but as a last resort I tried to heed Gandhi's advice yet again and "become the love I wanted to see in the world." But before I could get out the first selling point for why I might be in the one percent of unboring, undull men, she stepped up the assault, now personalizing it.

"Why don't you work on Mondays?" Why was this so fucking important to her? Was Monday the day she wanted to back the car into the lake and drown the kids and didn't want me around to witness? Her affair day?

"I think because I always hated having to go to school Monday mornings, and waking up early in general, so as an adult I have fashioned a career and lifestyle where I don't have to work on Mondays if I don't want to and I don't have to wake up early. I mean, if I'm on a deadline or I can only shoot on Mondays because of a location, then of course I do, but I try to protect them so I don't have to, and I pay bills and do little chores that I don't want to do on the weekend. So I kinda work. Just not writing."

"EMDR would cure you of that. You should really go. Clara and I see the world entirely differently now. It's amazing."

"Would it make you feel better about going out with me again if I did IMDB?" Internet Movie Database for Eye Movement Desensitization and Reprocessing. The joke had worn out its welcome at this point. I had used it 1,284 times in the three days I had known her, in response to the 1,284 times she had sung her new therapy's praises, pushing me to go there to get "fixed." She used the pretense that it was just a "gift" she wanted to give me to augment my already-rich emotional recovery.

"I know you've been sober for twenty-three years and do all your yoga and meditation and therapy and have worked hard on yourself, but it's clearly not very effective because you're still completely crazy. EMDR will cure you." For the greatest emphasis I could muster I paused, looked down, took a deep breath, paused again, looked her dead in the eye, and in the most calm, deliberate this-comes-down-from-God-himself-so-you-need-to-trust-it-like-the-gospel-that-it-is tone I had ever said anything in, I said, "I am the most sane person you now know or will ever know in your entire lifetime," she scoffed and looked away, cataclysmically uncomfortable with my sincerity. "I know you think my ability to make such a statement only further corroborates your theory that I am indeed the craziest person you know, but at some point—it may be in twenty years or it may be in five minutes—you will, if you're lucky, realize that it's true. And that all my nuttiness and eccentricity and blah-be-de-blah-blah, has nothing to do with the fact that I am completely grounded and present and evolved in a way you can't understand right now. And I'm not saying that IMDB wouldn't be an interesting thing to check out and I will do that if it's that important to you but—"

"That's all I'm saying."

"Fine. Next."

"Next what?"

"What else do you need, to feel like you want to have another date with me?"

"Can we walk? I'm afraid I'm going to be late." She was softening. My willingness to go to IMDB seemed to open her up. We might be able to have Scientology babies yet.

"Sure. Let's walk." We strolled onto the running path that circles the reservoir, home to one of the prettiest views in the world: the still lake in the middle of Central Park framed by the stately prewars and Frick to the east, the San Remo to the west, and the modern and postmodern skyline holding hands like brother and sister to the south marking the end of the forest, the beginning of midtown in front of us.

"I feel guilty walking here because when I run I always hate the people who use the reservoir to walk like we're doing now."

"This is the last time I'll say it, I promise, but EMDR would fix that."

"I just spit on them as I run by, pretending it was an accident and they get the message. I don't think IMDB could possibly be more effective than that." She rolled her eyes.

"No, I thank them because they're my teachers. I learned that from Bhagavan Das; do you know who he is?"

She nodded. "The musician who sings Sanskrit chants?" I said.

"I know who he is. I go to Jivamukti, too. Remember?"

"Right. Anyway, he told me to just say 'thank you, I love you' whenever anyone annoys me. They're my teacher, showing me my own self-hatred. So I actually don't spit on them. My first thought is, 'They should get the fuck off the running path. Can't they see it's for people running?! There are a million other acres in the park they can use for walking!' And then I realize there's no law against using it as a walking path as well and I just say, 'Thank you, I love you,' and run around them. Sometimes I give myself the finger just for fun as penance for the initial angry thought." April sighed and gave me a look like, "If you only went to EMDR, you wouldn't have to go through all those machinations."

"It's already off the table. I'm going. But just so you know, we have a fundamental difference of opinion, see, I don't think I need to be 'fixed.' I like how my mind works." She threw me a look like, "Okay, we'll see."

"I mean I'd like not to be terrified to fly."

"That'll be gone in two sessions."

"Okay, great . . . So what else do you want from me?"

"Well . . . If you could just slow down and not be so intense, you know? Just be normal." I stopped and kissed her. She went limp. I don't know what EMDR did for this girl, but I knew what kissing her did. It shut off her mind and she dropped into her body. Runners ran by. "Isn't there any other place in the fucking city these two could find to make out?!" I thought for them as we kissed. She thought of the climate, I thought of hate mail. We were ill conceived but trying our damnedest.

"You're whole face changes when you sink into yourself."

She smiled and looked really pretty. "I know." She looked like a different woman. Older. There. Here.

"And you look really pretty." She blushed.

"Thank you."

My 'phone rang. "I'm sorry. Let me just see if it's work." It wasn't. I stuck the wire in my ear and pressed in the scroller once, so the phone picked up. I had the conversation looking at April, to include her.

"Hey, Lexi."

"I left her a message."

"Thanks, but I called her and we're together now, kissing in Central Park."

"Get out of here!"

"Hi, Lexi," April yelled.

"I'll call you later."

"Okay. I'm so excited for you. Call me and tell me everything." I pressed in the scroller, hanging up, and kissed April again.

"I'm glad we're back together," I said.

"Me, too."

"When can we have a proper date?"

"Friday."

"Friday?! I was thinking tonight after your dinner."

"I can't. I have to wake up early. I'm editing chapter thirteen and am on deadline, and I have plans every night this week. It'll be good for you to wait until Friday. Remember, you're not going to get all crazy. Let's just be normal. If you back off, I'll be staking out your apartment building. Trust me."

"Okay. I'll see you Friday." I turned to head back north toward my house.

"Aren't you going to walk me to my dinner?"

"No. I'm gonna go for a run. You know, just a nice, normal run." I smiled mischievously and then rubbed it in. "I'll see you Friday." She tried to get me back by returning my nonchalance.

"Okay. Have a good run." It almost worked, but with all my might I didn't get insecure. I turned with a wave and started walking the other way. So I wouldn't have the chance to turn and look back at her, I hung a left into the woods leaving the reservoir path, and disappeared. My phone beeped three seconds later. I had a text.

"You looked handsome walking away with the city behind you." I guess I should listen to her. She was telling the truth about how she played the game. She liked to play games. I didn't, but would indulge her for a little while longer. She was smart and had a good heart, but I had a profound hatred of her severe judgment of me and feared it would ultimately destroy our chances.

I walked home past the bench on Ninety-third Street. I used to get stoned there during fourth and eighth periods and after school. Most of the kids were rich at Columbia Prep except for me and a couple of others who were middle class or on scholarship. The wealthy kids judged me as April did, but pretended not to. They were her people. Getting stoned helped with things like that. On the surface at least.

High School, College, Donny, and Melinda Rent-a-Fuck
After tenth grade in Vermont, I moved back to New York City a whole new man. Gone was the insecure boy who was extorted for all his belongings by his best friend. I was seventeen, a star basketball player, had great drugs, and was the new kid in an Upper West Side private school system filled with hot Upper East Side hippie chicks. It was 1978. Disco, cocaine, a ton of teenage sex, and five-star camp—an "invitation only" camp for the best high school basketball players in the country. I was invited. I had a terrible week and didn't play well. Having long hair and being short and white didn't help, either. I wasn't going to be recruited, so I quit my dream of playing in the NBA, one I had worked for ten years to achieve. I fell deeper into my drug and alcohol addiction. In eleventh grade, I was smoking pot every couple of hours whether I had school or not; I either went to the bench in the park or just blew the smoke out of the bathroom

window. Every night we drank rum or vodka or gin or Jack Daniels, and my friend Ronald, who lived on Eighty-eighth and Madison, would steal anywhere from one to five hundred-dollar bills from his stepfather while he was in the shower. How much coke we bought depended on how many bills he got that night. We'd do amyl nitrate, acid, downers, speed, and anything else we could scrounge up, and listen to Joni Mitchell, the Beatles, Elvis Costello, and Joe Jackson.

It was a wonderful time of overlapping musical cultures. The hippie in us listened to classic rock, Led Zeppelin, the Stones, Jimi Hendrix, and Deep Purple. The New Wave in us listened to the Talking Heads and Devo. And the great R&B of the early '70s hadn't left yet, so Kool and the Gang, Al Green, and Bill Withers were on the turntable as well. Bowie and Stevie were as much staples for us as booze and drugs were at seventeen. I'd do bong hits when I woke up, a joint on the way to school, and then down enough alcohol to take the coke edge off so I could go to sleep at night. The only thing I hadn't done yet was shoot heroin.

Since my basketball career was over, I needed a new one to aspire to. I wrote my first play, which I produced, directed, and starred in, as a senior in high school. My classmate Ally Sheedy played an old lady, Esther. Ally wasn't yet famous, but she was in a Coke commercial that was pretty cool to all of us.

The play was a huge hit even though, at one inopportune moment, my right ball fell out of my bathrobe costume for a brief second. Unfortunately, I was used to this kind of public testicular embarrassment but, unlike in seventh grade, I could now just get smashed and laugh about it. In spite of the accidental flashing, I felt the love from the audience and decided show business would be my new passion.

I went to Bard and somehow managed to graduate in four years. How I ever did is a testimony to my wily guile and gumption since I spent a vast majority of my time cutting class and drinking Jack Daniels and shooting cocaine. While most kids spent their days much as you would imagine a normal college kids' days would be spent, mine were spent getting drunk in the local redneck bar in Red Hook alone, chain-smoking Chesterfields, listening to sad songs on the jukebox, lamenting whatever girl had broken my heart that week, and waiting for night to come. Nights were usually some version of this, give or take a slightly inaccurate drug-warped memory or two. But trust me, pretty damn close: I would first find Melinda Rent-a-Fuck. She was a hot blond chick who had one fake breast and was a witch. A good witch. And she didn't mind her nickname at all. In fact, she liked it. She got it because, as rumor had it, she had been an escort for a time in New York before college. Back then, 1984, that was a cool and very unique résumé line.

I slept with her within her first week at Bard. It was much fun, and I couldn't tell she had one fake tit, they both seemed excellent to me. One night a few weeks later, jacked from shooting many grams of jazz musician coke (which I dealt at that time, I mean really, really good coke. Uncut. High 80s pure), I went home to my house in Tivoli, a small bizarre town near Bard built on a Native American burial ground. It had the reputation of having the highest incest rate in America. I don't know if that's true, but I do know it was a sketchy fucking pueblo with a plethora of Zippy the Pinheads wandering around. I got home at about three A.M., desperately downing gulps of JD in an effort to counteract the effects of all the coke racing through my veins so I could try and sleep. I looked into my bedroom and noticed something weird on my bed, which was made. I never made my bed. There was something on my pillow. I slowly crept toward my bed, my heart beating even faster than it had been before, and the thing on my pillow got clearer. It was a wooden handle? I threw back the covers and, there in my bed, laying right where I usually lay when I slept, was a long shovel with dirt on it.

What the fuck?!!!!

Someone had broken in to my house to put a shovel in my bed? What did that mean? OH MY GOD!!! My grave is dug out back!!!! Mongoloids, my redneck landlords whom I owed months of rent to, unknown demons . . . somebody was going to kill me tonight, and this was my warning. I raced out of the house, jumped into my car, and squealed out of the driveway. Unlike the stupid cunts in the horror movies, I had enough evidence and didn't need to look around my house to see if the people who put the shovel in my bed were still around . . . to, like . . . chop my head off and shit.

Cool, off-campus me drove back to campus. Back to all the uncool, dorky babies who lived in nice, cozy dorms devoid of hangmen and voodoo zombies keeping them up all night with fear of being mutilated and buried out back. But on the way, I had a revelation.

I bet Melinda Rent-a-Fuck could tell me who did this!

She was hooked into all the witch and warlock shit at school, which consisted of one, maybe two tripping Goth chicks chanting over a goblet of red wine once in a while. I had fucked one of these marginally scary characters one drunken night and she was convinced I had killed her cat, which I hadn't, I just didn't want to fuck her again and she was hurt so she wanted to sully my good name by calling me a cat killer. I was sure she was behind this.

I went to MRAF's room but she wasn't there. She hung with my crew and might be found in the mods (modules), these really ugly stilted dorm shacks in a ravine below the dining commons. I ran through the big field that guarded them, and went to Diller's room. I had sold him the last of an ounce of coke, four grams, and he and a couple of other guys were probably shooting it there. SRAF liked to be around the coke, and we liked her around us because she was an excellent fuck and took pride in that fact.

I got to Diller's room and pushed the door open to find Diller freaking out, Bart mumbling in the corner, and Chase fixing with a half gram in the register about to boot. MRAF was there but not looking her best. She was slumped in a chair, motionless and blue.

"What the fuck?!" I said.

"I know! What do we do?!" Diller screamed.

"Is she dead?"

"I don't know! Should we dump her body?"

"Fuck her first at least." Bart mumbled.

"Shut the fuck up, asshole! This isn't funny!" I screamed. We were all panicking. Eric Stoltz was nowhere to be found, and the only needle was in Chase's arm and he wasn't giving it up. *Pulp Fiction* didn't have shit on our college experience. Finally I got a bright idea. "Do CPR on her, Diller. You're a fucking science major! "

"Right, right. CPR," Diller said.

Chase chimed in with a play-by-play of his focus, "Check registerrrrr . . . boot," and shot himself with the syringe of coke, oblivious to Diller, who was now blowing air into MRAF's mouth and pumping on her fake tit in an effort to save her life. After a couple of attempts, MRAF came to, and the first words out of her mouth were, "You're a good kisser, Diller. Fuck me, baby." She was back. "Melinda, before you fuck Diller or die again, do you know who put a shovel in my bed? Was it that other witch I fucked who thinks I killed her cat?"

"She thinks you killed her cat," Melinda repeated as if I hadn't just said it.

"I know."

"Someone put a shovel in your bed?" Chase asked.

"Yeah."

"You got anymore blow?" he asked me. Priorities.

"No. I'm kinda freaked out about this. Melinda?" Diller had her skirt up and was fucking her, which she was enjoying. "MELINDA! Who put a fucking shovel in my bed?!"

"Don't worry. Fuck me after Diller, and you'll feel better. I'll put a spell on you so no one will hurt you."

"Thanks. You got anymore of my coke left?" I asked Chase. Priorities.

"A little."

"Can I have it?"

"Welllll . . . "

"Just make me a hit, you cheap fuck." He did. I shot it. We always shared our coke, and we always shared our works. It was the fall of

1984. AIDS had broken out three months before but no one thought anyone except gay people got it, and even that was kind of a mystery. We didn't know you could get it by sharing blood. Luckily, none of us got it. And I never was murdered and buried out back. I guess Melinda Rent-a-Fuck's spell worked. That was your average Bard evening fun. Managing not to die or kill anyone else, I walked in cap and gown in the spring of 1984.

After I graduated, I came home to New York and for the next eight years worked eighty-hour weeks. I drove the cab for forty, and wrote twenty screenplays in the other forty when I wasn't sleeping. None of them made me a dime other than the Molly fiasco, which paid me three thousand dollars. I was about to turn thirty and was getting disillusioned for the first time in my life. I always have had a tremendous will to win, a resilience in the wake of defeat that has me up and at it again, determined to succeed. But at that point in my life I wanted to quit. I mean, TWENTY screenplays. EIGHT YEARS. I was turning THIRTY. A lot of scary numbers. And I had the tremendous fake-out of the Molly experience, thinking I was getting my turn only to have the rug pulled out from under me.

Shortly after I was born, my dad quit show business and became an academic. My mother quit show business as well and became a social worker. The bright light in both their eyes was extinguished a bit when they decided to abandon their dreams. Performing had always been their first passion. I didn't want to quit as my parents had. I felt I would be a loser. A coward.

But after getting my heart broken over and over and over again for nearly ten years, I just couldn't take it anymore. I knew I had as much if not more talent than those getting cast for parts and chosen to direct and write films, and I had a hard-working agent, but I just wasn't getting anything. I realized that I wouldn't be a "quitter" if I chose to stop bashing my head against the rocks. I would just be making a choice to let go of a painful career. I could continue trying if I wanted to, but I could also choose to try something else that might bring me more happiness. It was a huge epiphany not to view myself as a failure if I stopped.

Then, in 1992, a movie called *Laws of Gravity* came out. It was made by some guys I knew who started filming with thirty-five thousand dollars. They shot enough with that money to raise the rest and get the film distributed. It was the first super-low-budget indie movie that made it into lots of theaters and made a big splash, at least that I had been aware of. *Return of the Secaucus Seven* had been out there, *She's Gotta Have It*, *Metropolitan*, *Stranger than Paradise*, a handful of acclaimed indie films that, while made on very low budgets, didn't get the bulk of their publicity from that fact. *Laws* got a huge buzz when it opened at the Waverly on Third Street and Sixth Avenue.*

After watching *Laws*, I thought that if they could do that for thirty-five grand and get it in a theater, I could do it, too.

I moved home with my mom, into my childhood room on Riverside Drive, and started saving money to make a movie. It was a very special time. I was thirty years old, nearly ten years sober and living with my mom when I actually wanted to be. We built a warm, loving, friendly relationship for the first time in our lives. She was much

---

* The Waverly was also the original home of the *Rocky Horror Picture Show* movement, of which I was a part and remember fondly for its inclusive spirit. A club for freaks and geeks and nerds and druggies and anyone else who felt estranged. I have always been in search of a clan. People who fiercely love you, unconditionally accept you, and adopt you as one of their own. I think that's why the Mafia has such an allure to me. They love you so much, they kill you if you try to leave them. The Jews, the Irish, the fucking PTA for that matter. Groups. It's also why I can hate and judge so harshly. Because I wish I felt part of a club like they do. *Rocky Horror* was the first thing like that for me. Organized sports came close but, because I wasn't a complete jock, I was never totally part of them. The druggies came close, too, and the theater people, but, again, because I've never been just one thing, I wasn't granted citizenship by any of them, and still ultimately felt alone.

So the Waverly held a special place in my heart and sense memory. It was the place where I first experienced a feeling of true belonging and from that cultivated a self-esteem and confidence that anything was possible. Funny how a supportive family does that for you.

better at being a mother and I was much better at being a son. It was charming. I would meet her in the middle of the night as we both sleepily shuffled to and from the refrigerator to drink apple juice. Half asleep, she was really cute. Small and soft in her cotton nightgown, she patted my face as she passed. "Are you okay, sweetie?"

"I'm fine, Mom."

"Good night, honey." And she'd disappear around the corner of the tall standing kitchen cabinet and I would bask in the light from the fridge, drinking Motts out of the bottle. I could appreciate her now for the kooky, wonderful woman she was. Loving, tender, enthusiastic, and outrageously supportive. I could now love her unconditionally, and have only compassion for her brutal childhood and hard life of sacrifice as she tried to raise both of us, me and herself, without a manual. And she had done a fine job. I knew right from wrong, could tie my shoes, and was a nice man. And although I resented that she hadn't let me go on the field at Shea to get a clump of grass when the Mets won the World Series in 1969, she had taken me there and I was one of the fifty-two thousand people who got to witness and participate in the celebration of that miracle in person. And it was probably wise that she forbade me from joining the euphoric wilding that was rampant on the diamond that day. I *was* only seven. I now am able to see that both she and my dad, having limited emotional resources at their disposal to raise a child when they were twenty-six and twenty-four, respectively, (Amazing. Consider where you were emotionally when you were that age. I was a basket case), did the best they could, which was excellent. I am forever grateful to both of them for all the gifts they gave me. Not the least of which was life itself.

A few years ago, I finally learned the obvious lesson that forgiveness is the key to my and the world's happiness. It's been my new toy ever since. It's our only hope. I cease being the victim and you cease being the perpetrator. It's win-win. Because I'm you anyway. Whatever I condemn in you, I've done or am still doing. Whatever beauty I see in you is the beauty in me, as well. The world is empty. I give it meaning.

It's my choice. As hard as it is, with my subversive ego battling that truth, I try whenever possible to remember it.

In 1991, I ran into a guy I knew from the neighborhood, Donny. We were the same age and, although he grew up on 99th Street, and I on 104th, we didn't know each other as kids or even in high school. We met when both of us stopped drinking and doing drugs in the mid-'80s and had tremendous mutual experience. We had hung out at all the same parties, knew all the same people, and had written graffiti as kids, but just never happened to meet. He was in the same boat I was, having bounced around as a bartender trying to make a film and acting career happen, but having very marginal success. He said he would help me make a movie, and so we partnered up.

We hung out at his beach share in Sag Harbor in the summer of 1992, and wrote *My Life's in Turnaround*. It flowed easily and effortlessly and was a blast to write. We laughed and wrote and got rejected by girls at the beach (well, I'll speak for myself. I know I did, he probably had a girlfriend, I can't remember). We wrote it in one month and, when it was finished, got some very sage advice from a filmmaker friend who told us to "pick a start date and DO NOT change it. Your best friend will come to you to try to convince you to move off it. DO NOT CHANGE IT." So that's what we did. November 3. It was Election Day, 1992. We figured it would be a perfect day to start. Either we would be ecstatic because Clinton won and could celebrate by starting our first movie, or devastated that Papa Bush was getting a second term (My god, there's been two of them. That's somehow just now sinking in. Scary. I've apparently just awoken from my happy denial.), and we would need to have the hope and inspiration that living a dream-come-true would produce.

John Sayles had played Donny's great-grandfather, Ring Lardner Sr., in *Eight Men Out*, so we wrote him a letter appealing to that and the fact that he was the godfather of independent film, and asked him to be in our little sixteen-millimeter movie, playing an asshole producer. He said yes.

I'll never forget the magical feeling of driving to the set that first morning. We were in Donny's sister's old, beat-up metallic blue Dodge Omni, trying not to spill our cups of diner tea while devouring bagels with cream cheese at five A.M. A green Mafia garbage truck was blocking Ninety-fourth Street, so we couldn't make a left onto Broadway and head downtown to our set. When I was a cabdriver, I would get furious when they would have the gall to block the street for the five minutes it took them to pick up the garbage from whatever restaurant they were servicing, but not this morning. I wasn't driving a cab now. I was a feature film director ON THE WAY TO MY FUCKING MOVIE SET!!!!! WAHOOOOO! I sat patiently and waited for them to finish, a rich smile on my face. I turned and looked at Donny. He didn't notice any of it, he was busy ripping the plastic lid of his tea in half, making a drinking hole. He never got mad at things like the garbage truck blocking the road, anyway, so he didn't care. I was grateful God had put him in my life to be part of this outrageously wonderful moment. Tears welled as they often do when I feel the presence of God. When I know there's God—

Okay, it's now been three fucking minutes and they're still not done; "You guys couldn't just pull up five fucking inches to let the traffic get through?! You have to stop right there?!" I screamed and my serenity and God-consciousness was completely obliterated.

"Eric, you really think that's going to change anything?" Donny said calmly. "We're making movies now. Who cares?"

"Excellent point. We're feature film directors now." We giggled like children as the garbagemen finished.

We made the left onto Seventy-sixth Street from Broadway, heading for JG Melon on the corner of Amsterdam, our first location. There was a little white-paneled truck with people offloading light stands and equipment. *Is that for our movie?* I couldn't believe it. I mean, I knew we had hired this English guy and his "team" of NYU students as our crew (When I say hired, I mean allowed them to work for free and be in charge of the seventeen thousand dollars we cobbled together from family and friends), but I had no idea they would get there before us and be setting up lights and cameras and things. I knew how to write and act and direct but I had never set foot on a film set before. I figured you hired other people to do the technical stuff. I just couldn't believe it was all actually happening.

John Sayles's scene was the first one we shot. It was amazing. He was sweet and generous and helpful and supportive and brilliant. We finished the movie in fifteen crazy, wonderful days and even survived the English "team leader" taking the film negative, unbeknownst to us, to his house instead of the lab every night for "safekeeping" in lieu of seven thousand dollars he said we owed him. The day after we finished filming, Donny and I went to the lab to screen all the footage and found out there wasn't any there.

On alternating days, either Donny or I wanted to get the film back by any means necessary, but luckily neither of us felt that way on the same day. One of us would talk the other down off that ledge and convince him that, although excruciating, we had to wait it out until we negotiated with the guy at a sit-down with a lawyer.

We agreed that he had spent three thousand dollars out of his own pocket, money we would have gladly paid him without his blackmailing us with our film, and in the end it all worked out and we got the film developed.

The film opened at the Angelika in the summer of 1994. It was ridiculous. The Rangers had just won their first Stanley Cup in a million years, the Knicks were in the finals, and we had a movie opening in our hometown. Janet Maslin had given as a good review in the *Times* and there was a little buzz happening.

Nothing could get me down. Not the fact that our opening night was the OJ Bronco slow-speed freeway chase, not John Starks going 2 for 18 in game seven, killing the Knicks' chance of a championship, not even Ed Koch telling me he hated the movie after I followed him into the bathroom after the premiere screening to get his opinion. Queen Latifah said I was funny, and that was much more important to me than the curmudgeonly ex-mayor's endorsement anyway. Everything was amazing. I had a hit movie in the theater, and I was living with the girl of my dreams. The third of my Aquarian trilogy: Wendy. The girl I had the "search for the great American winter misadventure" with. And I could finally stop driving the cab.

The Cab

It was 1991. I hadn't been in love since Molly and hadn't had a proper girlfriend since Grace, a couple of years before that. I would soon be on my way to L.A. to try to drum up some interest in If Lucy Fell from some producers Boyd had scheduled meetings with, and writing Turnaround with Donny was still a year away. I was back driving the cab full time but feeling pretty hopeful. The cab was more like a lover you keep breaking up with and going back to, than a job. I was twenty-nine and had to adjust to the shock of being behind the wheel again after having just lived a magical three months with Molly on Mulholland, thinking my cab days were over. I was actually succeeding and enjoying myself quite a bit.

The cab was an amazing place. Not so much for the reasons you might think. Nothing crazy or bizarre happened with any regularity, but as an observer and lover of people and life and New York, I got twelve hours a day to indulge, anonymously, from my yellow car. People in the backseat seemed to think, though I was only three feet away, that I was lost in deep thought or too stupid to understand the meaning of their conversations or just assumed "Eric Schaeffer" (printed visibly on my hack license), white and clearly American, didn't speak English, because they would talk about the most intimate things as if I wasn't there. On the street, people look past cabs. They'll steal cars, have sex in doorways, mistreat their wife and kids, all with a feeling of anonymity if my cab is the only thing around. Of course, I also bore witness to the loveliness of humanity as well. All from the invisibility of 6GG3.

I also drove a Checker for a time, one of the last twelve that existed. That was fun. They're built like tanks. I felt very powerful. They did bring out "the shit people" for some strange reason, though. The one truly bizarre phenomenon that occurred during my cabbing days.

It only happened twice and I know three makes a trend, but the exception is anything to do with shit. With shit, two makes a trend.

The first time, I was driving an ancient, effete man to Carnegie Hall. I picked him up on Park Avenue and Eighty-ninth Street. He was with a woman in her sixties; he had to be eighty-five. She was either a friend or a caretaker, I couldn't quite tell. They were both dressed for an elegant evening out, except for his interesting choice of a beige fur coat. I had never seen that look. A beige fur coat atop a tuxedo. I mean not since *Animal House* or some bad Russian espionage movie on Channel 9's *Million Dollar Movie* in the '70s. I went with it. I figured he knew better than I. But the problem was this disgusting stench emanating from him. Could it be from the coat?

It was made from a beige animal, not the usual mink or raccoon. I couldn't place the fur. Lion? Had he killed the king of the jungle while on safari in the '40s and had a coat fashioned from his prize? Whatever. It smelled really gross. I didn't want to make him feel bad but I had to crack open the window even though it was February. He didn't seem to notice. He paid me and got out. As he turned to throw his legs over the seat and decab, I scrutinized the coat, trying at last glance to detect its origin and understand why it smelled so awful.

The olfactory evidence was suddenly plain as day. A four-inch-long, two-inch-wide smear of some kind of feces in the center of his back.

He had shit on his coat.

How had he possibly gotten shit on the back of his coat? Was it human shit? His own shit? Had he fallen down backward onto some dog shit in his house or on the street? He looked completely fine, except for the shit on his back. I didn't think he fell. Did he have Alzheimer's and his coat was next to the toilet and he thought it was toilet paper? It *was* a light color and soft, like Charmin. He got out. His female companion followed behind him and she didn't seem to notice, either. *Was* it shit? I looked hard again through the window as he waited to close the cab door after his lady friend, his back was nearly up against the front passenger window. I quickly leaned across the front seat and rolled down the window to get the definitive look. Oh God, it was horrendous! It definitely *was* shit. He heard me roll down the window and after a momentary delayed reaction felt me staring at his back. He was confused by my actions.

"Did I give you the right amount of money?"

"Yes sir, thank you very much. No, I was just wondering . . . how that . . . shit got on the back of your coat?" I didn't say that.

"I was just wondering . . . who's playing tonight?"

"Yo-Yo Ma."

"Oh, wonderful. Well, enjoy."

"Thank you." He shut the door, and he and his friend went into Carnegie Hall. I felt a little bad for him, but he seemed strapping and happy and healthy and very proud of his coat, so who was I to say.

The second fecal incident was in the East Village. I picked up a Hungarian woman on Sixth Street and Avenue B. She was in her fifties and seemed stoned on Thorazine. Shelley Winters meets Nurse Ratchet. She wore a stained floral housecoat and carried a small purse. She only wanted to go a few blocks, to Eighth Street and Avenue A. That seemed a little weird, but not nearly as weird as the paper-mill smell emanating from the backseat. If you've ever smelled a paper mill, you know that it's one of the foulest smells that exists. A perfect bouquet of four-day-old egg remnants left in the sink in the summer, and bird shit. I opened the window. I wasn't afraid of offending this woman; she was wasted anyway.

She sat deerlike, still, staring forward. Was there a new paper mill in Brooklyn whose odor was wafting west? It wasn't going away but getting stronger as we drove. I always drive fast but I floored it on Seventh Street along the south end of Thompson's Square Park. I needed this woman out of my backseat. I think I hit 80 mph, barely made the end of the yellow light on Avenue A, power duck-tailed as I took the right like in a car chase movie, and screeched to a stop at Eighth Street.

"Three seventy-five please, Ma'am." I watched her closely in the rearview mirror, again searching for any clue to the origin of this maliferous odor. She dug around in her purse for what seemed like hours. Finally, when she produced a five-dollar bill, she also produced the evidence that solved the mystery. The smell was cat shit. She had a small baggie which contained three little logs of the cat shit in her purse for some reason. The cat shit was also on the five-dollar bill she handed me. Pet peeve number one under any circumstances, let alone when you carry cat shit with you: have your money ready at your destination. Did you think the ride was going to be free? I have other trips to make besides yours, thanks. Help a little and have your little change purse located and open already. And if it's not too much to ask, please have the fee be feces free.*

---

* While we're on it . . .
Other cab pet peeves:

1. Do you think you're the first person today who said, "'Eric Schaeffer?' Are you an American? You're the first English-speaking cabdriver we've had!" And if you know you're the hundredth, can you come up with another opener, so I don't want to cut you and your family's throats and then take my own pathetic life because you're so fucking unoriginal?

2. No, it's not okay for me to just "hold the meter" while you run upstairs or into the store or into your office or grab your friend in the restaurant or do whatever the fuck it is you're planning on doing. It's not going to take "three minutes"; it's going to take ten at least. At twenty-five cents every forty-five seconds of holding time, that's $3.25. I could have made a new meter drop of two dollars and a long eight-dollar fare with tip. That's twelve dollars, or at least two shorties of five dollars each. Either way, I lose sitting around waiting for you. Limos get fifty bucks an hour to wait for you to run your little errands. Although you think that you're "taking care of me" with that big, extra, dollar tip, try an extra fifty dollars if you wanna "make it worth my while."

3. No, I won't slow down. If you want a scenic trip or have "time to kill," take the Circle Line or hit a peepshow.

4. No, I won't slow down. I'm sorry you have a bad back. Hail an ambulance next time.

5. No, I won't slow down. If your kid feels sick from the circus, have him puke onto your lap and wash up in the maid's bathroom in your classic six and if ANY of it gets on my car, that's a hundred dollars. (A kid once did end up puking all over the back floor and door of my cab, in the ashtray and nooks and crannies of the door handle and moldings. The father happily told me to go fuck myself, since he had warned me if I continued to drive fast, his son would vomit.) *continued on next page*

To try to right my bad cabby karma, my atoning rule is: *the more annoying the cabby, the more I tip him.* One of the greatest barometers of my spiritual state is how I treat cabdrivers. How I behave on subways is a good one, too, but cabs are even better since I was him. Am him.

I once asked this middle-aged Pakistani driver to go faster because I was late, which wasn't the truth. I was just annoyed that he was driving too slowly—you know, the speed limit? Not in danger of killing anyone? Annoying. He sped up a tiny bit but that freaked him out and he slammed on his brakes at a car that was pulling out about three blocks ahead of us on Broadway. I don't have any idea how he even saw this guy, he was so far in front of us. It was one of those

---

6. Yes, it is legal for me to eat pizza while I drive. (I once had a man try and withhold payment of the fare because I was eating a slice during our little trip.)

7. I know pedestrians have the right of way, but this is New York; get the fuck across the street already. Your friend doesn't give a shit about the point you're trying to help land by slowing down for emphasis. I don't, either.

8. I know the "rule" is that I have to take you anywhere you want to go. I don't care. It's rush hour and I'm not going across any bridge or through any tunnel and getting stuck in traffic losing an hour to make it back to Manhattan, the only place I have any chance of getting another fare, just so you can catch your shuttle to DC or make it back to walk your roommate's dog in Queens before heading back into the city for acting class. Work harder like I do, and spring for the Manhattan rent.

9. Yeah, whatever. Take my number and report me. I'll see you in taxi court. (Of the thousands of people who whined and did take my number, none of them ever actually did anything. Only one silent woman ever reported me. She won. She said I pulled away before she was out of the cab and the door hit her leg and caused a bruise. She was probably right. She was putting on makeup or some shit outside the door before shutting it, so I thought I'd be helpful and take off; the right-hand turn would close the door for her. I must have clipped her a little bit. Whatevs. Sorry. $350 fine. A week's salary. Happy, bitch?)

10. No, I won't turn the radio down, I'll close the partition. I'm a human, too, and am working here. It's not all about you.

11. No, the customer is not always right.

Those were the most glaring. We don't have time for the whole list, or we'll be here all day. Of course, years later, I see what an asshole I was, and am paying for my cab karma every day in the form of cabdrivers who refuse to obey any of my commands, especially to turn off the French news that apparently HAS to be heard RIGHT now and won't EVER play again.

herky-jerky, stop-start rides, and he didn't understand that if he turned the steering wheel to the left or right, it would initiate a turning of the car to the left or right. Although only ten blocks long, straight down Broadway, it was the worst cab ride of my life.

He pulled over at Seventy-ninth Street, next to the church basement I was heading for to try to get closer to God and mankind. The ride hadn't helped. Or so I had thought.

But then the moment happened, as it does more frequently the longer and more devotedly I practice a spiritual discipline. The moment when the Great Spirit graces me with a small window of opportunity to reach down and yank my higher self out before I am completely drowned in the bile of my lower self. This time it came in the form of a simple thought.

"Look at him."

So I did. I leaned up and pressed my face through the hole in the open partition so I could take in this man more completely. We had just pulled over and he had just turned off the meter. He sat back against his beaded seat cushion and let out a massive sigh. It was crystal clear to me in that moment that he had just gone through the most harrowing experience of his entire lifetime. The brain cancer he had beaten, the loss of his dream of being the first Pakistani astronaut, and the realization that his best shot at life was to move to New York and be a cabdriver, the murder of his entire family at the hands of civil unrest in his homeland—none of it was more deeply disturbing to this man than just having had to navigate that car down Broadway from Eighty-ninth to Seventy-ninth. That was the sigh.

He was sweating and scared, like a baby bird thrown from his nest. He felt me looking at him and turned to face me. He couldn't even think of taking any money from me at this point. He was just so happy to be alive and not having to drive an automobile for a few moments. He smiled at me warmly, looking for some empathy. His eyes were big behind thick, magnifying glasses. He looked like a cross between a Middle Eastern Mr. Magoo and that sad little French boy in the cheap card-stock painting my mother bought me when I was seven, which they still sell to the tourists along the Seine across from Notre Dame. Tears started to flood my eyes. I deeply understood him and so identified with his fear. About everything. About living. I'm afraid of everything, too. I smiled back.

"Good job. Thanks." I handed him a five. "That's for you."

"Thank you very much, sir."

"Take care. Drive carefully." I meant it sincerely. I was worried about him. I wished I was rich and could give him a job as my assistant or personal chef or something, anything to get him out of that cab. I got out.

"I will. It's very hard."

"I know. I used to drive a cab, too. But you're doing a great job. You're an excellent driver."

"You used to drive?" He was excited. For the same reason I get strength to surmount my trials and tribulations by bonding with others like me in church basements, he felt calmer knowing I really did understand what he was going through and had lived through it and come out okay.

"Of course. You're doing great. It'll get easier for you."

"Thank you, sir, have a nice night." And I was saved. Once again. And he never was aware of the nasty judgment I had previously had for him in my head. He only knew me to be a kind man.

That's the difference between living now and then. I used to think the world should judge me for my intentions, which deep down were always good and loving, even if my actions were heinous. Now I understand that, regardless of my intentions, I must act out in loving kindness to have any chance of happiness and a peaceful, helpful life, which is the only goal.

I heard Geshe Michael Roach speak at Jivamukti last year. He spent twenty years studying to be a Buddhist monk, and is one of the few Westerners to have been given that title after completing the intense study.

"How would you behave if you accepted the truth about yourself: that you are an angel standing on a billion planets able to help everyone in the universe."

Not a whole lot of room for, "Why won't the fucking guy drive faster," huh?

There were many wonderful times in the cab. I felt that anything was possible and that I was paying the obligatory dues of the presuperstar. I was going to acting class, living hand to mouth, and working my ass off.

I intentionally picked up groups of black kids from the Lowe's movie theater on Eighty-fourth and Broadway at midnight, knowing they were going to Harlem. All other cabbies, black and white alike, would pass them by. One time, three kids piled in after seeing *Terminator 2*. I had KTU 92 pounding RUN DMC on my ghetto blaster in the front seat.

"One forty nimph and Lennox," the first baseball cap said.

"You got it." I floored it. Their heads flew back from the force like the Concord taking off.

"That's what I'm talkin' 'bout," the second baseball cap said.

"Yo, how come white cabdrivers don't pick up black people?" the third baseball cap said.

"I'm a white cabdriver and I picked you up."

"Word. But usually they don't."

"I guess they're just ignorant."

The nodding of their heads in agreement of my theory transitioned seamlessly to the nodding of their heads in time to the music and we rode to Harlem, silently understanding we were doing our part to change the world the only way we could. By doing something rather than just talking about it.

The post-Molly cab period was different. I knew I was a better man for having gone through what I had and having had a taste, like a bit of the disease in the vaccine, I still felt driven. I was cured of my short anticlimatic depression. I picked up Phoebe Cates and Sarah Jessica

Parker in my cab during that period, both of whom ended up being in movies of mine. I was still single and couldn't meet anyone, but was soothed by cold, late nights on the barren, frostbitten January streets, watching abandoned Christmas trees swept across Canal Street by the wind like urban tumbleweeds. I had a couple of dates with some very nice girls whom I just didn't click with. That always made me sad. The death of the hope of love. One girl messengered me a box of Yonah Shimmel knishes in the middle of a nine-inch snowstorm on my birthday. I was out making snow angels in Riverside Park and came home to them. It was one of the coolest gifts I ever got. She was my kind of girl, just unfortunately not enough. The next week I dropped off the cab and went to Kennedy to fly to L.A. for the If Lucy Fell meetings.

For some reason, God speaks loudly to me when I travel. The episodes in the cab both as driver and passenger, subways, road trips, and planes.

The previous summer, there had been this hot girl in a Gap ad on the side of buses. I was convinced that if I had her my life would be perfect. Why couldn't I meet her? That was the kind of girl I should be with. I got on a plane a week later and sat right next to her. She was boring and still fucked up from the night before. She took a sleeping pill and slept for the entire flight. Thank you, God. The gift was a different one than I was expecting but a wonderful one just the same, and I was grateful. But I seem to forget those lessons, which are countless, a few seconds after they occur. Luckily, God doesn't give up on me and just keeps them coming. My timing was off. His timing was perfect. I *was* meant to meet my next girlfriend on a plane, just not that girl and just not that plane.

Wendy

So I boarded the back of the plane on my way to L.A. to try to set up If *Lucy Fell*. My radar scanned for pretty girls. I wanted to erase the bad vibe of the drugged-out Gap ad chick from my previous plane trip because I had always liked the idea of meeting girls on planes and didn't want her to have ruined it for me. On a long plane trip you could have five hours for a proper conversation, provided you weren't sitting next to a passed-out model. It was like a blind date, set up by God and American Airlines, replete with the auspicious rule of opting out at any time without being thought of as rude. "Oh, the movie! Are you gonna watch? No? Okay, we'll talk again before we land," and on could go the earphones. And unlike any other dating situation in your life, if you weren't having a good time on a plane and wanted it to end, like a baby you could just take a nap. Could you imagine if that was allowed on a regular first date at a restaurant? "So listen, I've had a nice time talking with you so far, but I think I'm gonna skip the main course and take a quick nap. Would you please wake me up when it's time for dessert? Thanks." But I had an excellent feeling about this plane trip. I just knew it would yield better results than the dead Gap chick flight.

Uh-oh! Hot redhead a couple of rows back. I was right! Feeling her eyes on me, I futzed around with my overhead baggage, posing, pretending to be looking for something important. The plane wasn't crowded, so I wasn't blocking the aisle. I took an exorbitant amount of time to do nothing to my bag. I tossed my hair and gave her my best clinched-jaw profile while pretending to look all around her, past her, as if looking for something or somebody very important in the back of the plane (What? A stewardess to help me with my little baby bag? A pillow? My mother who was supposed to be sitting with me but had gotten lost on the plane? Who knows. I was just giving this girl a chance to dig me if she was going to and it seemed to be working, as I could sense her continued interest). I sat down and quickly considered my strategy.

Two minutes later, I rose with resolve, and made a beeline for her. She was on the other side of the plane, on the aisle in the middle row, so I had to cross over through the bathroom passageway in the middle of the cabin. She watched me as I went, but then, as all women do who have just stared at you harder and more searchingly then they would at their newborn baby for the first time, she pretended I didn't exist as I got closer to her. To further the ruse, she feigned intent interest in her *Vanity Fair*.

"You're an Aquarian, aren't you?" I blurted out as if I already knew her.

"When did you figure that out? When you were taking ten minutes to put your one little bag up, posing for me?" She parried with a crackle.

I was in love.

We talked the entire trip. It turned out she *was* an Aquarian. Usually if I'm overwhelmingly attracted to a woman, she's an Aquarian. Wendy was funny and smart and really pretty. Half-Jewish, half-English, so she had the best part of the WASP thing going on without the stuffiness and repression. She was the one who I had told April about who sat on my lap in the bathroom while I was number 2ing and mentored me on the delicate nuances of the advanced experience.

She worked in advertising, was twenty-seven (I was thirty), and was a girl who said yes to life. Optimistic, adventurous, sexy, and witty. As we passed over Palm Springs and turned right heading for LAX, we realized the ride was almost over and I think we were both surprised by the emotion we felt. Tears actually welled in her eyes.

"This is amazing," I said.

"I know. I just met you." She smiled and wiped her eyes.

"Why are you emotional?"

"The same reason you are."

"So where are we going to dinner?"

"I can't tonight. But tomorrow I can."

"Okay."

"I know we have this amazing connection, but I feel I should tell you that I just started dating this other guy?"

"So. That's done now."

"Well, I like him."

"How long have you been seeing him?"

"Three weeks."

"Three weeks?! Am I alone in thinking that we have some seriously crazy thing between us?"

"No, we do. For sure. But I always jump into things really fast and then they crash and burn, so I'm trying to go slow and just be normal for once."

"You can't possibly have the same thing with the other guy or this wouldn't have happened."

"I don't know. I do like him."

"What does he do?"

"He's a pilot. From Sweden."

"Oh, please!" I said incredulously.

"What? My father flies planes."

"Oh, okay, so that's it. He reminds you of your dad so there's a bond that has nothing really to do with him. Know that and move on. Life's short."

"I want to date both of you."

"You've only been dating the guy for three weeks. Just send him away. Come on. Don't be scared by this. It's magic. Just be happy it happened."

"Why can't I date both of you?"

"Because I don't do that. It's bullshit. I don't want to fall in love with you and then be the loser in six months, when you pick him. Just because we met five hours ago doesn't mean shit. Connections like this happen so rarely. You have to trust it. If you don't, then play out your Swedish pilot and call me when you're done and maybe I'll be here and maybe I won't."

We sat in silence for a moment. The steward broke it broadcasting scratchy instructions for the final approach.

Wendy had a black town car waiting to take her to Beverly Hills. I had an orange Budget bus waiting to take me to the Budget store.

"It was nice meeting you." It felt so strange to send my wife away with a cordial pleasantry. Divorced before the first date. It made me sick to my stomach. She was very sad, too.

"Are you sure?" She looked into my eyes, trying to convince me that if I stayed it would turn out well for me.

"Yeah. I'm just not made that way. If you're ever single, call me. You have my number."

"And you have mine, if you change your mind."

"Okay. Take it easy." She got in her car and was gone.

I don't know how people do that dating-more-than-one-person-at-a-time thing. I've since tried it being on both sides because in some mythical dating handbook "they" say you're supposed to, but I'm just not cut out for it. I can appreciate its rationale, but I just get too attached and too hurt when things end no matter how short they are. While I am willing to risk heartache, I still want the landscape as primed for my success as possible. Starting the game with other competition already in place seems like a recipe for disaster.

And when I've been on the other side, dating a few girls at once, or saying I need to be open to it even if I'm only seeing one girl, it's always been a vain attempt to convince myself I like the girl I'm dating more than I do because, if I really liked her, there's no way in hell I would ever introduce the idea of any scenario where other people were involved. I would only want her and want her to only want me. It's not that I'm lying to her, I'm lying to myself, having good motives, hoping it'll change and I'll start to like her more, but deep-down knowing inevitably, it's not going to happen.

Three months went by. I had written a play that I was producing and directing off-off Broadway. I thought about Wendy every day. I called her up and invited her to come to see the play. She did. It was as if a minute had gone by since I last saw her. Nothing had changed. We still looked at each other exactly the same way we had on the plane. It was after a Saturday matinee, so we went to Central Park and lay in the grass in the shadow of Belvedere Castle.

"So what's happening with Mr. Pilot?"

"We're still dating. It's going well."

"But you're here."

"I know."

"Wendy. Life is so short. Don't you owe it to yourself, to him even, to see if this thing between you and me could be the whole deal?"

"Yeah, but you don't want to date me if I'm dating him."

"So send him away."

"I don't want to."

I sighed deeply, frantically thinking. *There has to be a way around this.* And then, inspiration struck. I could hardly contain myself. This was one of my best ideas EVER! Wendy caught my huge grin.

"What?"

"You've been seeing him for three months, right?

"Yeah?"

"See me for three months."

"What?"

"If he really, really loves you, he'll understand and wait for you. What's three months if you're going to spend the rest of your life together? But if after three months with me you know I'm the one, then you're saving you guys from a bad, unfulfilling life or a year of dating and then a bad breakup, and gaining the man of your dreams. If you find out I'm not the one, then you go back to him, no harm no foul. It's win-win for you."

She paused, looked up and to the left, her creative mind going a mile a minute. I was shocked she was even considering my crazy proposal, and got really excited. I applied full court pressure.

"Come on, the fact that you would even think about it means you're not going to marry this guy. I mean, God bless him but you're lying in the grass with me after meeting me on a plane three months ago and being three months deeper with this guy . . . it's not gonna happen. It's not happening! If you were in love, you wouldn't even be considering it. You wouldn't even be here."

"Shut up. Let me just think. So what do I tell him? 'I like you a lot but I need to go date this other guy for three months to see if he's my soul mate. Can you just hang out and wait?'"

"Yeah, you could say that. Or you could say you need some time away from the relationship to figure some things out. That's not a lie. You're just not telling him you're going to see someone else during the time."

Her mind was racing, jumbled with the possibilities. She shook her head, trying to shake sense into herself.

"This is crazy. I can't do that!"

"No. It would be crazy *not to* at this point."

"I have to go."

"Wendy. Come on. Ninety days. Will you think about it?"

"No. Yes. I don't know. Maybe. Yes. I'll think about it."

She walked away, discombobulated with elation and terror. I smiled. I had her. I didn't have a fucking clue how, like when the Mets were down to their final out in game six of the 1986 World Series. There was absolutely no way they could win that game, but I knew they would. And they did. That's how I felt watching Wendy pass the Delacorte Theatre as she walked away from me on her way out of the park.

I didn't hear from her Sunday. Monday, the phone rang. She was at her office in midtown. I was writing.

"Hello?"

"How about thirty days?"

"Deal."

"Okay."

"What are you gonna tell him?"

"I'm just going to tell him I need some time apart to think about things, and I hope he understands and will be there when I'm finished thinking. I don't think it matters whether I'm seeing you. I'm deciding if I want to be with him. That's all he needs to know."

"I'll pick you up at work. When do you get off?"

"No! Not tonight."

"Why not?"

"I need to talk to him first."

"So talk to him and meet me after that. What time?"

Pause.

"Ten o'clock. Where?"

"Wo Hop. Mott Street."

"I'll see you there." She was so cool.

And so, we were off.

We ate Chinese food late in Chinatown. We played golf in Mohunk and ate blueberry cobbler at the bed-and-breakfast before. We went to movies and plays and made love and wrestled and laughed. We even got past the psychosomatic foot cramps she got in the middle of sex designed to stop it. She danced to the opening theme music to *NYPD Blue* on my couch, and we fell in love. Then, it was the last night of the month. A Friday. It was a fait accompli. Just to make it official, jokingly I asked, "So, am I the winner?" I knew it was no contest.

"Can I think about it over the weekend?" I couldn't believe she was serious.

"You need to think about it?"

"I just need to let everything settle for a couple of days. It's been such a whirlwind. Is that okay?"

"No. It's not. If you need to think about it after that month we just had, then forget it. It's bullshit." And I left her house. I was sure she'd call. She didn't. Out of foolish pride and hurt, neither did I.

Six months went by. Donny and I made *My Life's in Turnaround* and got it in the San Francisco film festival as the opening-night film. The first person I thought of calling to share the amazing news with was Wendy. Even though I was devastated by her indecision after our amazing month, on an ordinary Tuesday night in the middle of the summer, the only person I wanted to go for a walk with was Wendy. I wasn't angry anymore. I just liked her. And I've liked so few women in my life. So few people. I didn't care who she was with, I just wanted to see her and have her in my life.

"This is Wendy," she said, answering the phone, preoccupied at work.

"Hey."

"Hey. What's up?" She was equal parts cool and happy to hear from me, but knew it was just a matter of time before she agreed to see me.

"What are you doing?"

"Working. What are you doing?"

"I want to see you."

"I'm busy tonight."

"You still with the pilot guy?"

"No. I never saw him again." *She hadn't picked either of us?*

"You didn't pick either of us?"

"No. I just needed time to think after that."

"So you're not going out with anyone now?"

"No. I've been seeing Adam."

"Who's Adam?"

"My high school boyfriend? Adam? I told you about him." *Oh, your "high school boyfriend Adam." Your warm-safe-I'm-almost-twenty-eight-and-don't-want-to-be-alone-so-I'll-just-date-my-high-school-boyfriend-Adam-Adam. Yeah. I'm not too worried.* And I honestly didn't care. She could have been married to the pilot. I just wanted to know her.

"Oh, great. How's that going?"

"Good. He's really nice. It's easy. We've known each other since we were little."

"Great. So when are you free?"

"Are you seeing anyone?"

"Nope."

"And you don't care that I'm dating Adam?"

"Nope. I just like you, Wendy. And I've missed you and want you in my life. I don't give a shit about anything else."

"So we're just going out as friends?" *That's why I liked her. She was one of the few women in my life who didn't play games. No hidden agendas. She just answered when asked and asked when she wanted to know something. Exquisite.*

"No, I don't care that you're dating Adam."

"Okay. I'm free Thursday."

"Done and done. I'll see you Thursday."

It was only a matter of time until Adam was history. He was a place holder. I mean, God bless him, he's a child of God and all, but he was no match for the fate that was Wendy and me. He also hadn't made a movie and put his story with Wendy in it as a backup, just in case fate was getting a rub and tug that day and was out of the office.

I flew us to San Francisco and we went to the opening together. We had been hanging out as "friends" for a month, at that point. We went to a drugstore in the Mission. She needed saline solution for her contacts. I tried to nonchalantly buy rubbers at another counter while she was lost in aisle four. Suddenly she was over my shoulder plopping down a Bauch & Lomb bottle.

"HELLOOOOOOOOO. You're not gonna need those this weekend, Sparky."

"They're not for you."

"Oh yeah? Who else are you hoping they're for?"

"I don't know. I do have a major motion picture premiering here tonight. You never know." She made a sardonic "yeah, right" face and turned to leave.

The writing was so on the wall. I was so attracted to Wendy. She had childlike puppy dog eyes and a crooked smile. Angular features but soft edges. She had shoulder length red hair and an athletic 5'5" body. She had a great walk, which is so important.

We consummated round two of our relationship that night at the Landmark Hotel, a majestic old joint on a hill overlooking the east bay. It was the icing on one of the most iridescent days of my entire life. That morning Wendy and I had rented a car and drove up the coast to Mendicino. We hung a right inland and got lost on the most magical winding country road. We seemed lost in a time capsule. This was Ireland somewhere. Lush green, little stone houses hidden among huge trees. A dirt road with no other cars on it. We drank coffee and listened to the radio and knew we would spend our lives together. It was getting late and we had to get back for the opening. We had at least a two-hour drive and no idea where we were or how to get off this magical road, "God Road" we called it. Suddenly, around a bend, we came to a paved road. Taking a guess, we made a left. A mile along was a highway with a sign that read "San Francisco—149 miles." I drove fast and there wasn't any traffic. We pulled up in front of the hotel, with ten minutes to make it to the theater just down the hill. We spent five of it seat dancing to that slamming Whitney Houston song that I can't ever remember. In the video she was wearing leather and metal claws or something at a futuristic fashion show? Very BD/SM sexy. The song was smoking with an incredible hook. Lady Marmalade hot. It was the best seat dance of my life. I love seat dancing to ridiculously loud music in a car. It's one of my favorite things to do especially since I'm much too old to dance in clubs now. Naked in my living room in the middle of the day works, too.

The movie was a great success, after the projectionist finally got the film to play correctly. The first two attempts were misfires. The first one upside down; the second, backward. Luckily, the entire audience was drunk from the preparty and cheered his efforts no matter what image ended up on the screen. Donny and I, of course, were having heart attacks.

Wendy and I went back to the hotel after the after party and had amazing no-pyschosomatic-foot-cramp-to-corrupt-the-intimacy sex, and Adam was out. No additional thirty-day plan to immortalize in the sequel, no "friend" tag to have to endure while secretly pining for more, just Wendy and me. Boyfriend and girlfriend. Finally.

We moved in a year later and lived together for one more after that. Her sex issues were long cleared up, but mine, unfortunately, were just beginning. I never could make love to women I loved. It had historically been like that. I mean I could have, my dick worked, but I just didn't want to. Sex was always incredibly hot in the beginning. I'd fuck my girlfriend five times a day until I knew she loved me and thought I was the best sex she ever had, and then I would become frigid. I would love her very much and was very affectionate but anything sexual, even kissing, made my stomach turn, yet I was completely hot for every other woman on the face of the earth. (Not acting on it, of course.)

I turned down every advance Wendy made and then, after she went to bed, masturbated, thinking about all the women I wouldn't cheat on her with. That had been my pattern since I was in high school. I hated it, but felt powerless to change it. I was working on it in therapy, so Wendy was trying her best to be understanding. We had sex one time during the last year of our relationship. I loved everything about living with her, the warm feeling of sharing a home and a life with a wonderful woman who loved me and everything that came with it. There was no better feeling in my life. But unfortunately, I just wasn't ready. I was too scared to be that close, so I ended it.

Donny and I had written a pilot for a TV show for Fox and jumped from William Morris to CAA. We got three deals to write and direct movies the first week there, and I had signed Sarah Jessica Parker and Ben Stiller to be in If Lucy Fell. I ran into Sarah at a party and she had remembered my picking her up in my cab years earlier and we now had the same agent at CAA. Donny and I had met Ben for one of our other movie projects so that's how I got him. The last part left to cast was for "Jane," my character's love interest in the film.

As deeply as I loved Wendy and as much as I truly wanted to live the rest of my life with her, I just couldn't go on faith that I would find fame and fortune wanting. I had waited and worked for ten years for this moment. The eighty-hour weeks sweating in the cab, writing screenplay after screenplay, and now it was about to happen. I was going to have a network TV show and my second film released by TriStar and the last part to cast was being sought by supermodels. I had to be single. And I wasn't going to cheat on Wendy, fuck around in Hollywood for a few months, realize it was shallow, and go back to her a liar. I had to do the right thing and risk losing the woman of my dreams. It seemed a surreal choice, "I love you but I have to send you away?" But I had to. So, heartbroken and frightened, I did.

I wondered if I was fundamentally incapable of ever really getting close to a woman and if this excuse for leaving Wendy was just that, an excuse to not have what I always said I really wanted. I didn't know. I was doing the best I could at the time. If I could have done better I would have. I hated hurting her feelings far worse than hurting my own.

Donny and I finished shooting the pilot of our sitcom for Fox in L.A., and I returned to New York to find the apartment empty. Most of the stuff in it had been Wendy's. It looked almost as it did before we'd moved in together the previous year. It was Thanksgiving, and gone was my dream of a family with Wendy. She wouldn't ever cook her famous chili for our Super Bowl party again. Gone was the patio furniture. Gone was the couch. Gone was my girlfriend. I sat on the dusty floor and wept.

Demi Moore Again

I cast Elle MacPherson in the role of Jane, a move that led to a lot of heat from critics who said the only reason I make movies is so I can cast supermodels as my leading ladies. That accusation is preposterous for two reasons. First, if the best person for the part happens to be a supermodel or any other very attractive woman for that matter, of course I'm going to cast her, what moron wouldn't? Would I cast a pretty girl who wasn't right for the part so I could have a chance to go out with her, jeopardizing the quality of my film and millions of dollars of my and other people's money? Of course not. And second, I got more trim as a cabdriver than I have ever gotten as a writer-director-producer. Please! In this PC day and age? Gone are the days of chicks wanting the middle power guy. Now you either have to have Bill Gates money or be the scruffy Ethan Hawke–looking second grip. Who does Julia Roberts end up with? A director? No. The assistant cameraman. I get power lashback from women: "Fuck him. Just because he's the director-writer-star, I'm gonna go out with him? No way!" Even girls who might have liked me on an even playing field don't consider me, because of my job. When I was a cabdriver, shit, I was just lovable, nutty, "Eric the cabdriver." I met girls everywhere. On planes, trains, my cab, the gym, subways, the street.

Now my love life consists of receiving e-mails from girls on dating Web sites, telling me that the ten-year age difference between us is scary with the average "life expectancy" what it is today, and you wonder why I've been driven to professional hand jobs and golden showers?

While making *If Lucy Fell*, I started dating a girl, we'll call her Demi Moore again. It wasn't really Demi Moore this time either, nor was it even a member of the Brat Pack, but that's what we're gonna call her. And unlike the Molly Ringwald thing, I'm sticking to my guns in this case and maintaining her anonymity because the real girl was living with a man when we were dating, and this book isn't tabloid kiss-and-tell or designed to hurt anyone. It's about your identifying with me so you feel more united with humanity and less alone. That's why I'm writing this book. In this chaotic, fractured world, anything that can make us feel more a part of, more bonded, is of the utmost value. This is my humble attempt at a contribution to that end.

Molly was single when we hung out, so no one was injured by the telling of that story. Except for the wounds it reopened in me for a moment . . . and of course my chronic sexual sneezing. In this case, innocent people might feel hurt, so the woman will remain Demi.

Demi and I fell in love. It was hot. She was one of the most beautiful women I had ever seen, but more important, I liked her a lot. We had fun together. She was funny, dug and accepted me, and we had ridiculous sexual chemistry. It was an insanely romantic relationship. I once sent her a thousand roses when she was in Spain. They didn't have enough on the mainland and had to ship them in from the Canary Islands. I took the Concord to Paris to surprise her for dinner and we spent the weekend at the George V. It was a fairy tale. Although it was so not my MO to get involved with involved women, I had to go for this. It felt like a once-in-a-lifetime kind of a thing. And I got the sense that the relationship with her boyfriend was open or something. I think he was fucking around on her, and she on him. I can't be sure, and I never talked to her about it but I felt justified in taking my shot. I honestly thought there was a good chance that their thing was going to end anyway, whether or not I was in the picture, and that there was a real chance for us to have a lasting relationship.

It's what I've always wanted, since I was a kid. I never ever have had a time in my life when I said, "I'm just interested in fucking around and being single." I've always wanted a serious relationship. That's not to say that I haven't had dalliances along the way but after college, they've been relatively few, and, on the first date, my intention was always for something more. If it seemed not to be going that way, for whatever reason, and we both wanted to get laid, then I was sometimes up for it. But as I've gotten older, I can't seem to do that anymore. Women get all the press for it, but like them, I get way too attached way too quickly if I have sex. And if it's before I know the girl well, I can get close through the sex with a girl I don't like very much and then I get really confused and hurt when it doesn't work out, even though we weren't a good match anyway. So, my new plan (if it doesn't work out with April, of course—I already fucked up the new plan with her, having sex on the third date) is to not even kiss for something crazy like, I don't know, ten dates. Like a "saving-myself teen" or whatever they're called. Although those kids are giving head and rim jobs on the first date, from what I hear. As long as no cocks go in any pussies, they're "sticking to the covenant." Facials, pearl necklaces, sodomy, tea-bagging, tit jobs, those are all okay, just no intercourse.

The Demi period of my life was made even more enchanting because it was in conjunction with making *If Lucy Fell*. The budget for *Lucy* was tiny by Hollywood standards, but compared to *My Life's in Turnaround* it was epic.

We had big trucks, union crews, and thirty-five days to shoot instead of fifteen. I had an assistant and a cell phone (It was 1995, so they were those huge NASA flip ones that doubled as toaster ovens). I was stylin'.

Although Ben Stiller and Sarah Jessica Parker weren't the mega-stars they are now, they were still fancy to me. We shot in February, my favorite time of year. It was bitter cold and snowy and amazing. I was in a torrid love affair and making my second film. It was sick.

Page Six, the gossip page in the *New York Post*, wrote a story about how I was fucking Elle MacPherson in her trailer and filming was going to be shut down because I was so lovelorn over her finishing shooting and going off to be with her boyfriend in London. None of it was true. I had never had sex with Elle in a trailer on the set, and I was completely fine with her leaving to go do whatever she was doing in her life when not contracted to be working for me, and I was excited to be filming the scenes she wasn't a part of. Elle and I had a close friendship and she was professional and easy to work with. Enthusiastic, humble, and gracious. But Wendy read the piece and showed up on the set to ask me about it. We had broken up under the auspices of my figuring things out and maybe getting back together. She asked me if I still loved her, to which I replied the truth. I did, but not in the way I think she wanted me to love her, and I didn't think we were going to make it. I told her the thing in the paper was a lie but I didn't get into my relationship with Demi. That relationship had nothing to do with our troubles, and would only have hurt her to know about. There was absolutely no reason to get into it. She left my trailer in tears and I was heartbroken for both of us, but I just wasn't ready for her and in retrospect had done the right thing by ending it because I did end up falling in love with someone else, who turned out to be Demi, as I had suspected I might.

Though an electric love affair, Demi and I broke up a few months later. I could no longer deny the reality that she was involved, no matter how shakily, with another man, and I didn't want to continue to be part of that scenario for the obvious reasons. I felt like a female character in a bad TV movie, living for the hope that her lover would leave his wife. It was pathetic, so I broke it off with her even though I was ridiculously in love. I told her if she was ever single, to call me. We hugged and I cried in her arms. I was grateful for that chance. It was one of the only breakups I've ever had where we got to end it in each other's arms. It was unimaginably painful but easier to get over because I knew no one was at fault and that there was tremendous love there; it just wasn't meant to be. My blaming and self-hating ego had no ability to twist the truth for its evil and corrosive purposes.

I bumped into Demi six months later at Sundance when *Lucy* premiered. She was there promoting a movie she was in. She was still with her boyfriend and although she wanted me to stay for the weekend with her in her cabin, I declined. It was one of the hardest things I ever had to do in my life. I went home to watch the Super Bowl on my birthday with Helen and my friends. I was learning to take care of myself at the expense of immediate gratification and with tremendous heartache, but in the long run, for everyone involved, it was the right thing to do. So, another big love was gone. I was thirty-six.

I went back to L.A. after the Super Bowl and resumed working on *Too Something*, the sitcom Donny and I had gotten picked up by Fox. We were in the middle of a twenty-two-episode order, but things were totally fucked.

We had shot the first thirteen and they had aired five. Our ratings sucked, and although we were in Fox's best time slot, between *The Simpsons* and *Married with Children* on Sunday night, no one was watching. The network started meddling with the original concept of the show, and I tried to save it by rewriting every episode. The show was becoming increasingly sitcomified and watered down, losing all of its originality and edge. There was a tidal wave of opposition against me, and even though I was the cocreator and costar, I ultimately succumbed and things got ugly.

Donny was silent, not wanting to rock the boat, and although I realized in retrospect he was using a diplomatic strategy that might have helped us at the time, I viewed his silence as not having my back and was deeply hurt. At one table read, after being insulted yet again, I lost it, something I had never done before, and went ballistic with white rage at our other coproducer, one of my oldest friends. Donny had to separate us when I went after him physically. Studio security was called. I left the set and it was all in the trades the next day how I had gone crazy and was a nightmare to work with.

I felt enslaved, disrespected, and abused. The writers on my own show, while very talented, felt writing epithets about me on the blackboard in the writer's room was a more productive way to spend their time than coming up with better scripts. Donny and I weren't speaking. I actually wouldn't talk to anyone on the set, although we were still in production and making shows every week. I walked off the show and went home to New York. I quit a job that paid me $35K a week—and, believe me, I needed the money—but it wasn't worth how I felt I was being treated.

My coproducers, the writers, and the studio rejoiced. The evil seed was gone. They hired another kid to replace me, but unfortunately Fox didn't see it the same way and told them to get me back or they would sue the studio for the cost of the remaining six episodes. In turn, the studio threatened to sue me if I didn't come back, so I did, and finished out the string. It got really bad after I returned. During rehearsal of an episode, Henry Winkler was directing (the sweetest man I have ever met and my hero, Fonzie? Come on!); he had me use this long rolled-up carpet as a tool to unwittingly knock my costars down as I turned around, a physical comedy gag straight out of the Three Stooges. The next day I got a memo from the studio telling me that they were aware I had "knocked down" my costars and that "no physical abuse" would be tolerated. That was how ridiculous it got. It was the fucking nightmare of my life. I finished the shows; sold my Porsche for half its original price, losing a ton of money I couldn't afford to; left the scary gay castle; and went home to NYC. I had lost my best friend, my TV show, and the woman I was in love with. Not a good winter. But at least I had the opening of If Lucy Fell to look forward to.

Because it slayed at Sundance and got great reviews out of the festival, TriStar was going to open it on one thousand screens in March. In 1996, that was a big opening. Not huge, but big. And compared to the two screens My Life's in Turnaround had opened on, it was gigantic.

I went to the Cayman Islands to get rejuvenated (tan and thin) after everything that had happened and to emotionally prepare (get tan and thin) for the Lucy opening and the filming of my next film, Fall, which I planned to shoot in May, regardless of how Lucy did. I was rested (tan and thin) and excited beyond belief. The immense disappointment I had just gone through on every front was replaced with a will to win and a feeling that everything would soon turn around. I went to the premiere at the Sony Lincoln Plaza on Sixty-ninth Street. Helen was my date. It was red carpet and star studded and at my neighborhood theater. I told the "wood chip pile/running in Riverside Park/getting arrested" story as my opening speech before the movie began. Most of the people couldn't have cared less and wanted me to shut up so the movie could start and finish so they could go to the party that Elle was throwing at the Fashion Café. A few soulful guests loved the story and were glad I told it.

As has been the case with all of my films, Lucy got mixed reviews and didn't do well at the box office. My work is very polarizing, much like I am as a person. Love or hate. Negative reviews seem to be predicated on the reviewer's skewed perception of my lifestyle and/or intention for making a film. They have little to do with the content of the movie. I can live with a well-written review by someone who doesn't like one of my films if the reviewer makes salient points relating to the subject matter or the artistic choices I've made as the writer, director, producer, or actor in the picture, but too often my bad reviews are obvious stone-throwing displays by people who don't have the courage to do what they really want, which is to pursue their own artistic dreams.

These malcontents hate me for laying myself open, cleaving my heart for all to see. It scares people. It has my whole life. But I only know one way to live. The people who it doesn't scare become my friends, lovers, and fans. Again, that's not to say that there aren't many amazing, smart, heartfelt critics and others alike who don't like my work; there are, and that's fine, as long as they don't like it for the right reasons. It's just not their sensibility or their sense of humor, but not because they can't admit the truth of their own self-loathing that I then become the scapegoat for. And when it's critics, it's morally reprehensible because it kills my films and, as a result, many people don't get to see them, and that's unfortunate. It's about the message, not the messenger. A critic's job is to critique art, not the artist.

The critics who have raved about my work have never cited my haircut or who I've slept with in their reviews as reasons for their adoration. The critics who have killed me, have led their reviews with both.

As painful as that year was for me, I still have to remember that it included the deep joy and satisfaction of knowing that millions of people enjoyed a TV show and a movie I made, having my heart broken that meant at least I had loved and been loved, and getting to play basketball with Michael Jordan. (It could have been much worse and, believe me, I never ever discount my good fortune and thank God every day for all of my many blessings, and always am aware that my problems are luxurious ones comparably.)

During the time I was making *Too Something* on the studio lot, Jordan was shooting *Space Jam* and getting himself in shape to come back to the NBA after his baseball experiment. He had the Long Beach State basketball court trucked onto the lot in sections, reassembled, and housed inside a huge white plastic dome. Every day the buzz wasn't what movie star was filming, but what players Jordon was having run with him in his daily afternoon games. Bird? Magic? Barkley? The entire UCLA team?

I had to get in there. The head of lot security and I had bonded over our Porsches, and he said he'd get me through the front door but that then I was on my own. I practiced all day for my big moment. I didn't think Clooney had played with Jordan yet so I would be the first TV guy on the court. At five o'clock, after we were done rehearsing, and I had shot around on ER's hoop as often as I could during breaks, I went over to the dome with the security guy. He got me past the two huge bouncers and I was in.

It was like Oz. Huge booming speakers pounding rap from every angle. Hot chicks of every ethnicity, white, black, Chinese, scantily dressed, drinking iced tea on plush white sofas next to the court. Everyone from Chicago Bears football star Richard Dent (he had his own ball no one was supposed to touch) to L.A. Clipper Pooh Richardson was there. I walked over to the court. I was wearing sweats and a T-shirt I had been given from Nike. They give anyone with a TV show free rein in their warehouse, so at least I looked the part.

There was Jordan. He was on the free-throw line, engaged in a friendly wager with Urkel from *Family Matters*. No-look, left-handed foul shots for ten bucks a pop. And Urkle was matching him shot for shot! I rebounded and passed the ball back to them after every attempt. Because you see Jordan so much, you're desensitized and feel like you know him. I had to pinch myself. I had just thrown a chest pass to Michael Jordan. I was about to explode in giddy nervous laughter. I knew Jordon was a gambler, and my fantasy was to offer to play him a one-on-one game to five for $5K. It would be so worth it to me, but I was apprehensive. It seemed a little weird to ask.

I don't regret much in my life. I take most risks, 99 percent of them, but I didn't end up asking him, and that I regret. I did talk to him, and he was gracious and warm and told me I could come shoot around whenever I wanted.

I took a ball and went out past the three-point line on the side. He and a couple of other guys were shooting around. I was the only short, white guy there. The only white guy at all, for that matter, so although everyone was being cool, they were curious as to who I was and why I was there. I had been playing this moment over and over in my mind all week, shit, my whole life . . . my first shot on the court with Michael Jordan. I rose up and shot. Now, I'm a very good shooter, but as soon as that ball left my hand I knew I had just put up the biggest brick of my life. If it hit the rim, I would be lucky. If it clipped the side of the fucking backboard, I would be overjoyed. I mean it was a duck. As it flew toward the basket, seemingly in slow motion, my heart sank. I was sure Jordan would pretend not to see or care or wouldn't really see or care, but I was crestfallen anyway. All my years of practice, and in one shot, I would be the laughingstock of all who had ever played the game and would let down all the people I represented that day. Those who had a similar dream but would never get to live it. That shot was for all of them, too, and I had disgraced them all. But miraculously, providence lent a hand.

The shot was so off that it banked in. And because I was on the side of the court, I could have planned it. If I had been straight on it would have clearly been a radical miss, but from the flank, hell, I was fucking Larry Bird with a bank shot. Eyebrows raised a little and a guy grabbed the ball and started to dribble away.

"A little respect, please," I said and raised my hand so he was clear, so the entire gym was clear, on who had just stuck that twenty-two-footer. *Yeah, that's right. ME BIATCH! Now throw me the fucking ball!* For all the unfair treatment and lack of respect I had gotten at the hands of black basketball players on the city courts my entire life because I was short and white, even though I was better than many of them, I was willing to take credit for what I knew was the chuck of the century masquerading as designed perfection. Hell yeah!

The guy cracked a smile and threw me the ball. Jordan chuckled. I shot again and missed. I retrieved the ball near where Michael was about to shoot. I lunged at him pretending to try to scare him. He shot an air ball.

"That's that Schaeffer defense," I said dead seriously. He rolled his eyes and with a playful grin said, "Yeah, right." I just forced Michael

Jordan into an air ball, whether he would admit it or not. I retired at the peak of my game, having been a lifetime 50 percent shooter and all-star defender. Not that I *wanted* to retire, but I was aided by a very thin, tall black guy with a whistle around his neck who approached me out of nowhere, put his arm around my shoulder and neck a little menacingly, and started walking me off the court.

"Excuse me, who are you and what are you doing here?" I guess he was in charge of "handling" any players who were better than Michael Jordan and might continue to show him up on his own court. I puffed out my chest.

"I have my own TV show, *Too Something?*"

"That's terrific. Are you in the NBA?"

"No. I—"

"Because this court is for professional basketball players."

"I understand, but I have a show and I just thought—"

"Right, but are you a professional basketball player that plays in the National Basketball Association?"

"No, I'm not." My chest was no longer puffed up at this point, in case you were wondering.

"Okay."

"I just wanted to watch." I had somehow gone from Big Man on Campus to Bitch Man on Campus in a heartbeat. The infinitely less desirable BMOC.

"Fine. You sit on the side and watch. You don't come on the court again." My moment of revenge and vindication was over, and order was restored in the basketball kingdom. It was all alright. I had my moment. Michael knew. And Urkle showed me respect on Clooney's court for the rest of the summer. But none of the *Friends* girls cheered for me courtside. Not even any of the *ER* girls were there. I was still alone and wishing I had a girl watching. My girl.

so I'm allowed to have my tongue in your ass but can't pee with the door open?

"So I'm *allowed to* have my tongue in your ass but can't pee with the door open?"

"I would vote no for either actually."

"But you get my drift. I just had my mouth all over you and will very soon have it on your ass but—"

"Could you please not say that again. Really."

"Really. You really can't hear anything about the ass or shit or—"

"NO!" She was mad.

"Are you really mad?"

"Yes. I don't like it."

"Fine. No scatological humor of any kind."

"Thank you."

"And you can't look at me and smile while I'm eating."

"What?"

"That's one of my things. Your strange quirk is no scatological humor and no discussion of anything pertaining to the butt, mine is you can't look at me and smile while I eat. Especially dessert or my after-dessert drink of cold soy milk."

"Why is that?"

"I don't know. Maybe because my father used to look at me and smile with this emotionally intense look, and it just bugs the shit out of me."

"Have you called Tabitha yet?"

"Who's Tabitha?"

"EMDR? I e-mailed you her number. You so need it."

"Why don't you do IMDB on your ass phobia?"

"Because I don't think it's inappropriate that I don't like scatological conversations, or something I need to change."

"You don't think it's a disconnect that in the bedroom I can do way more intimate things to you than peeing with the door open, and you're fine with it?"

"No."

"Are you hungry?"

"Yes, please."

"Shall I make us a huge yummy salad?" She smiled and nodded enthusiastically. I left the bathroom doorjamb I had been leaning against during the previous inane conversation and headed for the kitchen, kissing her tenderly as she leaned against the bedroom doorjamb further up the hallway. I was trying to bring some comforting closure and reconnection, not wanting our postcoital sense memory to be a fight but rather a reconciliation and bonding. She seemed to want that, too. The kiss was gentle and sweet. I playfully slapped my own ass as I walked through the living room and tossed an over-the-top "I'm so hot" look at her back over my shoulder. She wasn't smiling.

"Are you gonna put some clothes on?"

"No, I'm making us the salad, I thought, unless you want to go out?"

"No, I know. Were you planning on making it naked?"

"Yeah. Is that not allowed either?"

"I'd prefer if you put on some underwear and a shirt or something."

"You're kidding, right?"

She paused, deciding if this was a battle she wanted to fight right now. She opened her mouth to speak but then closed it.

"What?"

"Nothing. It's fine."

"Apparently not. Say it."

"No, it's fine. Really."

"You can't do that. Say it."

"When I was growing up, we never had any money—"

"Don't you live in the same two-floor mansion on Fifth Avenue you grew up in?"

"Yes, but that's only because my dad bought it in 1958 or whatever. He was a teacher. We didn't have a lot of money but they always loved elegance. Even though they were middle class . . . I just don't want my children to have a father who doesn't wear a shirt at the dinner table."

I paused. I couldn't even respond. I acquiesced.

"Okaaaaaay." I was livid and my stomach was burning. I grabbed my shorts from the chair in front of my computer. They had come off fast on the way to the bedroom when she'd first arrived an hour before.

"I think you need to be rejected in order to like someone." She was on a roll. What part of her IMDB ass had she pulled this one out of?

"Excuse me?" I couldn't hide my disgust any longer.

"You're doing all these things to push me away."

"Peeing with the door open and cooking naked?"

"Uh-huh," she said with this sanctimonious smile that made me want to throw her off the roof.

"I disagree. I just think you're shut down, repressed, superficial, and self-hating, so you're finding minutia wrong with me because you can't imagine a guy as decent and available as I am would be interested in you. Do you like avocados?"

"Love!"

"Cucumbers?"

"Uh-huh."

"A hummus-tabbouleh-balsamic vinaigrette?"

"Sounds delightful." Again I had taken full advantage of her complete desire to avoid having any conversation that was real and honest, changing the subject to a much more palatable one . . . salad. I was getting far too used to this bad habit, though.

We sat on my couch, eating the salad. She really liked it. Nothing to fight about there. Oh, sorry, spoke too soon. I forgot. I was sitting cross-legged with shorts on. Not underwear but midlength Gap short pants, which, even when sitting cross-legged and riding up my leg as a result, still revealed nothing but my upper inner thigh. That was disgusting, distracting, and completely inappropriate to her.

"Just so you know, I like seeing you naked. In bed, out of bed. Having sex, cooking, eating, on the phone. Wherever. I like your body. And I like you no matter how you sit, clothes on or off. Just for the record," I said. She turned red and broke out The Voice. I guess that was too much affection and honesty.

"Noted. I'm going to go."

"Why?"

"It's getting late and, since I'm not going to stay over, I'll feel less like a whore if I'm the one to say I'm leaving and you don't kick me out."

"I thought you liked the whole 'having our own wings in the mansion and hanging out in the kitchen once in a while' thing."

"I do. But I still will feel like a whore if you kick me out after we've had sex, so I'm going to go."

"Okay. I'll walk you down to get a cab."

She didn't seem angry and I was glad that she was being proactive in taking care of herself emotionally so I wouldn't needlessly take the misguided wrath of her insecurity twenty minutes from now for saying that although I was having a great time, I wanted to watch SportsCenter and she needed to leave.

She had instructed me to lie whenever I wanted to part ways and just say, "I'm tired" rather than tell the truth that I actually wanted to engage in an activity that didn't involve her. This seemed oddly contradictory to what I thought was one of our strongest commonalities, the need for a lot of space.

I will love my wife and want to do many things with her, but I will also need a wide berth. Most women see that as a threat to intimacy; I see it as a builder, a strengthener, a protector of intimacy. Hey, my longest relationship has been three years, so what the hell do I know, but I feel fairly certain that for me at least, I have to think outside the box to have a chance at a successful relationship. Six out of ten marriages end in divorce, and I don't want to add to that stat. When some women have the superficial, clichéd reaction to me of, "You're forty-four and haven't been married yet? You have intimacy issues, for sure," my reply is, "I would rather take my time and get it right when I finally do get married than have been married and divorced twice already, with a couple of kids having come from broken homes."

Out of the four remaining couples that don't get divorced, how many do you really think have mutually loving, emotionally evolving, happy, healthy, sexy, fulfilling relationships that aren't riddled with infidelity, alcoholism, rage-ism, or are just shut down, uncommunicative, and dying? One? Maybe two? So that means most people don't have a clue. Whatever "book" everyone's using isn't working. I will want to be closer to my wife than to anyone else on the planet, but if we don't have enough money to have a huge mansion where I cannot see her for a day every once in a while, if I'm so inclined. I don't think it's a crazy idea to keep my office/apartment at Spuyten Duyvil as a place I can watch Monday night football alone upon occasion if the mood strikes me. Or she can, for that matter. Again, I don't think an idea like that is a threat to intimacy, I think it's a way to ensure that real intimacy will last because I'll be honest and know I'm loved unconditionally, with all my quirks, as I will love her unconditionally with all her quirks. We will compromise and know we have each other's back in a real way, about the important, hard issues. Not just "poker night" and "girls' night out" bullshit, but the deep things, which can fester and cause resentments that become the cancer that kills relationships that otherwise wouldn't die.

For instance, I've never been a good sleeper. I toss and turn and, on my best night, get five hours of undisturbed sleep. That's alone. And I go to bed late, at three A.M. Then I'm up and down, peeing and eating, until five A.M., when I can finally fall asleep. So my only real sleep is between five and ten A.M. If someone is getting up to go to work at six or seven A.M., banging around the house, forget it, I'm done. I'm just not a good sleeper. And although I like the idea of sleeping with my wife and enjoy the cuddle, I really just want a huge, king-size bed of space to myself. Sex, cuddling, talking, a kiss, and then "Good night, see you in the morning, I'm off to my bedroom." I don't think that's so weird. And not every night. And you know what? I might change and turn into a smothering cuddle monster who never wants to leave her arms through the entire night, I don't fucking know. I just want to know I can be the real and complete me with the woman I'm going to spend the rest of my life with, because she will definitely be able to be the real and complete her.

April actually agreed with me philosophically about the whole "apart/not apart" thing and, after I felt assured it wasn't because she was trying to build a wall of distance because of a fear of intimacy she had, I was ecstatic that I had found a woman who saw it as I did, as a good thing. It was one of the only things we agreed on, but it was a huge one.

The cab door was open, and the driver eager to get going.

"I had fun. Thanks for coming uptown."

"Sure. I did, too. Thanks for the salad. It was great."

"Did you have fun in the bed?" She turned red again, nodded, and in The Voice said, "Hm-hm."

"You know. I understand you're not as forthcoming as I am—"

Amazingly, she dropped back into her regular voice. "I'm trying. It's just very hard. I don't know why. It's just very scary. I've never met anyone like you who really listens and sees me, and [she couldn't hold out anymore and went to The Voice for the punch line] *it's terrifying.*"

"Well, I just want to tell you that in the same way you like to hear me say nice things to you, I like to hear them, too. I want to know that you're liking this and me."

"I'm trying."

"Okay. Thanks." I kissed her and she got in the cab. As it pulled away, she looked back and waved. I waved back and crossed the street, heading back to my building. In the elevator, my Blackberry light blinked. She had texted me.

"I rented *Fall*. I'm watching it tomorrow."

"I thought you hated it," I texted back.

"That was ten years ago. I thought I should watch it again."

"Good idea."

"Good night."

"'Night."

The next day was Sunday. Donny and I were walking west through the park, returning from the spiritual meeting on the East Side that we usually go to every Sunday night before eating chicken and rice and beans at Flor De Mayo. My Blackberry rang. It was April.

"Hello?"

"What are you doing?" she asked eagerly.

"I thought you had all your fancy plans at the Soho House or whatever tonight."

"I canceled them."

"Where are you?"

"In your lobby."

"Really? How long have you been there?"

"Twenty minutes or so."

"I'll be there in ten minutes."

"Okay." I hung up.

"That girl just showed up at my lobby to surprise me."

"Really?"

"Yeah."

"That's good."

"Yeah. I like it. Let me go obtain her. I'll talk to you later."

"Obtain me later with all the proper discussions." I jumped in a cab. April was waiting for me outside my building when I arrived. She was wearing a yellow sundress, white frilly blouse thing, and flip-flops. She seemed older, calmer. And her face looked different. Content. Quiet. She looked very beautiful. She was holding a bouquet of flowers, a card, and a manila envelope.

"What's up? You have many things."

"Yeah, well. I've had an intense day." I kissed her and went upstairs.

I got us both a glass of ice water. It was an August-in-June day in New York. HHH. Hot. Humid. Hazy. As she gulped . . . well, she didn't gulp. A normal person as thirsty as she was would have gulped. She control-gulped so as not to give the impression of gulping but only drinking quickly. But not too quickly. While all of that was going on, I put the flowers in a vase.

"Cut the stems. They'll last longer." I guess that's why one doesn't gulp. It would be too hard to interrupt a gulp to criticize. But when appropriately drinking quickly, one can still easily stop to bark instructions without choking or spilling.

"They're Korean stand, baby. One day and out."

"No. If you trim off the bottom of the stems, they'll last for a week." Not true, but with this girl I was definitely picking my battles and this was not going to be one of them.

"Okay." It *was* okay, anyway, because I liked having a reason to use my scissors. Cutting things is fun. And chopping. That's why I love making salads. You get to chop. Any cutting or chopping, I like. Except for the first time I "groomed" my below-the-belt area two years ago. Everything was going fine, grooming, trimming, grooming. Then I pulled the hair on my testicular sac taut so I could get a closer cut. A few years previous, I had gone to an eye doctor to investigate a slight blurry condition that had suddenly beset my lifelong perfect eyesight. He put mean drops in my eyes, which made them a million times more blurry than they had been before I went to him, and made me look at a thousand charts. "Better, worse, the same?" Change. "Better, worse, the same?" Change. "Better, worse, the same?" Then he scribbled on a pad, tore off the top sheet, and handed it to me.

"What's that?" I asked innocently.

"Your prescription."

"I need pills for my condition?" I asked, horrified. "I thought for sure it was because I just became vegan last month or, knock on wood, a brain tumor or something." He laughed. He thought I was joking.

"It's none of that. You need glasses."

"Excuse me? I have perfect eyesight." I wasn't joking.

"How old are you?"

"Forty."

"That's when it happens."

That's when it happens? That's when it happens?!!!! That's when what happens? My fucking eyes go blind, you cunting cunt?! And he walked out of the room, my youth and manhood with him. Glasses? I don't think so. I filled the prescription with the cheapest pair of peach-colored Charles Nelson Reilly frames I could find, since I was never going to wear them again after the test. As soon as the drops wore off and I could see again, I experimented by putting the heinous things on and looked at the CitiBank sign across from the Cohen Optical, where I had gotten them. Everything was indeed much clearer, so I took them off, stuck them in a drawer and never took them out again. And I never will. I hate having anything obstruct my view. Especially glasses. Sure, words are clearer, but at the expense of my sanity. I just don't feel like myself with them on. I can't think. I hate everything about them. The tradeoff is I have to hold labels—and apparently my balls—at arm's length now, to see them clearly? Big deal.

SNIP! AWWWWWWWWWWWWWWWWWWWWWWWWW!!!!!!

I had snipped a small chunk of my nut purse in a perfectly cylindrical design. Scrotal origami. Wasn't fun. So maybe just for groin grooming, at least, I'll start wearing the glasses.

After that, whenever I use the scissors with the red plastic handle, which I got at Duane Reade, I twinge just a bit from the memory. This mission went off without a hitch, however, and April seemed satisfied with the job, except for how I arranged the flowers in the vase, of course; that took some adjusting. I tried to remember if this was how all relationships with women were or whether it was endemic to just this particular one. I had a nagging suspicion most men would tell me it was all relationships, but I have never been one to sign up for deep and frequent annoyance in mine. I would rather be alone, or hold out.

The jury was still out on April. It would be coming back in very soon and wasn't looking good for her, but still out for now.

"That's much prettier don't you think?" No, I don't.

"So, what are your other things there?" I said, referring to the manila and card-size envelopes.

"Well . . . Where do I start? This is a play I wrote when I was fifteen. It's about my sexual abuse when I was five, and no one has ever seen it or read it, and I want to give it to you. I watched *Fall* today and I cried for four hours. I realized that, like the girl in the movie, I lost myself years ago and have been living a life I don't want to live, and I want to get myself back." Wow, she was making a huge comeback. I had always suspected this battle was raging in her, and I had been holding out for the other April to emerge. The one who valued having a man who cared for her in the bathroom, more than whether the door was open or not. Hearing her admit it seemed like a breakthrough and was very promising.

"So there was that. And then I had two epiphanies. The first is that you were right. You are the sanest person I know. And two, falling for someone is like getting food poisoning." I was happy she was opening up, but a little concerned at the sudden about-face. I mean, she had just confessed she was falling in love with me. Even though I liked hearing it, I don't like instability and inconsistency. It scares the shit out of me.

"You go from zero to one hundred in a second once you throw the switch, huh?"

"Uh-huh." She put her arms around my neck.

"Why do you put up with me?" she asked. It was her clumsy way of trying to get closer to me instead of just saying she was insecure, having just opened herself up more to me than she ever had to any man. She wanted some reassurance.

"Because I like you and had an idea you were in the middle of that kind of war with yourself, and *really really* like you when the old April you want to reclaim wins." We kissed. Again, I wished it was more in sync but it just wasn't. Even when she was in her body, we just didn't have kissing chemistry. I mean, if there was ever a time for a kiss, this was it, and it just didn't land. She had a flickering, withholding tongue. It was a passive-aggressive tongue. She would lightly send it in but then withdraw it suddenly, then bring it back and flick your tongue with it quickly but shallowly. It was like those pseudolesbian hetero porn stars who aren't really into girls so they kiss without putting their lips together and just flitter their tongues at one another, except April would at least have her lips on mine. I'm sure, to many men, she was the best kisser in the world, just not to me.

I picked her up, carried her to the bedroom, and tossed her on the bed, trying to jolt her out of her head and into her body. I jumped on top of her and started grinding. I whispered in her ear.

"Can you feel my cock?" Silence. *Maybe she didn't hear me.* "Do you like how I feel against you?" Silence. I like talking dirty in bed and find that most women love it. Did she not like it?

"You want me to fuck you soft or hard?" She broke into hysterical laughter.

"I'm sorry. You just sound so ridiculous."

"You don't like talking dirty?"

"No. It just seems foolish to me. I have to laugh."

"Okay."

"Is that a problem?"

"No. Not at all." It was a huge problem. This girl just was not turning me on. She had wanted to have sex on the second date and I had declined, wanting to go slow. If I like a girl and think there's potential, then I like to try to wait as long as possible. At least three dates. Conversely, if I'm on a first date with a girl and it becomes clear that there's no chance of anything long term, then we can fuck in the bathroom at the restaurant.

"Are we going to have sex?" she asked as matter-of-factly as if I were the keynote speaker at a 1956 AMA symposium on human sexual behavior and it was the question-and-answer phase of the evening. This was her version of dirty talk, I guess.

"I'd still like to wait," I said sincerely.

"But it's the third date."

"I know but I want to know you better. I would think you would like that."

"Is it because I don't like dirty talk?"

"Of course not."

"Come on. Just fuck me." Her request seemed odd and forced.

"There's always some reason guys won't fuck me. I'm not Jewish. I'm too successful—"

"I just want to go slow. I thought that's what you wanted."

"Okay, we can go slow." She started to get up off the bed.

"So, no making out unless we're going to have sex? You're turning high school boy on me?"

"Yeah. Kinda." I was lost in this sudden role reversal. I wasn't pre-pared for it at all, and was confused by the power exchange. What was I supposed to do? I got scared. When in doubt, fuck, I guess. I grabbed her, flipped her on her back, hiked her skirt up, unzipped my fly, and started fucking her. In silence.

She wouldn't touch my dick. She wouldn't even unbuckle my pants, but she was very wet. It was the only hint she liked what we were doing or that I turned her on, because I certainly wouldn't have known it by the way she wasn't touching me. I rolled over on my back and pulled her on top of me, thinking she might be able to cum that way since she wouldn't let me go down on her. When I had kissed below her belly button on our second date and she got the idea where

I was headed, she jumped up, nearly breaking my nose with her pelvic bone, and said she didn't feel comfortable with me doing that yet.

Lying on top of me she seemed to be enjoying herself and moving toward coming. I tried to lift her up, cowboy style, so I could stroke her breasts and see her face. She wouldn't budge. She was glued to me, her torso pinned to my chest and her face turned away. I whispered, "Sit up."

"Why?"

"Because I want to see you."

"No. I don't like to be seen."

She got close but didn't cum and then told me the window had shut; she wouldn't be able to now and wanted me to cum, so I did.

"Am I allowed to go to the bathroom naked?" I said jokingly.

"Of course."

"I want to work with you on this. I just want to know exactly what I can and can't do naked."

"Anything but cook or watch TV."

"Okay."

"Or, you know, lounge around in the living room, talking."

"So basically I should only be naked in the bedroom or bathroom."

"Yes."

"Okay."

In the bathroom, I took off the condom and filled it with water like a water balloon to make sure it hadn't ripped or wasn't defective. It was my routine. I didn't really have to do it with April because I trusted that her last HIV test was authentic, and she was on some coil contraceptive, but I checked it just the same. She meekly called from the other room in The Voice.

"I wish I was a different person, if that's any consolation."

"Why?"

"I don't know. I know I'm difficult."

"You're great. You should be you." I went back and joined April in the bedroom. She was under the covers but fully clothed.

"How did you get clothes on so fast?" She smiled. I kissed her. It was slightly better. More relaxed. She let her tongue lay more heavily on mine, which was nice. She didn't try to move it away.

"Can we go onto the balcony? It's so nice out."

"It's hot out there," I said. We were in the middle of the longest streak of getting along we had ever had, and I wanted it to continue. I feared it would end if we went onto the veranda and she launched into her "no patio furniture?" trip.

"I know, but it's nice," she said. I carried two folding wooden lawn chairs I stole from the Bard graduation, and two ice waters out onto the balcony.

"Are you *against* having patio furniture?" She wasted no time. Straight for the jugular.

"Absolutely not. If you want to give me some as a present or if we get married and you want to have whatever out here or on whatever balcony we have, then I'd be totally up for it. I don't care enough now. I either just walk around or bring chairs out or blankets to lie in the sun. It works fine." She considered my response while she drank her ice water. She wasn't pleased with the answer or maybe very pleased, actually, because she had some more ammunition to use against me.

"So, I want to talk to you about something," I said seriously but with tenderness.

"Okay."

"I'm totally fine with being p . . . understanding about your sensitive sexual issues and . . . "

"You were going to say 'patient.'"

"Yes, I was."

"Then just say 'patient.'" She was tense.

"I was trying to find a word that didn't seem—"

"That's how you feel; just be honest."

"Okay. I'm totally fine with being patient about your sexual issues but I'm just wondering why you never touch me below the neck. You said you like oral sex but just aren't comfortable yet with me going down on you, which is fine but it seems like there's a no-touch zone below my neck, too, and it makes me feel like you're not attracted to me, or do you really not like oral sex, or—?"

"It's so funny that you're saying this to me, because in the past I've always been the more sexual one and, for some reason, with you I feel shy and . . . I don't know. No, I'm extremely sexually turned on to you. I will say, though, that when you asked me last week if I liked you better thinner—?"

"Yeah. You said you didn't care." I had asked her if she thought I was more attractive now, or fifteen pounds thinner, like I always am when in a movie. She had said she had no preference and she thought I looked "great."

"Well, I will say that, seeing you in *Fall* again today, I was hit with a visceral schoolgirl reaction like, 'Wow, he's hot.' And it's your body and you should do what you want with it, but I will tell you that I am more attracted to you when you look like that."

"It's kinda weird that you're bringing it up at this point of this conversation because, before you had even seen *Fall*, which you just rewatched today, you didn't want to touch me, back before you had any thinner image of me to contrast against what I look like now, so why are you bringing it up at this point of the conversation? Are you saying *that's* the reason you aren't interested in doing other things with me?"

"Well, maybe a little bit."

"How much does it affect your attraction to me?"

"Well, let's just say that if you were fifteen pounds thinner, I would have gone down on you by now." I couldn't believe my ears. *She did not really just say that out loud.* I felt like vomiting and crying on the spot. I looked at her to confirm that she had really just said what I thought she had said and, again, with that churlish grin and non-apologetic shrug as if to say, "I'm just sayin' you kinda disgust me and I don't care that saying it is going to tear you up. That's actually the part I like best," she stared back.

"You asked me to be honest." *Yeah, but not in a way that would gut me.* Was *intended* to gut me. I took a deep breath, got up, went inside to the bathroom, and shut the door. I guess she was going to get me to do it one way or another.

I am very rarely speechless but in my entire life, I had never *ever* had someone say something so mean to me. I was reeling. I looked in the mirror to make sure I was still there. I was, barely. I splashed some water on my face, toweled it off, and sat on the toilet lid, staring at the white tile wall. I couldn't even imagine what I was going to do or say next. I was just trying to get my bearings. I heard her creep toward the door.

"Eric? Are you okay?" she said in the smallest, most contrite voice.

"Yeah, I'll be out in a minute," I said as if nothing was wrong. *I'm just in the bathroom admiring my blue eyes in the mirror rather than trying desperately not to disintegrate.*

"Okay." She retreated into the living room, leaving me to take a few more deep breaths. It was all I could think to do. Could you imagine if a man had said that to a woman? He would be strung up in Times Square and stoned to death. Exiled, never allowed to have a girlfriend again, blacklisted for eternity by all women.

And rightfully so.

"Uh-huh? Good. Thanks for the honesty, April. And while we're on the subject I have just a few things . . . If your ass wasn't so boney, I would want to fuck you more. If your legs weren't disproportionately long for your torso, making you look like a midget giraffe, I'd want to fuck you more. If you didn't waddle like a duck, your cankles announcing their disgusting selves like a new giant inflatable cartoon character called Canky-Cankles in the Macy's Thanksgiving Day Parade, my dick might get harder than the demibone I can only muster by imagining fucking your crazy sister. If you knew how to kiss, if you had a clue how to be sexy or sexual in any way, I might want to fuck you more or even just kiss you. If you were prettier and not just kinda plain looking I'd be more turned on to you; I mean you're not ugly but you're just kind of boring and you put yourself together well, which makes you seem prettier than you are. If you had sexier feet, if you didn't have a semiretarded appearing arched back and arms that are too long for your body . . . If you weren't a mean-spirited, repressed, fucking cunt, I might want to be around you for two minutes after I cum and not want you to get the fuck away from me like the heartless cunt you are."

If you're not Molly Simms or that French guy Diane Lane fucked in that movie before Richard Gere smashed his head open with the glass orb, you have a list of defects. And even they have a list, trust me. A much shorter one but they have one, for sure. Doesn't mean you tell the other person what theirs is. You deal with it silently. And if asked, you reply honestly but with tact and grace: "I am wildly attracted to you, Eric. You make me feel sexier and cum harder than anyone has in my life, and if you didn't change a fucking bit I'd want to do nothing but be chained to a radiator and used as your sex toy for eternity . . . but if you did want to lose fifteen pounds, that could be fun, too." Something in that ball park. Like you know, ladies, how we can't even say ANYTHING TO YOU IN THIS AREA OR WE'RE DEAD FOREVER?! Not even something with the most amazing disclaimer like the above example? NOTHING?! Yeah, well, surprise, we're kinda the same but may be able to take it just a little bit more. But use some common sense and don't push your luck.

Even with April's list, I still could have fallen in love with her and enjoyed fucking her immensely for eternity and certainly never ever would have mentioned any of the items on her list to her, even if she begged me for just one. And that doesn't make me dishonest. It makes me kind . . . and wise. Because, ultimately, whatever misgivings I had about her body would have been easily trumped by my love for her, and those same flaws would have been transformed into attributes . . . because they would be *her* flaws. The flaws of the woman I loved, and therefore, not even flaws anymore.

The point is, it was lose-lose with April. Either she didn't really mean what she said and just wanted to push me away, or she did really mean it and was just feigning contrition in an attempt to change her fundamental nature for me, which wasn't going to happen long-term.

But I wasn't thinking about any of that now, I was just devastated. I took one last deep breath and returned to the living room, where April was sitting on the couch, legs crossed Indian style. I sat across from her, Indian style as well. She would just have to suck it up and live with my unsightly upper inner thighs exposed.

"That was the meanest thing anyone has ever said to me in my entire life."

"I'm so sorry. It came out wrong. I didn't mean it." She crawled over to me and put her arms around my neck.

"I honestly don't know if you can ever recover from that."

"What if I were to blow you right now? (a) Would you view it as me just trying to prove I'm attracted to you and didn't mean what I said, and that's the only reason I was doing it, not because I wanted to; and (b) would you care." I cracked a little smile.

"Let's go to the bed and talk about it . . . But my initial sense is no and no." She jumped up and took me by the hand. It was by far the most initiative she had ever taken sexually. I fell back on the bed and she went straight for my belt buckle, undoing my pants. She pulled them off, jumped on top of me, and kissed me. I was trying to force myself to let it go and forgive her, hoping her newfound sexual aggressiveness would assuage my fears that she was Beelzebub, but it wasn't coming easily. My heart was still broken and my stomach queasy from having been skinned alive moments before. I stopped her and looked searchingly into her eyes. "Do you really want to do this?" She paused for sincerity and said, "Yeah. I really want to do it," and then gave me a surprisingly good blow job replete with wandering fingers, which was very hopeful. Before, this girl wouldn't touch my tit and I hadn't even been allowed to acknowledge the existence of an ass or anything that comes with it, and now, at first blush, she was fingering the outside of my asshole? Zero to one hundred. I guess I just had to trust her and let her find her way and it would all work out in the end (pun always intended). I just didn't know if I could live through the process, though. I'm not built for abuse. I'm very, very sensitive, and if the cost of her coming out of her shell would be judgmental comments like the one she had just made, I might not survive to see the girl I wanted and knew was in her.

She swallowed. Another good sign. When I was growing up it was a given, but these days, it seems, few and far between are the girls who love to drink you. I understand the added health risks in this era but still, even in a committed relationship, it seems there are just less women who like it. And based on what I knew about April, I figured she wouldn't let my cum anywhere near her mouth, let alone take it down. But she liked it and that was really sexy and very intimate, which made me feel we might have a chance.

"That was really amazing. You instinctively do everything I love."

"Really?" She was genuinely pleased and proud.

"And the finger about to go into me? That was surprising and wonderful."

"It was okay? Some guys freak out." I gave her a stern look. She had forgotten one of our games. She caught on.

"I'm sorry. From what I've *heard* from my girlfriends. Obviously I've never been with anyone else before, but they tell me some guys don't like it."

"That's only closet gay guys. All straight men embrace the joys of a good buggering."

"My nails are a little long."

"All the better."

"Really?"

"Absolutely."

"Good to know."

"Although 'get the Earth Balance' doesn't have the same ring to it. Even though I'm not vegan anymore, I still use that instead of butter."

"We'll cross that bridge if we get to it."

She said it was time for her to go, and I walked her to a cab. While I rode the elevator back up, she texted me.

"You taste good."

I got hard. We really might have a chance.

"That blow job was outstanding."

"When am I seeing you again?"

"As soon as you get a manicure."

"Perfect. Tomorrow night then. xo a"

The pain in my stomach was replaced with butterflies. They were flying in the dark, but they were there.

I woke up with the same hard on I went to bed with, and immediately checked my e-mail. It was 10:30, an hour before my usual wakeup time of 11:30. April usually had a message waiting for me, but since I changed the schedule there was nothing. I e-mailed her.

"You up for me saying something sexy?" I asked, wanting to take her temperature and not make her feel like a cyberwhore, something she said she felt like when I would just e-mail her sexy things out of the blue.

"Yes . . . " She wrote back. She was becoming someone I could fall in love with.

"I'm just curious. Could you not tell from my physical response last night when you were doing things with your left hand while your right hand was on my cock and you were blowing me, that I was not only loving the blow job and everything the right hand was doing but equally loving what your left hand was doing and eager for you to go further? Or was it just the 'nails' thing, or you just weren't into doing it all on the first time? Just wondering."

I eagerly awaited her response, thinking I might even jerk off to our little cybersex talk. I grabbed the olive oil from the kitchen cupboard. I started using it last year when, in Vermont one weekend, I ran out of Vaseline and Number 4 Hawaiian Tropic Coconut Sun Tan Oil, and olive oil was all that was left. I realized it was probably healthier to have on my dick than either of the other two anyway, so I've stuck with it. The only problem is the sense memory. Now, whenever I sauté, I think of jerking off. I mean the Molly-cat thing is enough. I can't be tossed about like a sex puppet by my unconscious all day long.

No response was forthcoming. It was odd, usually she was quick on the trigger. Maybe she had gotten a call. I started to get worried. She couldn't have flipped again so fast. Back to the crazy April?

"Helloooo? Did you get my last e-mail?"

"Yes. I don't think I'm having the response you hoped I would have."

Oh Christ, what is it now? I wiped the olive oil off my quickly withering dick with the paper towel I had hoped would be used for something more fun and called her.

"What's going on?"

"Why do you always have to lead with something that *didn't* happen?" She was really pissed.

"April, I was just wondering honestly if you couldn't tell that I was liking it by how my body was moving, or if you just didn't feel like doing more. I told you how amazing the blow job was."

"I know but yet your lead was me disappointing you. Not doing something to you that you wanted. Jesus, can you just be patient? Does everything have to happen all at once? Can't things unfold at all?"

"Of course, they can. Again, you know I loved last night and I thought that we were past this. We joked about it. The fingernail thing? You were laughing about it and fine. Why are you sliding back into assuming I'm not happy with you? This is your stuff. You look at every-thing as if you're inadequate from the beginning and I'm going to be displeased. What should I have said?"

"Why couldn't you say something like 'I couldn't get the vision of seeing you on top of me out of my mind'?"

"Are you kidding? That might have set you off, too. 'How could you say that to me?! You know I don't like being watched when we have sex! Are you trying to be mean? Drawing attention to something I don't do that disappoints you?'"

"That's a stretch."

"I don't think so. You don't like to be watched, so if I had said I can't get the vision of seeing you out of my head why wouldn't you freak out? I don't think it's a stretch at all. Look, if you really think I'm the kind of person that is always disappointed by you and only wants to use you to fuck you and isn't interested in you for anything else, then this really isn't going to work because I really think I have evidenced myself to be far from that person. You should think about it, April."

Pause. I could hear her mind prattling a million miles an hour. I had seen it before. She disappears, almost going into a trance. A mortal flashback, an avalanche of fear that envelops her in a black hole? Who knows. She becomes a different person. It's scary to watch.

"Oooookay. I'm going to walk the dogs and do just that." I was right. Her voice confirmed it. Deliberate, distant, already out the door.

"Okay. Bye." Even though she had been possessed by her demons, I thought her dog walk might exorcize them enough that we could continue the talk in a more rational way when she returned. She usually rebounded well and was more lucid after she took a little time to process things.

After a quick shower, I heard the synthetic "*tchunk*" signaling the arrival of an e-mail. It was from April.

"Eric. I'm so glad we met. Unfortunately, it seems the downs still outweigh the ups and we're causing each other too much pain. I've learned a tremendous amount from you. Good luck with your book. All the best. April." *What the fuck?* "*All the best?*" *Is she out of her mind?* I called her. The machine picked up.

Beeeeeeeeeeeeeeeep.

"What the fuck is this? Pick up the phone. Pick up the phone. April?"

Her cell phone. *Beeeeeeeeeeeeeeeeep.*

"You're going to break up with me over e-mail and not even talk to me? Nice. Classy, April. Yeah, 'all the best to you,' too."

I was squirrelly with anger but deep down had a sneaking suspicion—similar to the one I had many times during the previous week, which felt like ten years—that I was dodging a bullet and should let her go.

* * *

"Hi honey! How's it going?! I'm so glad you guys are in luuuuuv and gonna get maaaaaaaarried." She was in full Lexi mode, apparently unapprised of the developments.

"She just sent me a break-up e-mail." I said into the phone.

"What?! Why?"

"I don't fucking know. She said really mean things to me last night about my body and how she'd blow me if I was thinner—"

"She did not say that!"

"Yeah."

"Oh my god, that's awful."

"But then she did blow me."

"Oh, she did? Well, that's good, right?"

"Yeah, but then I joked with her about putting her finger up my ass, which she was gonna do but didn't because she needed a manicure, and then she flipped out and accused me of always being disappointed with her."

"Lemme talk to her."

"No. Fuck it. I think she's got too many issues. Just don't do anything."

"Are you sure?"

"Yeah."

Then three days of similar calls to Lexi, Fred, Donny, Helen, Caroline (the new addition. My "girls are the new boys" friend) and my mom and Bill.

Should I call her? No. Yes. I like her. She has potential. Don't fall in love with "potential." She needs to make the move this time. Do you want to be right or happy? Fuck your pride, call her. No, fuck her, she's got too much shit and you don't deserve to be treated like that. Come on, she's young and a little inexperienced, cut her some slack. She's a cunt! I'm an asshole! Life's too short to deal with this shit. Life's too short to let go of something so fast; you rarely meet people you like. Why do you want to be with her if she treats you so badly? Because I see an amazing inner fun, wacky spark, and she said herself she wants to change back to the girl who lives from that place and not her Spence–Park Avenue–Cocktails-on-the-roof-of-Soho House–put–on–thing. Just call her.

I wrote her an e-mail but didn't send it. I didn't like how the last phone call had ended, so even if we weren't going to get back together I wanted to tell her some things. I prayed about it, meditated on it, and decided not to send it yet. *One more day. Let's just see what happens.* Lexi called me and told me that April had e-mailed her and had said she was sad and missed me but didn't know how we could ever get along. My heart was softening, and my will to win and inspire us both to choose love over fear was building. I woke up on day four of the second breakup and felt a powerful voice say, "Send it now." I pulled the e-mail up on the computer. My finger hovered dangerously over "send." I was about to press it. *No turning back. For eternity you must live with the decision to press "send."*

Then, a little voice said, "Hit the God button instead." The "God button," of course, being "delete." *No. I must send it.* I took a deep breath and pressed "send."

Subject header: Unfortunately
You see no furniture . . . instead of a gorgeous deck overlooking the ancient Hudson River, the majestic George Washington Bridge, stoic St. John's Cathedral, proud Central Park;

you see an insecure, emotionally stifled, unrecovered, borderline bipolar child you must babysit.

and no costume, no pretense, no address, no therapy, no change he could make could change that truth in you. and for that I am sorry because we could have so much fun together and I could be your rock and support you like a tidal wave.

If you ever get enough self esteem to be loved by me, or even liked, call me. Until then, you'll always find a reason why not. one day, I hope you wake up and say yes. that day, the man of your dreams will appear. i wish that for you. whether it's me or not.

I know you at your soul, that girl you lost and long to get back. her cruel judgment of me is an imposter, a ghost I can easily see through, but a smoke screen nonetheless . . . it masks the mirror in my eyes, which, if she could see, would reveal her own brutal self loathing. I know it well, but deal with it in other ways than hating you. Than finding fault with you. I see it for what it is and I command it be gone when it tries to take me from love. I am not ruled by it. I am informed by it.

I see the potential and hope and inspiration in your journey and forgive you all your choices and only root for you. I would have been and maybe one day still can be your biggest fan . . .

but you can't see me right now . . . whether I put a shirt on or not.

I wish you saw in yourself all the beautiful things I see in you . . . then you wouldn't hate me for seeing them.

light, easy, breezy. that's all perfect. but it has to be with a woman who knows how to respect herself profoundly, so she can in turn know how to give me the profound respect I deserve. you don't, so you don't. i would like to get a chance to find out whether i could know you for a lifetime.

become the love and change you want to see in me and then find me. i hope i'm still here.

namaste, xo e

Suddenly, a superloud "TCHUNK!" My speakers had been turned up to max from when I was in the shower listening to Aimee Mann from my iTunes before I sent the letter, and I had forgotten to turn them back down. It was an e-mail from April. It arrived EXACTLY at the nanosecond I pressed "send." We had pressed "send" at precisely the same time. My stomach immediately plummeted as if I was on that horrific ride where the centrifugal force pins you to the wall in that spinning room before the floor drops out from under you. *Fuck me.* I opened her e-mail.

> Hi Eric. Let's not break up. I would like to go slow though if that's okay with you and just start out as friends, seeing each other once a week or so in the beginning to see if we have fun together . . . " *Okay, she still sounds kinda nuts but let's see where she's going with this?*

> I've attached the Kushner family 4th of July weekend events schedule and you're invited to any and all of the plans. No pressure but it will be Jacki, me, and my mom and dad attending. It's our tradition to do things over long holiday weekends together. Let me know. Again, no pressure.

> <u>Tonight, July 2nd - Dinner at Le Cirque.</u>
> <u>Tomorrow, Monday July 3rd - "Superman 3" at Union Square</u>
> <u>followed by Dinner somewhere casual nearby.</u>
> <u>Tuesday, July 4th - Brunch at the Four Brothers Diner at</u>
> <u>11:30. Cocktails (nonalcoholic beverages for you, of course)</u>
> <u>at the Soho House at 4 and a fireworks party at Emily's at 9.</u>

Of course, I had no idea who Emily was.

Okay, so she's totally crazy. Go slow, let's see each other once a week except for every day with her parents. Whatever. I liked her. But I had just killed it with my e-mail. I jumped on the phone. She didn't pick up. I left a message.

"Hey. Okay. That's just too weird. As much as I meant everything in my e-mail to you, I probably would not have sent it had I gotten your e-mail, so, that is what it is. Call me back, please. We need to talk."

I felt calm somehow, I think because I had stood up for myself and said everything that was important to me. I went to Spuyten Duyvil to write. I turned on my laptop and waited the eternity for it to boot up while eating my peanut butter–on–spelt bread sandwich and an apple. My Blackberry rang. I picked it up excitedly. It was her. I launched before she had a chance to say anything.

"I think we should just get married already. Just fuck all this bullshit, fly to Vegas tonight; we'll have to miss one dinner on your fifty-plan itinerary but we'll back in time for brunch at your family reunion tomorrow." She was laughing sweetly. I felt in that moment, just hearing that laugh, that she would be my wife.

"Do you think it should be this hard in the beginning, though?" She asked, desperately hoping I'd have the right answer.

"Why shouldn't it be? That's another one of those myths propagated by all the people who don't know how to be in relationships. Why shouldn't it be hard in the beginning? Maybe that's when it should be the hardest. Who made up the idea it should be easy in the beginning? Is calculus easy in the beginning? Is childbirth easy in the beginning? When you don't know someone and you're figuring them out, why shouldn't it be hard? It gets easier when you know them better. Who the fuck knows?" I was on a roll and wanted to believe what I was saying, because it was our only hope.

"Maybe you're right," she said, trying not to be submerged by the cinderblock I had tossed overboard to her as a life preserver.

"And I'm not with any of the girls who I hit the ground running with, so what does that say for 'it should be easy in the beginning?' Are you?"

"No."

"Okay, then . . . We pressed 'send' at exactly the same time."

"I know. That's really weird." She sounded really good.

"What did you think of my letter?"

"Well, I kind of skimmed it with my eyes half closed, standing ten feet away."

"Excellent."

"From what I did get it kinda of felt like a punch in the solar plexus."

"It wasn't meant to be. It was the truth."

"You think I'm filled with 'self-loathing'?" Maybe she wasn't so good.

"Yeah. And I said I identified with it, having it myself. Look, if you read it carefully with your eyes open, I think you'll see it as a gift and not a punch."

"My writing partner liked it. She said I have to put on so many faces for so much of my life, it seemed like you were someone I could be messy with and that would be good for me."

"You can. What did your sister say?"

"She thought it was the biggest piece of masturbatory crap she ever heard and that I should tell you to go fuck yourself. But I take everything Jacki says with a grain of salt."

"Yeah, well, God bless her but she couldn't understand word one of that letter. If it's okay with you, I'll pass on dinner tonight but I'd love to do the movie and dinner afterward with your parents tomorrow."

"Okay. Great."

"So, 'going slow' is four dates in a row with your parents along before I've even seen your apartment?"

"I never said I wasn't crazy."

"What time is the movie?"

"One, but Jacki and I will be there at noon to get seats. My mom fell skiing and hurt her hip so she's moving a little slowly these days. Where do you like to sit?"

"Middle middle."

"Okay."

"Is your father nice?"

"He can be. He's brilliant but I hate him sometimes. I just learned this term 'rage-aholic'? That's what he is. Have you heard of that?" I had to laugh.

"Yeah, I've heard of it."

"That's my dad. Nice one second but you never know when he will fly off the handle and go ballistic."

"And your mom?"

"You'll see when you meet them. She's complicated, too."

"Okay. So I'll see you around twelve forty-five then?" I said, employing my final "get out of uncomfortable conversation with a WASP for free card." I don't know why I played by her rules in that moment. I really was interested in her family history and her feelings about her parents. They were ultimately the reason behind why she treated me the way she did, so I certainly wanted to investigate, but things were going so smoothly that I just wanted to help her not drift into a scary place by oversharing too quickly.

"Lovely. I can't wait."

"Me, too."

So much made sense to me now. On April's list of things she hated about me were two items that had seemed so outrageously misplaced, expenentially more so than the other ordinarily misplaced ones. The first was her fear that I was secretly a rageful person that couldn't be trusted; and second, her fear that, because I was twelve years older, I would become an invalid and she would have to take care of me.

I have raised my voice in anger five times in twenty years and have always been an athlete in great shape and hopefully always will be, God willing.

So basically, she was making me out to be both her mom *and* dad.

Wow. I'm really fucked.

I found them all in the back row of the lower section in Theatre 13 at the Union Square multiplex. They were chattering away like the happiest, closest-knit family on earth of course. I felt a little shy and bumbly meeting the parents for the first time, but excited. April looked beautiful in her new blue strapless dress and kissed me sweetly on the mouth, which took me aback a little with her mom and dad looking on.

"This is Eric."

"Paul Kushner."

"Rose Kushner. Pleased to meet you."

"Very nice to meet you both."

They couldn't have been nicer on the surface but, like April's penchant for quick turns, and because of what she had told me about them, I was waiting for the other shoe to drop. They were both, her father especially, very proud of April and Jacki (who seemed to be on her best behavior around her parents and was almost tolerable as a result), and lavished them with adoration, loving looks, and physical affection. He seemed like a sweet, jolly, bloke; their mother, however, was much tougher. She walked with a slight limp due to her skiing accident but her injury apparently had taken nothing from her spirited personality and, in fact, had buoyed it. That obviously was pure conjecture on my part since I had never met her before and therefore had nothing to contrast her behavior to, but that was the sense I got. She was clearly a very, very strong woman. A tremendous fighter. It was interesting that he was the rager; and she, the caretaker. Upon first glance, you might have thought it the opposite. After the movie, we went for burgers at a local Greek diner. As opposed to all the non-Greek diners in New York. (For those of you who never have visited our great city, there are no diners in Manhattan that aren't run by Greeks.)

"They really like you." April whispered after she shut the door on her parents' cab. Jacki was hailing another one for us.

"I really like them." We kissed. We both thought it was going well, which was nice.

It had been seven years since I had even met, let alone cared to impress, a girl's parents. It felt good.

"Oh, I forgot to tell you my idea. I think we should make a deal that we're not going to break up today. It's Monday. The last two Mondays, we broke up," I said.

"Good point. And we're making it even tougher, including the parents meet and greet." She agreed.

"Exactly, but I feel by just throwing hell to the wind and going for broke, if we make it, it'll be a turning point for us."

"Okay, I'm in. No breaking up today."

"Good." We kissed to seal it. Jacki yelled for us to get in the cab she had commandeered on Broadway.

Dinner went off fine, as had the movie. Her parents had given me the bird's-eye view into April's makeup I was looking for. They were very loving, kind people, like April was, but both, in single quick moments, showed me where April got her anger and judgment from.

At the movie theater, on my right, April, Jacki, and her mom had been talking, leaving Paul (to my left) and I to chat about baseball, which was great. Farther down the aisle to our left, an extremely obese man was about to wedge himself into his seat. As he did, Paul made the most disgusted judgmental face accompanied with a sotto voce guffaw under his breath as if to say, "If it was up to me, all fat pigs should be shot and certainly not allowed in movie theaters with their fat asses in my face." It took me by surprise and unnerved me. That's what I read into his look. Maybe I was wrong. Maybe his look really was, "damn these rude theatres and their small seats! That poor man can't even fit into one. He paid good money, he should at least have a seat he can relax in." But having experienced April's critical tendencies and having been briefed on her father's dossier, I felt fairly sure I wasn't mistaken.

And then, at dinner, as I always do, I asked the waitress a lot of questions about what was and wasn't in my food, especially wanting to steer clear of any alcohol, lest I get accidentally dosed, which has happened a couple of times over the years and is very upsetting. Although I am determined to get answers, sometimes at the expense of brevity, most servers don't seem to mind, sensing that I'm respectful of their time and effort and am just adamant about getting it right, a goal they share.

We were on dessert, and I again asked the waitress many searching dietary questions, which she was completely comfortable answering. I knew this for sure because, earlier in the meal, we had shared a secret bonding moment when I had expressed my appreciation for her putting up with all my questions and needs for extra mayo and the like, and she had sincerely replied, "Don't be silly, it's my job."

After she left with our dessert orders, Rose said, "She's very nice."

"Yes, she is," I replied.

"Thank God we don't have any more courses for you to annoy her with questions about," and she laughed, trying to pass it off as a joke.

"No. She and I are cool." Not being one to back down from a fight, and wanting to show this entire table of Kushners that I didn't roll like that and if you want to play with the bull you're going to get the horns, when the waitress returned, I confirmed it for everyone's edification.

"Here you go. Two ice-cream sundaes and one banana split. Anything else I can get for you all now?" she cheerfully asked.

"No, thanks a lot," I said, even though I was the only one not having a dessert.

"Okay, great." She was about to leave but before she could, I asked, "Listen, so I wasn't annoying you with all my questions about everything, was I? Alcohol in this . . . extra mayo on that . . . " Rose started nervously smiling and mumbling that she hadn't really meant anything by it and we shouldn't talk about it.

"No, of course not. I'm allergic to all kinds of weird stuff myself, so when I eat out I always ask, too. No, we're cool." She smiled warmly at me. Rose thought it was over, but just in case it wasn't clear to everyone . . .

"Because I'm meeting April's parents for the first time and her mother thought I was being rude to you." The waitress looked at Rose.

"Oh, no. Not at all." The other three were dealing with this in true WASP fashion by imbedding themselves in the ice-cream sundaes and pretending our conversation wasn't happening. The waitress smiled at Rose and left. I smiled at Rose. "They usually like me," I said without any hint of "I told you so," and took a sip of water.

"I can see that," she said with a huge hint of "go fuck yourself," and took a spoonful of ice cream. April nervously stroked my thigh under the table in a clumsy attempt to bond.

I was part of the family.

I was pretty much shut down as we walked to April's apartment in her straggly, dorm-looking compound of a building on Spring Street. April had sold 3 million copies of her first book and they had just finished shooting the movie version of it with huge stars and although her second book hadn't done as well, she still had enough money not to live where she did.

"I need to walk the ladies. Will you come?"

"Sure." There was nothing I wanted to do less, but I couldn't very well sit in her apartment while she did it alone. We hadn't been dating that long and I *had* just met her parents, so we couldn't be apart. We needed to process together.

She opened the door and two very cute, fluffy, white Maltese things started doing their best demonic-miniature-Russian-circus-bears-on-speed imitations, jumping up and down on their hind legs like pumping pistons, smiling faces and tongues flailing. They were adorable . . . if not a tad unsettling.

We got back from the walk, a quick jaunt around the block, the dogs' little legs motoring in time with April's with such precision it was hard to tell them apart. When we arrived home, I got the tour. April's apartment was immaculate and tastefully appointed. It looked like something out of a magazine I don't read. Like the best suite in a fancy gay hotel, except for the shit and piss the dogs had released with impunity all over the house; the walks apparently being only for show. April said she was going through a lot when she got the pups, and their training had to take a backseat to her emotional recovery. No wonder she hated my house. She didn't want a home to feel like anyone lived there, unless you considered copious amounts of little-puffy-white-doggy excrement prominently displayed in the center of the living room floor, honey.

Like April, the little you could see in her apartment was shiny. Everything else hidden. (Excluding the dog urine and feces, which was quickly whisked away with a smile as if she were throwing away empty bottles of Evian she had forgotten to dispose of, not expecting company.) I'm sure behind all the closet doors and in all the drawers there were many interesting things, but when you looked around all you saw was nice, white, and perfect. And two cute dogs who, after the excitement of the ten minutes outside wore off, allowed their true personalities to emerge, which were frighteningly revealing about their owner's personality, as all dogs' are.

One was still happy and jumping and loving and kissing and licking and jumping and "Hi, I'm here, look at me, love me, play with me!" and the other one was sitting in the corner stoically, nihilistically staring out the window at the bleak Berlin night, contemplating suicide.

I slumped into a big cushy chair, codependantly upset over the sad dog. April was slumped on a sofa across from me petting the happy one.

"So you really don't read? What do you do?" I was ready for her this time.

"I watch *Skating with the Stars* and, even after saying out loud to myself, 'Dude, there's no turning back if you watch this, you still have time to save yourself. At least put on *Project Runway*,' when Bruce Jenner and Ty Babalonia hit the ice and tears welled in my eyes, I unashamedly watched every minute and will continue to."

"We better not talk anymore or we might not make it through Breakup Monday," she said in The Voice. Had I not been so emotionally spent I might have gotten mad, but she was at least trying to show she could have some distance by joking about it, and that was promising.

"Good call."

I was glad we had made it through Breakup Monday. I liked April. She was smart and sometimes funny, and would be funnier if she relaxed and didn't try so hard. She was substantive and successful and wrote thank-you notes and answered the phone "Hello?" with a kooky childlike-anything-was-possible spirit and was adventuresome. Although she was repressed beyond belief and rageful at the moon, she was trying to get better, and would, and I respected that. And she was a Leo, and I really, really like Leos. I had one other Leo in my life before April. Melissa.

Melissa

"Where the fuck is Wisconsin?" I asked Melissa. I was drunk on JD and flying on jazz musician coke. I was seventeen and checking out Bard to see if I wanted to go there the fall after next.

"I'll draw you a map," she said and grabbed a crayon that happened to be on the table we were sitting on. We were at a party in the art building, Proctor Hall. She drew the outline of the United States on the white surface, and I could not take my eyes off her. I hadn't been able to take my eyes off her from the moment I saw her across the room, and I couldn't take my eyes off her for the next twenty years. I still can't take my eyes off her.

Her long, kinky, dirty-blond hair was tied in knots and had beaten-up green toy soldiers and plastic flower barrettes stuck in it. She was alabaster, red cheeks and lips, deep blue eyes. She was sinister and snarky and the sexiest woman I've ever known. She would put her delicate fingers in my mouth when she kissed me and I would die.

She was a drama-dance major, like I was, and before she was finished drawing the West Coast I knew I was going to Bard. They had an "Immediate Decision Plan," which meant you wrote an essay, had an interview, and if you passed both you got into the college. They were looking for "creative people," not caring so much about SAT scores, which was good, as I got a combined 880 on mine. I got drunk and did coke all night, wrote the essay on "why essays are stupid," and met with a school interviewer.

I landed at Bard with a gallon of gin and a half ounce of cocaine. I started dealing so I could have enough money to buy the drugs and booze I wanted, and it was fun having the power. After the shovel-in-the-bed incident in the fall of my sophomore year, I moved out of that house into another one in the center of town. Melissa lived in the apartment upstairs from me with two roommates. I lived downstairs.

Melissa wouldn't give me the time of day during my freshman year. She ran with a different crowd, but we were thrown together when we were in plays or dance concerts. I was the best male dancer and there weren't too many others to choose from, so I was picked for most of the girls' dance pieces. They had no choice. Melissa had no choice but, even so, nothing happened between us all year.

Sophomore year, we were in two plays and six dance pieces together. All I remember were her hands on my shoulders and her feet peeking out from her ripped leg warmers. She relevéed, spreading her toes wide and, balanced, holding onto me. Her hair brushed my face and she smelled like love. She smiled at me. She was allowed to like me now, just not in front of her friends. I had felt that way my whole life. Like no one really liked me, not even my friends. They were maybe allowed to like me in private, but couldn't admit it in public.

Every night after performances were over, we would all go "down the road" to the only bar nearby. The drinking age was eighteen then, so the place was packed. It was an old split-level two-family house: the bottom floor, the bar and restaurant; the upstairs, home to the guy who owned it.

We would get ripped and dance until four A.M. "Brick house," "Psycho Killer" and "Rock Lobster" were the standards that brought the house down. Melissa and I would lead the slam dancing, and people instinctively would clear a small patch for us and watch as we battled. This was our fucking. And it was amazing fucking, at that. Sweaty, hard, intense, nonstop-for-five-hours fucking. We'd slam against each other and then back off, grinding, shoving, sliding, bashing our bodies until we were panting like dogs unable to fuck or fight anymore. Intermittently, we'd retreat to our table of friends to drink beer as if we didn't know each other and weren't in love. I would dole out small packets of coke to the trust-fund kids for ridiculous prices (but it was excellent coke. The best on campus.) and select a few lucky kids to follow me into the bathroom for lines off the back of the toilet. I'd dump a gram on the porcelain tank, smash it with my plastic Bard ID card, and we'd snort it with a dollar bill.

At four A.M, when the bar closed, I would grab a girl and we'd go to her dorm and, drunk fuck. I wanted Melissa, but she was always going out with someone and denied even liking me, let alone being attracted enough to want to sleep with me. But I knew the day would come. It took two years, but at the end of my sophomore year it finally did.

We were in a play together. Edward Bond's *Lear.* One night I was drunk during a performance, something I tried not to do, but upon occasion my daytime drinking just got the better of me and I had to muddle through half baked. Acting was easier in that condition than dancing was, since I didn't have to hoist anyone over my head in *Hamlet* but might have to in a dance piece. I once dropped a girl on her head; she wasn't injured but I wouldn't have given a shit if she had been. Or so I thought. Deep down, of course, I was devastated for having dropped her. I only ever wanted to just be a normal, nice guy who had friends he loved and who loved him back, did well in school, and was a good son. Drinking and drugging made that impossible. I lived antithetically to every value I held dear, but didn't know why or how to change.

In this particular performance, I was supposed to crawl out of the well with a stage knife (scary looking but dulled, and not really dangerous), take a quick look at Ophelia (played by Melissa) who was supposed to be sleeping, and then jump on Lear and kill him. Melissa had pissed me off, though. I was finished with putting up with her pretending she hated me when I knew she was sweet on me, and this was the moment I was going to get her back. I decided to change the script just a bit.

I knelt down over her and started playing with the wisps of hair on her temple with my stage knife blade as she "slept." I could see her breath get short and quick with fear. She knew I was fucked up and crazy and, though I had never been violent, she couldn't be sure what I would do. I could hear the stage manager whisper-shouting at me to stop it and move on to Lear. The audience rustled. They knew something was up. After a few moments, which must have felt like hours to Melissa, I got up and continued on with the play everyone else was doing.

In the hallway backstage after the curtain call, Melissa came at me with an empty beer bottle. I managed to duck out of the way as it smashed just over my head against the wall.

"*You ever do anything like that again and I'll fucking kill you!!!*" She was livid.

"Fuck you." I sneered a signature Melissa sneer and left.

"NO. FUCK YOU, ERIC!!!! FUCK YOU!!!" she screamed after me. She was out of control with rage and I loved it. She cared, and couldn't mask it anymore.

I went home from the bar early that night, three A.M. or so, and went to bed. A rare night of only drinking, no coke. Melissa hadn't been at the bar and there was a buzz all over campus about what had happened at the theater. At 4:15, I woke up from Melissa's car pulling into the driveway. I listened as the car door slammed. Only *one* door. She had broken up with Bravo, this tall, gangly musician guy she was seeing, and apparently hadn't picked up anyone else wherever she had been. The front door of the house opened, *she should start climbing the stairs to her apartment on the top floor . . . but she's not.* I heard her walk slowly down the hallway, toward my front door. I couldn't believe it. My heart started racing.

Knock.

Knock.

Knock.

I jumped out of bed and quietly scurried to the door. I opened it, and there she was. Her mangled hair like modern art, backlit from the streetlight, cast flickering shadows on my face. She leaned in close. She smelled amazing. I was about to lose it.

"You wanna hurt me, Eric? Is that what you wanna do?" she said, trying not to sound as shit-faced as she was. I was somehow suddenly stone-cold sober, even though I had polished off my usual fifth of JD before I had gone to bed a few hours before.

I was speechless. Entranced. I had dreamed of this moment for three years. Begged God for this moment. I was so in love with this girl.

"Do it then. Hurt me."

I kissed her and we fell into my apartment onto the floor. Strangely, it wasn't fueled by an eternity of pent-up rage, our lovemaking. It was gentle and calm and loving and sweet. I kissed her for hours and we made love until the sun came up.

I finally had her.

Melissa was mine.

I looked into her eyes and she smiled. After a moment she sat up, looked at me and said, "This means nothing. You know that, right?" She snickered. "This meant nothing." My heart sank. *Is she joking? If she isn't, I might die. Oh my god, what did I do? What did I do?* I had trusted her. And she had set me up. *Oh . . . my . . . god.*

"You were a fuck. That's all. A fuck." She got up and grabbed her clothes. I swallowed hard, fighting back tears. I clutched my guts with both arms and curled into a fetal position.

"And I didn't even come. Ha." And she went upstairs.

I had vowed I would never shoot drugs. That had been my limit. I started shooting heroin the next day. As hard as I was, I got harder the moment Melissa did that to me. I went under but vowed that one day, that girl would look into my eyes and say she was hopelessly in love with me and mean it. And I wouldn't stop until she did.

* * *

My friends, Harold, Steve, and I started shooting coke daily and dope when we could get it from the city, usually on weekends. They would stay up for days; I would somehow manage to drink enough to counteract the coke and fall asleep for a couple of hours a night in between binges. I was failing out of school, running small-time bank fraud scams in town to get money to buy more drugs, and bouncing checks at local stores to buy booze. Melissa and I didn't speak the rest of that year or the first semester of my junior year. She was a senior by that time, being a year ahead of me. My father told me if I didn't go to rehab, he wouldn't give me any money to go to school with, not that he was giving me that much; he was a schoolteacher, but he was supporting me along with my student loans. I told him to fuck off, I didn't need his money; I would just continue dealing drugs to get by.

I spent Thanksgiving night, 1982, basting a turkey with Steve in Tivoli, listening to *The Heart of Saturday Night* fucked up on a fifth of Jack Daniels, a case of Narragansett beer, shooting heroin. I was trying to pass myself off as a "cool" kid who didn't need to go home and be with family like all the other "losers." Secretly, all I wanted was to be with my family, but I didn't know it and couldn't admit it.

I went to rehab forty days later. January 3, 1983, during Christmas break, my junior year at Bard. I went to get everyone off my back. I had absolutely no intention of stopping drinking and drugging forever. I figured I would take some steam baths, chill out for twenty-eight days, and learn to control my drinking a bit. It was the dead of winter in New Hampshire, and I drove my beige 1972 Chevy Malibu to the joint and sat in the parking lot finishing a six-pack. It was zero degrees, pitch-black at four P.M., and snow everywhere.

The first day I woke up sober in that brick compound that looked more like a minimum-security prison than a cushy rehab, I knew my life would never be the same. I just had a feeling. A profound, peaceful knowledge that I was going to be okay, and never drink again. Of course, I immediately rebelled against the clinic's system that was designed to break me of my habits. They wouldn't allow me to sleep late or glom on to pretty girls to take the focus off what I was supposed to be doing there, which was to recover from a heinous disease that was killing me, so I left AMA (against medical advice) after nineteen days. I was grateful for the epiphany, but not interested in staring at nothing but my own insides for another nine days. I hadn't honestly looked at myself or my behavior my whole life; I figured, making it nineteen days in that kind of a place, where that's all I was doing, was pretty damn good. But I left there with a reverent zeal to stay sober, which I have maintained now for twenty-four years. I also left there with a dance piece I had choreographed for Melissa and me. It was a beautiful slow ballroom number to a Frank Sinatra song, and it would be my way of getting her back.

She met me at the Morey, a sawdust-on-the-floor joint in the center of Tivoli, famous for Brandy Alexanders and Bloody Marys served by the ancient proprietor, Mr. Bailey. He was 120, if he was a day. "Danny Boy" on the jukebox harmonized with the sound of the steel disk that slid along the rosined lane en route to plastic pins on the miniature bowling game in the corner and the symphony of electronic pinball bells that followed a strike.

She had a Screwdriver. I had a big glass of orange juice.

"You stopped drinking?"

"Thirty-four days without a drink or a drug."

She downed half of her vodka and OJ.

"I made a piece for us. Will you be in it?"

She looked at me hard.

"You fucking with me?"

"No. We'll just dance."

She looked at me hard again and downed the other half of her drink. "Okay."

She got up and left. She was mine.

We started rehearsing the next day, fell in love, and stayed together for a year. Really together and really in love. But then that evil cliché appeared. The thing that had plagued every love I had ever had.

Because I finally had her, I didn't want her anymore.

I hated that it happened to me. I didn't want it to, I had always feared it, I was sure it wouldn't happen with Melissa, but it did. In the twenty-two years since, I've worked it out and know for a fact it's dead, but then, unfortunately, I was still a slave to it.

Melissa and I broke up the following summer. I was still sober and she was still a drunk. I had a fantasy that she would get sober one day and we would get back together, convincing myself that the combination of her sobriety and my working out my intimacy issues would coalesce and we'd live happily ever after. Since I had first laid eyes on her, she was the first thing I thought of when I woke up in the morning, and I wondered if there ever would be a day when she wouldn't be. She had moved to New York after Bard, and I would see her around town here and there. She seemed to be getting meaner and drunker. She was dancing and playing bass in a band; I was driving the cab and writing screenplays.

One day I saw her outside the Plaza Hotel. She was waiting for the bus. I swung the cab over to the curb. "Melissa!" She came over to the passenger window.

"Where you headed?"

"Downtown."

"Get in."

She had a different air about her. Softer. One I knew she possessed but hadn't seen since we were together a long time ago. It hadn't ended well. She found out she was pregnant two weeks after we broke up. I was hurt and was an asshole and said some mean things. It had been strained between us since.

"I stopped drinking."

"Really?"

"I've been sober for three months."

"I'm so happy for you, Melissa."

"Thanks." It was what I had been waiting for. God had given me a second chance with her. She knew what I was thinking.

"But it doesn't mean I want you back in my life."

"Gotcha." And that was that. It seemed a fitting death. What I had feared most wasn't nearly as bad as I had thought it would be. I dropped her off, had a good cry and it was done.

I still see her from time to time. She married a lawyer and has two kids in Brooklyn. I called her a couple of years ago and said it would be fun to hang out in the park and I could meet the kids and we could talk while they played. Just mature adult exes now able to be friends. But I thought better of it and canceled. She's not the first thing I think of when I wake up now, but tears still well when I think about her saying, "You were just a fuck."

The Immaculate Cakeception

I usually feel better after a good cry. If I think of Melissa or Wendy or Liza or Grace or Demi and want to cry, I do. But sometimes I can't identify the sadness and it manifests in a mutated form, such as amorphous dread, anxiety, fear, or anger. Since drinking, drugs, cigarettes, and promiscuous sex are out, that leaves one thing.

Eating.

So if I don't cry, I eat.

Last night, I ate cake out of the trash again. Or was it vegan chocolate chips out of the cupboard with peanut butter, vanilla Rice Dream, and a soy milk chaser? It's usually a bit of a blur, my four A.M. kitchen rape and pillaging. I go to sleep at 2:30 or 3:00 A.M. after watching my third *SportsCenter* of the night, in between Howard Stern reruns, a late game from the West Coast, and Nerve whoring. Surprisingly, I'm anxious when my head hits the pillow. *All girls hate you. You'll never work again. You're going to die very soon because you're worthless, and God, who doesn't even exist, thinks you suck.*

At four A.M., I rise in a wonderfully familiar trance, one that carries with it the peaceful excitement of a child awakening throughout the night on Christmas Eve, and sleepwalk to the kitchen. If I'm in one of my "healthy" phases I eat an apple and, proud of my restraint, go back to bed. If I'm in one of my "unhealthy"—well, we don't like to judge ourselves too harshly, so let's just call it one of my "doing the best I can" phases— I open the cupboard where the vegan chocolate chips are. Let's clear this up right now because you really don't want to be one of those people I hate who say, "You mean carob chips?" No, I don't. Vegan chocolate chips are not carob. They are full-blooded chocolate; they just don't contain any dairy and are sweetened with malt extract rather than white sugar. They taste like regular chocolate chips.

I alternate mini handfuls of chocolate chips with little spoon-, fork-, or knifeful (in that order) of peanut butter. The weapon is contingent on what stage of dirty dish insanity I'm ignoring in my sink that has left the clean utensil drawer empty. I won't go to the final option of chopsticks, though; even I'm not that crazy. I'll wash a spoon before I'll do that. I alternate the chocolate and peanut butter, getting more and more parched, feeling more and more sublime, with my eyes closed, trying to stay asleep as if in a beautiful dream while I quietly devour a half bag of chips and a total of three tablespoons of peanut butter. (I negotiate amounts that are acceptable for my night eating so as not to make me fat, calories I've carefully banked by scantily eating throughout the day so I can cash them now.) More and more parched, salty-sweet, chocolatey-carby, like the best foreplay ever, all leading up to the last bite, which I finish chewing as I put the peanut butter back in the fridge, about to come as I grab the perfectly cold soy milk and, just as the last swallow goes down, with the precision of a NASA launching . . . cold soy milk. Gulp gulp gulp, pause, gulp gulp gulp, ahhhhhhhhhhhhhhhhhhhhhhhhhhhhhhhhhhhhhhh.

That's the good version. The not-so-good version goes something like this:

I'm a fucking grown man with willpower and I can have cake in the house and not eat it! This is during the "experimenting with moderation" phase. It emerges every six months or so, between the "healthy" and the "doing the best I can" phases. In this phase, after the "you can have cake in the house and not eat it in the night" voice has allowed unfinished cake to remain in the house, I wake up at four A.M. and head for the kitchen, as a fierce debate instantly begins: DO NOT EAT THE CAKE! You don't NEED it.

But I WANT IT! I'm a fucking adult; if I want the Goddamn cake, I can have it!

Don't you have any willpower?! Do you want to be a loveless, alone, fat piece of shit? One of those pathetic people who goes through life twenty pounds overweight just because they can't not eat cake in the night but they're not so fat that people point at them and go, "Look, there's a fat guy!"? The kind of guy who will never know how it feels to have washboard abs like Marky Mark?

Hey, I'm not twenty anymore.

Two things. First, you never had washboard abs, even when you were twenty. And two, Marky Mark is forty like you are and he somehow manages to figure it out! If you eat it, you'll have to spend an extra hour in the gym tomorrow on that evil treadmill. Remember the rule:, if you have enough energy to lift the cake into your mouth, you have enough energy to go to the fucking gym!

EAT IT!

NO!

YES!

NO!

Sometimes I eat it, sometimes I don't. When I do, at least I let myself enjoy it. Sort of. When I don't, I proudly march back to my bed, my stomach full with a glass of water, feeling like a fucking champion. Until the next night when, sure I've beaten it, I take to the kitchen again, and scarf every inch of cake I can find.

This leads to the LIGHTBULB ABOVE THE HEAD IDEA. A sign to everyone else in the world that reads "Turn and run away!" but I see as the margin of my brilliance. The idea is, if I throw the cake in the trash, I won't eat it because it's garbage now. Mensa, baby! I know whether I'm going to eat the cake out of the trash before my feet hit the floor. And if it's yes and I've spoiled it with detergent, I eat around the detergent. If, believing it isn't safe in my internal apartment trash, I throw it in the communal trash in the hallway, I still eat it. Once, the service elevator door opened and the porter, looking to steal away my trash bounty, caught me in full bite, chocolate smeared on my face, when I didn't want to waste the time to go back inside and eat it. He just looked at me with a steely stare, "You done?" Pointing to the stinking industrial can of the seventeenth floor's waste, more affectionately known as my evening dessert. I made sure I got all my cake out. "Take it. And then just the check, please." I didn't say that last part.

So, I rummage through the communal trash until I find my cake and take it back into my apartment. The only way it's off limtis is soiled with detergent, mutilated into crushed bits, and scattered among other people's garbage. It has to actually be touching my neighbor's decaying chicken carcasses, not only safely touching my own decaying chicken carcasses in the womb of my own trash bag, or it would be totally in the game. Kind of like how you would touch your own (inner) child's shit if you had to for some reason but no one else's.

The last line of defense is the "keep absolutely nothing in the house" strategy. Knowing the refrigerator and the cupboards are bare, I will always ransack them anyway, hoping to find some forgotten gem from whenever ago. In twenty years of reconnaissance I've never found even a single chocolate chip. But one night, right there safely tucked on the right side of the shadowy fridge, I thought I saw a sus-picious unknown plastic take-out container. *What the hell is that?* I knew everything in my fridge and that week I hadn't gotten any food that lived in one of those containers, for sure. I cautiously opened it. It was white on top. *Some old moldy thing?* Gross. I prodded it with a fork because I still wanted to detect its origin. The fork moved through the mold easily and softly. Strange. *Is that mold?* I turned on the light. I could not believe my eyes. *A fresh piece of Boston cream pie?* I don't think I had ever eaten a piece of Boston cream pie in my life. I'm not sure how I even knew what it was. All I knew was that that was a piece of choco-late pie with whipped cream on it. Boston cream pie, right? I quickly turned the light off in case it was a dream, I didn't want to wake myself up, and cautiously took a bite. *OH MY GOD!* It was the best-tasting thing I had ever tasted in my life. I ate it slowly, savoring every bite of this immaculate cakeception until only the graham cracker crust bits remained. I smashed them onto the back of a fork, finished them off, and went back to bed, truly feeling I had been visited by God.

A couple of days later, I realized the maid had been there that day and that she had left it, but unfortunately it doesn't matter. I'm ruined, because every night now I am sure I will find something.

Throughout my teenage years, I was pretty much pegged at 140 pounds. Youth, along with massive amounts of cocaine and Chesterfields, helped keep me at that weight. Since I got sober and stopped smoking at twenty-one, my weight has systematically fluctuated by forty pounds, depending on my work and emotional state.

In the cab days in my twenties, I generally stayed between 150 and 165. It wasn't too bad. Even though I was sedentary while I worked, either driving or writing, I ran a lot, and the mental energy expended in eighty-hour workweeks kept me from ballooning. My basic diet was an apple and almonds for breakfast at noon; a slice of pizza at eight P.M., eaten in the cab or in front of the computer if it was a writing day; and, for dinner at three A.M., a grilled cheese sandwich or lamb gyro and soup followed by three Nemos chocolate cakes and a pint of Ben and Jerry's New York Super Fudge Chunk or Chunky Monkey for dessert.

When I made *My Life's in Turnaround*, I was thirty-one years old and 148 pounds, my adult goal weight. I was svelte and could run six seven-and-a-half minute miles, which was my fastest. I felt great. My "barometer jeans" swam on me. I have four pairs. "Fattest," "medium," "perfect," and "high-school-ridiculous-sick." These were my "high-school-ridiculous-sick" ones. Torn and tattered, 28 years old. Completely unwearable except for barometer purposes. 30-30's. Sweet.

Wanting to be thin for my first movie, I worked out hard and ate scantily, mainly fruits and nuts with some peanut butter toast thrown in as a treat. Six-mile runs every day, and an hour at the gym lifting weights as well. Gone were the Nemo's, the Ben and Jerry's pints. That diet and workout regimen, along with the ridiculous stress and lack of sleep while making the movie, kept me at that beautiful weight.

After the movie was finished and the pressure to be "I'm-in-a-movie" thin was gone, I relaxed the diet and workouts a bit. A more chilled routine, combined with sitting in the editing room for eight hours a day for six months, made me gain twenty pounds, to reach 168. Over the next year, I got back down to 150 in time for the premiere of the movie, since it was important to me to look my best for my coming-out party. But after that pressure was over, I ballooned back up to 160 in a flash. You see the pattern emerging here.

Then Donny and I got the pilot for *Too Something*, and I got back down to 150 to shoot that. The yo-yo between 150 and 180 continued for eight years, until I was thirty-nine.

I always vowed that I would be in the best shape of my life when I turned forty, but four months before I did, just as I was about to go on my killer 120-day gauntlet of health to achieve my goal, my home was attacked.

My soul was slayed when the planes hit the World Trade Center. I love New York. It's been my only home since I was born in 1962, and my mom still lives in the apartment I grew up in. I live six blocks from her on the Upper West Side, where I've lived my whole life. I know the butcher and bodega owners, as well as their sons, by first name, and have seen the fathers pass the stores down to them. People whose names I don't know, I still keep track of by watching their hairstyles and girlfriends change as I pass them anonymously on Broadway over the years. They are my extended family, as is all of this city. The morning of September 11, 2001, when the attack started, I was in L.A., about to get on a plane. I sat in my hotel bed in disbelief, staring at the TV as if I was watching a movie. Every five minutes, I tried to get through to my mom on the phone, but the lines were constantly busy. Ten hours later, when I still hadn't reached her and it was clear no one knew when planes would start flying again, I rented a car and drove a hundred miles an hour straight home in fifty hours, stopping twice by the side of the road to sleep for a couple of hours.

People were camped on blankets on the floor in front offices of every Motel 6 on I40 East. It was chaos in the middle of the country; I couldn't even imagine what it was like at home, and felt angry I wasn't there and hadn't been for the attack. If anything was going to happen, I wanted to be there to help and protect as best I could.

I met my friend Jenny at midnight on Friday the fourteenth the second I got over the GW Bridge, and we went to a coffee shop on Sheridan Square and had bacon cheeseburgers and milkshakes. I had spoken to my mom somewhere in Nebraska on the twelfth, so I knew she was okay.

After seeing my first bus stop completely covered with homemade fliers advertising lost loved ones instead of piano lessons and apartments for rent, I broke down and sobbed in Jenny's arms. I couldn't take it. I still can't.

My little plan to get in shape was off. I cried for the next three months and was very shaky. I had been rocked to the core and, although still practicing yoga and trying desperately to have love and compassion for the perpetrators of this mass murder and have an open mind to all the angles and complications the situation presented, not the least of which was our own government's participation in provoking hatred against us, I still wanted blood in return. I'm not proud of it but that's how I felt. You fuck with us, we fuck with you.

Again, I know that my heroes, Martin Luther King and Gandhi, spiritual gurus I try to emulate along with the most profoundly truthful Buddhist teachings, preach nonviolence. I believe that's the only true path to repair our world but, in that moment, I wanted us to kill someone. I'm imperfect, of course, and human and ashamed of my weakness, but I would have pulled the trigger if I could have.

But I couldn't, so I ate. I wept and ate. I gained thirty pounds and on my birthday was a lifetime heaviest of 185 pounds, and felt disgusting. My feet hurt from carrying all my weight. I couldn't breathe. I couldn't lift my leg straight up to put on my sock; I had to sit in a chair and hoist it up sideways. I hated myself. I had two friends that had been away to this vegan fasting retreat cleansing place in the Berkshires, run by Seventh Day Adventists. They each had lost twenty pounds in ten days and, more important, glowed. They looked amazing. I knew it was gnarly and had never hitherto had the willingness to go, but now I did. I called up and got a room for the next day.

Your Home in the Darkness Mission was run by Practitioner Roland Davies, his wife, and their two daughters. They happened to be black, along with the six other clients, who happened also to all be women. I was the only white person and the only man, other than Mr. Davies. It was awesome. I loved the group and the Davies. I could tell from the moment I arrived at their completely self-sufficient compound in the woods, replete with organic garden, wood-burning sauna, and independent generators (they believe the End of Days is coming, and need to be entirely self-reliant) that I was in a loving place where a profound transformation was going to take place.

My room was in the main house where the Davies lived. It was the only room with a TV. I wanted to have peace and quiet for reflection and mediation but also needed to be able to watch *SportsCenter* and *Ally McBeal*.

There was also a guesthouse. Both were rustic New England–style three-story homes with wood-burning stoves and simple amenities. The guesthouse was home to the other six cleansers and the meeting hall, where most of our events took place.

The highlight of our day was at six every morning. It was the event that kept us motivated to stay strong throughout the day's rough times and long, foodless nights when you wanted to jail-break to the nearest 24-hour McDonald's.

The weigh-in.

Instead of sitting on my couch enraptured in a perverse rationale, crying with joy over the scale victories of *The Biggest Loser* contestants while shoveling copious amounts of cake and ice cream into my face but taking comfort because I was "not as bad as they were," I was now a brother in arms.

You felt both impending doom and impending glory when you stepped onto that scale and hoped against hope that the hell you had put yourself through the previous twenty-four hours would yield a result that would have made it all worth it. Usually it did. For boys, that was at least a one-pound loss per day, except for the odd "plateau day," which was seriously demoralizing, but nowhere near as bad as the even more obscure "increase day." I mean if you were going to fast and choke down drinks you wouldn't wish on your worst enemy, you'd better damn well be losing weight. But the wise and experienced assured you that the plateau and the increase days would be followed by massive loss days and that kept you hanging in. Usually they were right, so you learned to live with them as necessary parts of the process. Being a pound or two thinner put you in a very happy mood, and you'd go racing downstairs to Bible that was the first post-weigh-in event of the day.

The six women at the retreat, all Jamaican for some reason, ranged in age from twenty-six to seventy-one. They were also all Seventh Day Adventists. I'm not a member of any church but as a spiritual mutt and fervent seeker, I'm always up for learning about and discussing spirituality.

Like the Jews, the SDA believe that Saturday, not Sunday, is the holy day of rest. That seemed fine to me. They don't believe in homosexuality and abortion and premarital sex. That wasn't so fine with me, but I practiced forgiveness for them while they spouted that part of their religious dogma. I took what I liked, which was the "God is Love" part, and left the rest, which was the "God is hate" part.

The unpleasant teachings of the morning spiritual lecture were made even harder to swallow by its being the time allotted to ingest the first of our many mandatory daily potions, a half gallon of warm salt water.

It was served in one of those cheap, thick, glass wine carafes they give you at the Olive Garden that you get to keep as a "gift" and use as a vase if you order the salad bar. The salt water was by far the most heinous drink we had. Everyone employed different methods of getting it down. Some used the slow-sip method. Some tried to hold their noses while they drank it, which at first I thought was bullshit but then learned that much of taste is a product of smell, and it actually was effective in neutralizing some of the displeasure. Some would pour it from the carafe into plastic cups and drink that down, thinking it seemed more handleable in smaller doses.

I just gulped down as much as I could, usually half the carafe in one shot. I would barely stave off vomiting by breathing deeply, ignoring my gag reflexes' demands that I throw up, talking it down from the ledge with the quiet determination and expertise of a hostage negotiator. *You don't have to do this right now. You're fine.*

But I need to throw up NOW! HERE IT COMES! I'M THROWING UP!!!

Just relax. Think of how bad you're going to feel if you send salt water spewing out your mouth like an out-of-control fire hose, all over the sweet, little seventy-one-year-old, Jamaican SDA gay basher. Just breeaaaaaaaaaaaaaaaaaathe. Inhaaaaaaaaaaale. Exhaaaaaaaaaaaaaaaaale."

And it passed.

Then I would pour the remaining half carafe into a sixteen-ounce red plastic party cup. It barely fit. I could only get three gulps down at a time before having to back off, needing five minutes between each round. It would take four or five triple gulps to get that cup down. I usually finished just in time for the hymn, which signaled the end of Bible class and the call to assemble at the "dining table" where "breakfast" was served.

We each got a tray with seven cups on it. Some little, some big. The first little cup contained phosphorus, a syrupy green liquid that looked the worst but tasted fine. The second little one contained MSM crystals in an ounce of grape juice. MSM is a sulphur that is nasty tasting but excellent for your skin and bones. It was only a shot, so you could bang that back and use your hunk of lemon as a chaser to quickly eliminate the taste. The third shot was cayenne pepper in water. Excellent for your immune system and not nearly as hot as you'd imagine. A slight burning deep in the stomach, but nothing in the mouth or throat. Then came the truly vile one. The mission's specialty.

The mud drink.

This was a Dixie cup filled with a murky, salty, dense, claylike liquid made up of enzymes, minerals, and vitamins, with an ounce of water which made it viscous enough for the sludge to make it down your throat without choking you to death. It was all you could do not to heave it and everything else in your stomach back up. Still, though, having made it through the salt water, I knew I could do it! I gulped that shit fearlessly after letting out a couple of prefight yelps and self-administered face slaps. Then the lemon wedge before my brain could get too involved and try to convince me the only humane thing would be to vomit.

Having survived the first six potions, you were on easy street. You could relax and laugh with your compadres. While imbibing what seemed like a milk shake compared to the other fluids, psyllium husk and grape juice, we exchanged war stories of the near upchuck episodes we all had skirted by the closest of margins. The psyllium shake coagulated quickly, making it thick, which made it seem like a treat and a meal, so it was win-win. The only caveat was that you couldn't enjoy it for too long because, in ninety seconds, it got so thick it hardened like concrete and you wouldn't be able to drink it at all.

While emotionally and physically digesting the harrowing first two feedings, the salt water and the tray of seven cups, we sat around the table and bonded over how we had gotten fat and how our various food addictions manifested. The rule was, we weren't allowed to actually talk about food, so we'd just leave it out conspicuously.

"God, I know. I just love in the middle of the night to go to the refrigerator and . . . you know . . . ."

The rest of the afternoon consisted of a vegan cooking class, lectures on how our bodies worked, why our eating habits were killing us, and a sauna and subsequent roll in the snow. Three rolls in the snow, actually. Hot hot hot. Roll in the snow, roll in the snow, roll in the snow. Back into the sauna, back out into the snow. Back in the sauna, back out into the snow. Then a nap and the evening feeding; the same beverages as in the morning save, thank God, the salt water.

Beside the morning weigh-in, the most exciting event of the day was "the straining." We'd go out back with Richard, one of the helpers, and our big, white, industrial buckets. We were given them upon our arrival and informed that "everything that comes out of us, goes into the bucket." Once the salt water hits your system, a "flushing" action begins and doesn't end until you go to sleep. "Flushing" is an affectionate term for pissing out your ass, which is basically what's happening every twenty minutes for sixteen hours.

Into the bucket.

Thirty, forty, fifty, sixty years of all the bad things you ate, impacted in your colon all that time, rotting and putrefying, trapped, with no escape. Until now. Until you started drinking a half gallon of salt water every morning . . . and began "flushing" it out.

We became fascinated by "the straining." Not only *wasn't* it gross, it was what we lived for. A source of quiet pride if your daily batch was "cleaner" then your friend's. Not that you would openly gloat—we had more class than that and wished only the best "cleansing" for everyone—but it did make you feel good if your bucket didn't contain anything too "black," as that would denote cancer or a movement in that direction.

We performed the "strainings" for the first three days so we could sear our sense memories with images and smells of what our diets had done to our insides. It didn't make you want to run out of there and break the fast with a bacon cheeseburger and French fries, I'll tell you that.

In the evening, we had more lectures on diseases, preventions, and cures. We looked at our blood under a microscope, and at the stars in the cold night sky. While fasting I was visited by volatile mood swings, from euphoria to paralyzing hopelessness and everything in between. Epic bathroom sessions released not only unimaginably long ropes of stored decay but equally ancient emotional entanglements and memories from as far back as I could remember.

On days four, five, and six, we were fed real food. Only fruits and vegetables, all raw, nothing cooked, but by that point you saw God in a carrot stick. You would gladly trade your future sex life for a second apple slice. And, of course, you wanted to eat nothing but fruits and vegetables for the rest of your life because they tasted so good. Hell was the industrial bucket and heaven was the salad bowl. Then they took the food away, and the last four days was back to the triple daily feedings, the saltwater breakfast, and tray-of-seven-cups lunch and dinner. It was a master plan. The crack cocaine of health. They gave you a taste and then withheld, and showed you what you were in for if you ever strayed again. By the tenth day, I had lost twelve pounds and felt emotionally reborn. I called my mom and dad and offered to send them to the mission as a present, and extolled its virtues to all my friends.

I left with my Vita-Mix (the Cadillac of blenders) and a bag of supplements, MSM included since my complexion was amazing, and hit the road home to NYC resigned to be a strict vegan from then on. Not since I left drug and alcohol rehab eighteen years before had I made such a severe physical, spiritual, mental, and emotional metamorphosis, and it felt amazing.

I broke the fast with food completely against the recommendation of the mission. They suggested broth for two days, then a couple of days of steamed root vegetables followed by two weeks of completely raw fruits and vegetables. I felt like that was basically another three weeks of fasting and, while I was completely grateful to them for all the knowledge they had given me and proud of myself for making it through the program for ten days, I wanted a real fucking meal, whatever the cost might be. I mean, what, a little indigestion? I'd accept that trade. I needed to eat.

I had a bowl of lentil soup and tofu in tomato sauce with whole wheat bread. It was like a boulder in my gut for two days, but it was worth it to experience the cavalcade of flavors that burst in my mouth. It was scrumptulescent.

I was vegan for the next three years. The first year was great. I lost all the weight I had gained and was pegged at 150. Ethically, ecologically, and spiritually, I felt I was doing my part to help the planet while helping myself, and it felt really good. But then, over the next two years, I started to feel progressively tired and out of it. I felt foggy and my mental acuity was waning. I felt three steps behind, and that, I couldn't bear.

I was about to start shooting *Starved*, my most recent TV show, which was a black comedy about eating disorders, and I needed all the energy and mental stamina I could muster, so I decided I would eat a piece of meat to see if that would help me feel better.

I went to Fairway and bought two organic filet mignons. I went home, stripped butt-naked, seared the steaks quickly on the stove with some garlic and onions, and devoured them like a ravenous Survivor having won a challenge. From the first bite, it was as dramatic as shooting heroin in its immediate transformation of my mental and physical state. A tingling energy, vitality, and strength rushed through my body like a freight train that had been grinding steel on steel, off kilter, derailed, and was now suddenly on track again. I was locked in; the entire world came crashing in on me with a vibrancy and crystal-clear presence I had not felt in three years.

I feel badly being part of the meat-eating community again, but it's a compromise I choose to make and believe ultimately serves the universe's higher good. If I'm meant to be a servant for God and my fellow beings, I can't very well do that when I'm operating at 10 or 20 percent. As is done in many traditions, I thank the animal for its sacrifice, ask for forgiveness, and then eat it, knowing its life will help mine to help others.

I still eat mostly organic, and much of my diet is the same as before I resumed eating meat; I just substitute animal protein for vegetable protein at dinnertime. As annoying as it is, I call myself a vegan who eats meat, spiritually feeling more vegan than not.

Ever since my stay at the mission I go in for semiannual house-cleanings. Not back at the mission, that's too intense. I've found a much cushier place and, while the results are not quite as complete, they're still pretty good. It's much more chill and there's no warm salt water. At We Care Holistic Spa, they pump you out with a machine rather than using gravity and a nasty carafe of savory liquid, and they don't have a mud drink. There *are* potions, but they're much more benign. Dried green powder you mix with water. Enzymes and vita-mins. Vegetable juice and even a cup of hot pureed vegetable soup every night, so you feel as if you're getting a real dinner. And they use a different kind of psyllium at We Care than at the mission, which is more finely ground and has flaxseed and some other things in it so, when mixed with the apple juice, if let to coagulate (like I did with my Carnation Instant Breakfast when I was a kid), becomes very rem-iniscent of an apple pudding kind of thing and is quite tasty. I do that twice a day, creating the illusion of breakfast and lunch, and it's legal since it's all going to the same place anyway; mine is just thicker sludge than everyone else's. As long as I drink a lot of water with it so it doesn't clog me up too much, it's all good.

We Care has cable TV, massages, a pool, sunshine, and some B-list actor getting thin for the *SurrealWorld* or an equally interesting Hollywood type roaming around to break up the day of meditating, liquids, chitchat NOT ABOUT FOOD, and the highlight of the day (excluding the weigh-in), just like at the mission . . .

The release.

Except, at this place it's colonics, not an industrial bucket. It's a lot easier to lie on a comfy white massage table, wrapped in fresh linen, and have sexy Mexican-American young mom Angela rub your tummy while your colon is washed with water that's pumped in by a machine.

Through the brightly backlit tube that carries your latest trans-gressions from your body to the waste receptacle, safely out of view in the ground somewhere, you watch everything that comes out of you with piqued interest. It's much more civilized than the bucket.

It's the same equally rich conversation we had at the mission, only at We Care it occurs around the granite table in the main house where everyone hangs out, getting their drinks and comparing notes on the "success" of their "release session." What did or didn't come out. What was the weight difference after.

It was rumored that Courtney Love once saw a pink Barbie shoe float happily through the tube, exiting her life after thirty years of residence in her large intestine. Nothing that exciting ever came out of me or anyone else I've talked to in my five trips to the ranch-style compound in Desert Hot Springs. I just lose ten pounds of unwanted fat and varying degrees of unwanted emotional weight, which is plenty.

Battling my obsession with weight, what to eat and not eat and when, has been by far the hardest challenge in my life as far as substance abuse goes. Drugs and alcohol, you can just eliminate entirely. You don't need Jack Daniels or heroin to live. But you need food.

I'm ingesting the agent of my disease every day and then asking myself not to binge, not to restrict, not to get caught up in the mental Olympics of body image and self-worth connected with it. It's outrageously hard. It would be like trying to have two drinks, no more, no less, every day and not drink the whole bottle. Impossible. So I do the best I can. I'm willing to say I'll never drink again. I'm not willing to say I won't ever eat chocolate again. I mean, I don't drink, smoke, drug, or rage. I pray, meditate, practice yoga, go to spiritual groups daily, give up my seat on the subway, forgive, love, donate, and recycle—can I just have a fucking piece of chocolate cake once in a while?! Or five?

Burping up cookies in the morning and sleeping off maple sugar hangovers occasionally is disgusting, but they are compromises I'm willing to live with for now, to have a little comfort food from time to time. Of course April proselytized that IMDB would cure me of the desire to binge, another reason to stay away from it. What's the fun in one. It's the loneliest number for good reason.

five minutes before the miracle

7

"*So you really don't think* I'm unattractively fat? You just said that to try to come up with excuses why you don't want to be in a relationship with me because you're scared?" I asked April, wanting reassurance that her comment about my weight really was about her issues and not the reason she didn't want to have more creative sex.

"Yes. But I will say that I don't want you to ask me anymore if you're fat. If I wanted to field that question, I would be a lesbian."

"Fine, as long as you're assuring me that your laundry list of severe judgments against me, the peeing with the door open, the cooking with no clothes on, the ten pounds of fat—"

"Yeah. I don't care about any of it."

"The no patio furniture, the running in the heat—"

"I don't care."

"The no reading and no IMDB."

"Those I actually do care about."

"How much?"

"Ten percent."

"So our relationship is 90/10 in your mind? Good to bad?"

"Yes."

"Your displeasure with my not reading and not racing off to do IMDB accounts for ten percent of 'not good,' and the rest is happy, sexy, fun, niceness?"

"Yes."

"Awesome." Luckily, because April was again in her shut-down-never-ask-any-questions-about-real-things mode, I wasn't asked to give my assessment of the good-to-bad ratio of our relationship and therefore didn't have to admit the uncomfortable truth that I also saw it 90/10, but unfortunately the other way: 90 percent bad, 10 percent good. But giving us such a high score bumped her up to 20 percent, so I felt there was potential. Then again there's that saying, "Don't fall in love with potential." It's a good one, but hard to stick to. I always want to champion a person to have the courage to drop the fear and take the risk to shine. It's really hard for me to accept that some just won't have the guts in this lifetime. Liza was two and half years I won't get back. April and I were at three weeks with two breakups. *It's now or never.*

I kissed her gently, privately celebrating her victory and climb in rank. We were on the couch. She had just blown me. I had initially wanted her on her knees with me standing in front of the full-length mirror in the living room, but she had rebelled. That positioning made her feel too much like a whore, she said, but if I wanted her on her knees, as long as I sat she could accommodate. The nuances of emotional damage. Fascinating.

I had signed up and sat on the couch. The pillow Wendy made for me with the serenity prayer crocheted on it was under April's knees, providing her comfort (some significance surely. I can't quite figure it out. I'll let you run with that one) as she gave me an excellent blow job. The only downside was that April had glued her forehead to my stomach as she went down on me, never once lifting her head so I could watch her, part of her phobia of not being seen during any sex act.

"Do you want to hear some of my book?" I asked; my after sex ritual with anyone I didn't want to leave right away.

"Sure," she said excitedly.

"You know I've been writing about us."

"I figured."

"Do you have a problem with that?"

"No. As long as you tell the truth and change my name."

"Of course. I have no interest in breaking your anonymity, but I think it's valuable in a book about my being single up to now, to write about a girl who hopefully will change that." She blushed. "Really?" I was amazed she seemed so surprised.

"Do you not get that I like you a lot?"

"Sometimes, but not really."

"What do you think I'm doing with you?"

"I don't know." She really seemed not to.

"You understand I've been on three third dates in seven years, right? And the fact that we've been dating for three weeks equals the longest thing I've had in that time, which means it's very important to me?"

"I guess so."

"When I hold your face in my hands and say 'you're such a sweet girl,' you don't feel that I like you a lot?"

"No. My father used to do that and I hate it. I hate to be called 'sweet.'"

"Oh. Okay, well that might be part of the reason I'm over here trying to give you love and you're over there not getting it. See, I need to know things like that so I can give you affection in a way that you can receive it."

"Okay." She was utterly lost.

"Do you understand what I'm talking about?"

"Not really. I never talk about things like this with people I go out with."

"And you wonder why your boyfriends call you from work after living with you for a year and out of the blue, when everything seems fine, say, 'I can't do this anymore,' and break up?"

"That's not that abnormal. People change their minds." I was horrified again.

"*That's not abnormal?* Honey, that's a freak show. There needs to be some warning signs before someone just up and leaves you. That's completely fucked up. You think that's acceptable?"

"People change their minds." She seemed sadly resigned to that idea, repeating it like a mantra.

"Okay, would you give me more of a heads-up after a year of being together than that? Than suddenly one day just saying things weren't working and you were leaving?"

"Yeah, but—"

"So if you hate the word 'sweet,' what word makes you feel loved?"

"'Beautiful.' If you call me beautiful then I'll think you like me."

"Done. See? I need to know things like this."

"Okay, sorry. It's just so hard for me. I'm not used to talking about how I feel, or being with someone who cares about how I feel or really sees me or wants to listen to me."

I kissed her tenderly. "Well, I do."

"And that's why the sex is so hard for me. I'm fine if I hate you and you just call me up drunk in the middle of the night and want to come over and fuck me, but if I really like you and I think you like me, then, I don't know, it's just really hard." I kissed her again. I was getting turned on.

"See, I get hot when we talk like this. Honesty and closeness is a total turn on." I pushed her back onto the couch. "Is it for you?"

"Yeah, but it also freaks me out."

"Okay, well, because I'm nice and want to help. Just this once I'm going to give you a gift and offer some relief for the uncomfortability that's building as a result of the intimacy, since I know how hard that is for you . . . " I was smiling mischievously. She knew I was playing.

She rolled her eyes and smiled. "Yeah?"

" . . . and like what you're used to, detached, objectifying, dispassionate, and robotic . . . so you'll be more at ease . . . I'll let you blow me again but, this time, I'll watch the Mets game while you do." She hit me and laughed.

"Thank you. You're so generous."

"I'm trying. You know, being a forty-four-year-old-nonabsorbing-narcissist, it's not easy, but I think I'm slowly getting the hang of it, don't you think?" I jumped up.

"Where are you going?"

"To read to you."

"Oh. Hooray!" I booted up the book and gave her a disclaimer. "Now, you know that all kinds of stuff goes on in my head, and that doesn't mean I really feel that way, right?"

"Eric, I'm fine. Just read it." I trusted her somehow and launched into the introduction, reading about our first date in the park. I read it all, pulling no punches, even my unspoken thoughts about possibly thinking her the devil. I finished and cautiously looked over at her. She was beaming on the couch, speechless with pride.

"What?" I asked, confused by her reaction.

"I come off so well!" This was why, yet again, I was sure we could never make it. I was afraid she would get angry, thinking she had been exposed to the world (even as an anonymous character) as being the worst human in the history of humans, but instead she thought she was enchanting. "I'm glad you think so."

"There's a really nice thing you do. What is it? I can't remember, but I was telling my sister that Eric does this really nice thing—"

"Yeah, you might not want to start a compliment like that unless you can finish it. It kinda has the opposite effect than you're—"

"Oh, I remember."

She used The Voice. It must really be sensitive. "You really listen to me. No one's ever done that before."

"Voice," I reminded her.

"Damn it."

"Do you want me to stop telling you when you do it? I don't want you to feel like I'm badgering you all the time."

"No, I don't mind. I just get angry at myself for doing it. I find this all so hard."

"How have you handled relationships up until now?"

"By drinking, of course."

"Really." *You don't say.*

"Not getting drunk, but nice and tipsy, certainly. A couple glasses of wine. Everyone does that. I mean, I hadn't had sex completely sober in thirteen years until you. OH! And I realized why that yeast infection I got a couple of days ago won't go away. I've been drinking every night since I took the medicine, and you're not supposed to."

"Huh?" I said, desperately trying to process this new information with a spin that would produce a way of looking at it that might allow a chance of including April in my future. At worst, April had just detailed major symptoms of being an alcoholic; at best, someone who used alcohol in a dangerous and self-abusive manner. It was lose-lose.

"But you don't think you have a problem."

"No," she said, scrunching her face disdainfully for emphasis. "First of all, I only drink really in the summer. In the winter, it's too cold out, so we don't sit outside at long dinners, drinking wine," or something like that. I was in a bit of a daze, half-listening to her explanation for fear it would further indict her.

"And second, if I had a problem with drinking I wouldn't have that unopened bottle of vodka in my freezer or the unopened bottle of Crystal my publisher gave me as a present two years ago after my first book came out, would I?" *Right! Of course! Thank you for saving me. And yourself. Of course no alcoholic could have unopened bottles of booze in their house. You can't possibly have a problem.* I could keep going out with her. My codependant rationalization spoke loud and clear. Everything I knew about alcoholic denial leapt out of my head as quickly as I used to guzzle my first morning beer.

Whether April was an alcoholic or not, I don't know. She certainly didn't drink the way I had, but regardless, her reasons held no proof whatsoever. I had all kinds of strange fallback excuses for why I wasn't an alcoholic. My personal favorite was that I wasn't an alcoholic if I could still see my dick past my stomach when I peed. As soon as the beer belly protruded to the extent it obscured the ability to see my average-size flaccid penis, I would have to stop drinking. And I was fair about it; as I got fatter I didn't even jerk off a little before I peed, to create a demibone to sway the judges.

The fact seemed to be that April used alcohol to medicate herself, and more frequently than did the average person. Anyone who hasn't seen their lover's eyes sober in over a decade has a problem. But I, love starved and still hopeful, continued on my merry way.

"Good. Well, I'm glad you've thought about it and are on top of it."

Saturday, we went to dinner downtown at one of her places, "Très Bon Bon Trendy" whatever. It was all starting to feel very familiar, and a bit too quickly. April was in girlfriend mode; I could just tell by how she talked to the doorman when we came back from dinner. "We're so lucky, we just missed the rain. We forgot umbrellas. Good night, John." Yup. I was her boyfriend now. And the doorman needed to know it because I would be walking the dogs soon, when April couldn't and I was downtown for yoga or something and might be able to do her a "favor" and "swing by to take the ladies for a quickie. Thanks so much." She pressed the elevator button. "I loved the Brussels sprouts. Didn't you? Brussels sprouts are my absolute favorite. You like Brussels sprouts, don't you?"

"I try to like them but, as with eggplant, I just do not." I was getting a little queasy, having a sense somehow of what was about to come.

"Well, your girlfriend thinks—oops, sorry," she caught herself. She knew I thought it was too soon to say the word, even if in her mind it was what she was.

"No, it's fine. Excuse me, I'm just gonna vomit over here for a quick second."

The Voice. "Love-ly." She was hurt, of course always thinking the worst-case scenario. I put my arms around her waist and pulled her to me.

"I didn't mean because *you* would be an awful girlfriend, but just the intimacy of having *any* girlfriend, can, *at times*, make me sick . . . in a good way." I kissed her. "But I want it. You believe me, right?" I added sincerely. It was too much honesty for her, and her knees got wobbly. She was about to hit the deck but luckily was saved by the elevator bell. *DINGGGGG!* She had an out as dependable as a good corner cut man. Mindless chore chatter. The door opened, we boarded the lift, and she was off. "The ladies are probably going crazy. We really can't leave them this long. It's not nice."

"It's okay, they'll just go in the park that is your living room floor. They have impunity, what do they care." Damn it! I was once again seduced by the ditch-out-of-the-uncomfortable-but-necessary-intimate-talk-whenever-you-want rule. Though it held a nice immediate gratification, I knew it would bite me in the ass later, and I needed to kick the habit cold turkey. It had happened with Liza. When people don't feel fully heard, they hold their feelings in and quietly resent you until they blow up and suddenly leave you. Not suspecting that anything was wrong because no one ever said anything, you're surprised when the guillotine falls. *SWACK!* Your head's off, rolling around on the cobblestones of Gansevoort Street while she looks on from a street-side table at Pastis, laughing, a martini and her new hottie in tow, while you try to glue your head back on before all the blood drains out your neck. That's why, as gross as it feels to have those talks, I do it more often than not, as much out of love and hope for a positive resolution and closer relationship as out of selfishness, not wanting to suffer the hideous alternative.

But just this one last time, I'll let it slide.

"Stop saying that. They rarely go on the floor. They have little colds. Give them a break," she said, a little too annoyed.

"I have a little cold and you don't see me shitting and pissing on the floor," I responded, nonplussed, and opened her front door.

"YAP YAP YAP YAP YAP YAP YAP YAP YAP YAP YAP!!!!!!!!!!!!!!!!!!!!!!!"

"Hello, ladies. Wanna go for a walk?" I was as eager for the verdict as she was, so I made a beeline for the kitchen. April took the living room, bathroom, and bedroom, doing a quick once-around twice in each room.

"See. There were good little—" Her victory was short-lived.

"Hello! Kitchen! Shit and piss!"

"Oh, well. It's our fault for leaving them so long." She had it cleaned up before the sentence was finished. No body, no crime. "Will you walk them with me or you wanna stay here?"

"I don't think they need to rush straight out." I gently shoved April against the fridge and kissed her.

"They really should. And besides, I'm still burning a bit down below. I don't think anything should touch it."

"There are other things we could do."

"I think I'm getting a callus on the inside of my upper lip."

"There are other things we could do."

"Slow down there, Speedy. I have enough pain south of the border in the front, the back door is remaining shut, possibly forever, my friend, but certainly tonight."

"Wow, I'm both impressed and inspired that your mind went there. I wasn't even thinking of that, but good to know it's a future option. See, we're not that far apart."

"So what were *you* thinking, then?"

"Well, you could lie on your back on the bed and I could jerk off on—"

"My face? Is cumming on a girl's face the new blow job? It seems like it's rampant these days."

"That wasn't my thought but, again, very nice to see how your mind is working. I had a feeling once the floodgates opened—"

"So, what then?"

"If it would be sexy to you, you could watch me jerk off kneeling over you and I'll cum on your tits."

"Hmmm. Could be fun. I'll try it."

"You've never done it?"

"No, but only after we walk the ladies."

"Yeah, not gonna happen." I picked her up. She screamed in playful mock-protest as I carried her into her bedroom, threw her onto the bed, and jumped on her. The dogs subsequently jumped on me, were gently swatted to the floor and, taking the hint, retreated to the couch in the living room. April stripped off her T-shirt with one hand à la Samantha Mathis in *Pump Up the Volume* (one of the all-time sexiest moments on film, one Sam refused to reenact when we briefly dated in 1994). April loved to do that. It was so strange what she did and didn't feel comfortable with. I unbuckled my jeans and pulled them down to my knees.

"Do you think I'm smart?" The kind of talking April liked to do in bed was the kind that I liked to do at the dinner table . . . okay, never.

"Can we not talk about it right this second?"

"Answer the question. Do you think I'm smart?"

"Does no at least get me a blow job when your callus heals?" She rolled her eyes.

"Of course, I think you're smart; what are you, an idiot? You're a fucking genius; now squeeze your tits together and shut up and you can't get mad at that because we've already joked about it and you know I want you for more than just titty-fucking you."

"You didn't say titty-fucking. You said jerking off on them."

"Fine. Baby steps."

"And besides, my tits are too small to be titty-fucked."

"Baby, no tits are too small to be titty-fucked. And besides, you have perfect tits for every and all events." She did. 34B. Firm and pretty.

I kneeled over her and started jerking off. She suddenly got real quiet. She was watching intently, her face mostly in darkness like she liked. I guess since, technically, in her mind, I was the one who was performing the sex act, I was allowed to watch her watching me. I took her hand, which was idle, and put it on my balls. She took the cue and started gently playing with them.

"Are you liking this?" I whispered sincerely, trying to sound as sexy as I could without crossing the boundaries from normal speak into dirty talk and thus elicit an uncomfortable laugh. I was successful.

"It's surprisingly sexy. Yes, thank you for asking." Although the complete disconnect between what was happening and the sterile way she discussed it momentarily made me lose my erection, I soon recovered because she was actually able to look kind of turned on, and I came on her breasts a few minutes later. I cleaned her off with a warm towel, like her own little geisha boy. She grabbed a T-shirt from the closet, put it on, and we sat Indian-style on her bed.

"So you liked that?" I asked again.

"Yes. You looked beautiful kneeling over me." I was shocked by her openness.

"Thank you. You looked beautiful lying under me." She blushed. We kissed.

"Why do you like me?" she asked like a scared child.

"Because you wear T-shirts that say, 'Fuck me, I'm famous.'" She laughed. She had a great laugh. It was one of the few times she would allow her vulnerability and true nature to show, which was great.

"I'm serious. Why do you like me?"

"You're funny. You're smart. I like that you're successful. You're really, really talented. I like your whole 'put-together-WASP-Upper-East-Side-thing.' I like how you smell. I like your style. You're really sexy, and I see the potential to get even sexier, which is amazing. I like that you know you have issues but are dealing with them in IMDB. I like that you like to go out more than me and that will draw me out more, which is important to me. I think you're kind. I like your dogs and I love the way you answer the phone with childlike enthusiasm and wonder like anything is possible and it might be Willy Wonka on the other end of the line, offering you a trip to the chocolate factory." She was smiling and smitten, as was I in that moment. Tears welled in my eyes. I liked her so much when she was like this.

"How was that answer?" She had absolutely nothing to say for the first time ever.

"Ummmmm . . . Yeah . . . Good." She couldn't stop grinning and was turning red.

"I'm glad you liked it.

"I wish there was a word in between *like* and *love*," she said, amazingly not only not backing away from the obvious moment we were having but, in fact, running headlong into it and in her regular voice no less. "What do you say to someone when it's more than *like* but you don't want to say *love* yet?" She added.

"You say, 'I like you *a lot*.'"

"Really?"

"That's what I would say." She paused and looked me dead in the eye.

"I like you *a lot*."

"I like you a lot, too." I smiled. She was endearing. I did like her a lot, but not *a lot*. But by not emphasizing *a lot* I wasn't lying, well, maybe a little, because in that context I'm sure she thought I meant it in the same way she had even though I hadn't emphasized it. I felt bad but gave myself a break. I might have been slightly overwhelmed myself. Hey, it happens. I'm far from perfect.

"I'm going to go now. I'll feel like a whore if you kick me out so . . ." I said, jokingly invoking her rule while also respecting her desire for me to lie when the reason I wanted to end the evening had to do with *SportsCenter*. I was allowed alone time to meditate, do the dishes, even jerk off while thinking of other women (I had told April the story about the fight Grace and I had gotten in over that issue, and April said, "That's ridiculous. I would never set myself up by asking you that question." So, that's how I knew it was legal.) but there was something about that evil *SportsCenter*.

"Oh, okay." Beat. "I'll miss not having you here."

"Thanks for saying so." And with a kiss, I was out the door.

It was raining, but luckily a cab appeared outside April's building.

"Hi. One hundred and tenth and Broadway, please." And we took off.

I checked my self-esteem machine for a text. The red light was blinking.

I must say that staring at the upper right-hand corner of my Blackberry has replaced many of the mirror glances I used to take throughout the day. I'll have to add up that time and get back to you, but it's a painfully hefty number. One of my yoga teachers said she got rid of hers because she was tired of staring at her thumbs. I identify. But for me, it's more being tired of my self-worth being connected to the blinking red light like an umbilical cord.

It was blinking. It was from April. I pressed the scroller to boot it up.

"I can still smell you on my chest." OH MY GOD! I alternately wanted to never see this girl again and marry her. One was going to win out very soon, but which? "I can still smell you on my chest?" My heart and dick got big and warm simultaneously. They're inextricably connected these days. I called her.

"Hello?" she answered like she always did, with sheer wonderment, like she had no idea who was calling her even though she did. It was just the sweetest thing.

"Did you not know it was me?"

"No, I figured. But your number comes up as restricted. My mom's the only other one that does that but I didn't think she was calling me at two A.M."

"Did you have fun?"

"Did you get my text?"

"Yeah."

"Then you know I did." See, this is what I hated. I wanted to puke and my dick was now limp and I never wanted to speak to her again. We just were never . . . in . . . sync. I choked out a response, trying desperately not to be found out.

"Okay, well, I had a lot of fun and I just wanted to call." I pulled it off.

"Me, too. I'm glad you came over, it's just that I get scared that . . . never mind."

"What?"

"No."

"You can't keep doing that. You can't just stop in the middle. Tell me."

"It's just that I get scared that there'll come a day when I'll bump up against my limit sexually and you'll want to go further and I won't be able to."

"Listen, April, I've had maybe five fake cocks up my ass in thirty years; it's not like I need freaky sex all the time. When it comes down to it, I'm pretty traditional most of the time. The things we've done and are doing, which you're fine with, right . . . ?"

"Yeah?"

" . . . are perfect. Trust me. I'm not worried at all. Quite the contrary, I'm very hopeful it's only gonna get better and better, and it's great right now."

"But, for instance, there's nothing I would find appealing at all in a sex shop." She sounded very serious, bordering on angry. But this was important, so I forged ahead.

"Blindfold?"

"Oh, I have that in my underwear drawer," she said as if we were suddenly in a different discussion. One she liked and could be good at.

"Ankle and wrist restraints?"

"You can buy those at Bergdorf's." She continued with more and more ease. *Bring it on!*

"So, you wanna amend your earlier statement to 'I find absolutely nothing appealing at all about anything you would find in a sex shop unless you can get it from your panty drawer or overpay for it on Fifth Avenue'?"

"Yes. That's fine."

"Then I think we're good on that one. Anything else?"

"Could you reframe for me how you define the difference between *dating* and *being boyfriend and girlfriend*, because I'm sure you do it well and will make me feel better about it, because I sort of thought we already were boyfriend and girlfriend? I mean, we've slept together three times this week and I'm not seeing anyone else, so could you do that for me? I'd really appreciate it."

"Sure." I took a deep breath but didn't let her hear it. "Are you sure you want to have this conversation now, over the phone?"

"Yeah, I'd rather that than have to wait until the next time I see you."

"Okay. Well, it's weird because it's at an awkward stage. I really, really like you and am not interested in seeing anyone else; and the few girls I've met and even had a vibe from, I wasn't interested in. I mean, you're the bar and it's set very high, and I can't be bothered to investigate other girls unless I was really blown away, and I'm not really even open to it because I want to see what's going to happen with you, and I have a lot of hope about it." That was the truth. The only girls I had talked to were Nerve girls, and April didn't even know I had a profile up and, since she hadn't asked and we weren't "exclusive," this being that talk, I didn't feel the need to bring it up. Her nightly dinner parties and events were my Nerve.

"Right, so far that's exactly how I feel. I get asked out constantly but no one is . . . well . . . you."

"So lots of guys ask you out?"

"All the time."

"So you flirt and stuff, and then they ask you out and you say what?"

"Well, I don't think I flirt; I talk to them at parties and things, and then they usually give me their card and I say thank-you and take it."

"Why do you take it if you assumed you and I are boyfriend-girlfriend?"

"I don't want to be rude."

"Why don't you just say you have a boyfriend?"

"Well, because I wasn't sure how you felt. That's why I want to talk about it with you."

"Right, but if *you've* felt we were boyfriend-girlfriend then, what does what I feel matter to your stockpiling numbers or not?"

"Just finish what you were saying, please."

I had a bad feeling. I suddenly felt she was duplicitous, and it scared the shit out of me. I had never felt that about her before. Even with all my ambivalence, I had always trusted her. "Okay, but just let me get crystal clear here. Is there anyone else you want to go on a date with right now other than me?"

"No."

"And you haven't kissed anyone else since you've been seeing me?"

"No. Definitely not. Only you."

"Okay. So, I'm not into anyone else but it just feels too soon to say we're committed to each other exclusively. I don't feel like we've earned that level of intimacy yet, on the other hand, if you were to tell me you were going on a date with someone else I'd want to jump off the roof. So it's very awkward for me. I don't feel comfortable either way, so it's just this purgatory where you're technically allowed to date other people and so am I, but I would get sick if you did and certainly want to know if you did and if you were going to kiss someone else. . . . See, I can't even say it without wanting to vomit."

"But you want to vomit at the thought of calling me your girl-friend, too."

"Yes. Right now, this minute. Yes."

"Okay."

"I mean, I don't see this period going on for more than another week or so, and then I think I'd want to go to the next level."

"Uh-huh."

"Are you okay? Are you freaked out? Are you retreating?"

"I don't know. Everything you're saying makes complete sense to me. Let me sleep on it and we'll talk more tomorrow, okay?"

"Okay."

"Good night."

"Good night." I got scared. I didn't want her to disappear like she had before when she would do her sudden flips, but I also had to be honest with her. I thought about calling back and getting some reassurance, but decided not to. I hawked the Blackberry red light the rest of the way up Tenth Avenue and even through the end of *SportsCenter* at three A.M. Nothing. I went to bed resigned. Whatever happened would be for the best. I thanked God, as I always do, for everything that happened that day, regardless of appearances, and went to sleep.

April and I had planned to get together at my house the next night. I was going to cook and we were going to watch *Entourage*. I woke up to an e-mail from her.

"Are we still on for eight at your place?" Everything seemed okay.

"I'm looking forward to it," I wrote back, and waited.

"Me, too. I'm off to brunch with my parents. Of course you're invited, but I know this is sports/couch day for you, so I totally understand if you pass. Then a workout and massage and I'll see you at eight." Back to business as usual.

"Thanks for the brunch invite, but I think I'm going to watch the British Open instead. I'll see you later. Have fun."

It seemed like everything was fine, so I just went with it. I had my usual perfect napping-on-the-couch-intermittently-while-watching-golf-and-baseball afternoon, after which I walked across the park to a spiritual meeting and then shopped for dinner supplies at Gary Null's Uptown Whole Foods on Eighty-ninth and Broadway.

I was making my special cucumber-apple salad with a hummus-tabbouleh-balsamic vinaigrette, followed by whole wheat penne putanesca and, of course, the vegan chocolate–chocolate chip brownie cookies for dessert. I was excited. Sunday nights often felt lonely and depressing, and I was happy to have April coming over. As I started chopping, I called the inner circle—Donny, Fred, Helen, and Caroline—to help me figure out whether I was being scared, not wanting to go steady with April, or whether I was just honoring what I really felt to be the right thing to do for me. I always want to make sure I'm not operating out of fear.

The consensus was that I was being a pussy and, at this point in my life, after being sad for years because of not meeting anyone I wanted to date for as long as three weeks, I should just shut the Nerve profile down, not see anyone else, and make April my girlfriend. In a couple of weeks it would be clear what was going to happen with her and, if it wasn't good, then I could break up, but this half-ass thing was stupid. I kind of agreed with them but at the last minute thought of a compromise that would make me feel better.

An *engagement* to go steady.

We would not see other people and commit only to each other, but not call it being boyfriend and girlfriend yet. It was a step in the right direction, and it sounded fine to everyone, so that was going to be the play. I can sort of hear a collective sigh from some of you like, "Come on already! No wonder you're still single if you don't just make her your girlfriend without all these histrionics!" But don't forget, my friends, how crazy and mean she had been at times. This was far from a no-brainer.

April looked really pretty, as she always did, and smiley. "Hi." She kissed me and came in. There wasn't any weirdness in the air at all, which I was grateful for. I wanted to connect with her after our last conversation in the cab, and the best way I could get a sense of her emotional state was to make love with her.

"How's your woo?" I asked sexily, moving in on her. She laughed. "My woo?"

"Yeah, your woo," I repeated and motioned toward her pussy with my eyes. We were still standing in the foyer at this point.

"Oh! All better. Last night's good sleep fixed it."

"Come in here. I have something I want to show you." I took her by the hand and led her toward the bedroom.

"Aren't I getting dinner cooked for me?" She was into it.

"Can't you smell it?" We passed through my bedroom doorway.

"I can. It smells amazing." She dropped her bag and kicked off her shoes.

"Then stop your complaining," and I tossed her on the bed.

The sex was getting better every time. She was relaxing, and this time even sat up for a few moments while riding me and let me caress her breasts and look at her, but then she had to plaster herself to my chest again. At least we were making progress. She almost came but was still too scared to, and she still wouldn't let me go down on her. After fucking for a while, she asked me to cum because, although her pussy was fixed, it was newly fixed and was starting to get a little raw, so I did. After our panting subsided she whispered into my ear, "That was amazing. I haven't felt like that since Thanksgiving night, 1992."

That was the last time she had been in love. And the last orgasm that wasn't self-inflicted.

"Why don't you want to cum?"

"Because I'll imprint myself on you like a duckling, and I don't want to do that yet if we're not exclusive."

"You know, I've been thinking about that."

"Me, too."

"Okay, you go first."

"Well, I think it's a really good idea. I didn't at first, but then I started feeling closer to you, and I think it's because by not being boyfriend and girlfriend and therefore not feeling like I have to scrutinize everything you do to decide if you're going to be my husband, it takes the pressure off and I feel more relaxed."

"Okay, well, I'm glad you feel closer to me but I was thinking of kind of a middle thing. We commit to not see other people but not call it boyfriend-girlfriend yet. What do you think of that?"

"So, you get emotional security and I don't even get to be your girlfriend? Fuck that."

"That's how you take that?"

"Yeah. We're either exclusive or not, and if we are, you call me your girlfriend."

"So like being engaged to be married but not married yet, you don't like being engaged to—"

"Be boyfriend-girlfriend? No. That's stupid."

"Are you punishing me? I mean, last night you assumed we already were and then seemed to be upset when I said we weren't, and it's only been twenty-four hours and I've changed my mind and want to go steady."

"I'm not punishing you; I just think you were right last night, that we haven't earned the intimacy yet and should just keep doing what we're doing. I don't want to see anyone else—"

"You're sure? There's no one else?"

"No. And we'll just keep dating until we want to go to the next step."

"Okay, it just seems weird that you told me you're falling in love with me, right?"

"Yes. I am."

"And you haven't had sex like that in fourteen years."

"Right."

"Yet you want to be open to seeing other people?"

"So you want to take that off the table now?"

"Yes. That's what I'm saying."

"All right, let me sleep on it. I just got used to this new change and reframed it so I wasn't hurt, and this is just throwing me for a loop. Let me just think about it, okay?"

"Okay." I didn't have a good feeling about it at all. She had gone all *Sex and the City* on me. What a Happy Thanksgiving show that was. Created a legion of women who think it's empowering, sexy, cool, and smart to be superficial, mean-spirited, man-hating game players. As if somehow aligning with the minute percentage of men who are like that will teach all of us who aren't a lesson. Way to go, girls! That's the way to a happy, healthy relationship!

We ate, watched TV, talked, and she went home. It was perfectly fine. I was a little sad that she didn't want to celebrate my willingness to go steady or share my excitement for the idea, but we had a nice time and I had faith she would come around. But how wrong I was this time. In retrospect, it was like the last cigarette before the execution. I had no idea what was in store for me the next morning. I called her after I woke up.

"So have you thought about what we talked about last night?"

"Yeah I have and . . . well . . . the not-reading thing is still a big problem for me."

Oh my god, we're back on that?

"I mean, all my friends have read *A Prayer for Owen Meany*. We talk about it. I can't talk to you about it."

"Uh-huh." I was just trying to keep afloat while my mind raced for an answer to this shit again.

"If you hate books, how can you respect what I do?"

"I hate Brussels sprouts but I respect God for making them."

"You know how you installed your air conditioner wrong?"

"What are you talking about?"

"In your bedroom. The new air conditioner?"

"The one I got because you were too hot during our first kiss?"

"Yeah. You know how you didn't quite install it right, so the plastic things that spread out to reach the edge of the window frame don't reach and air gets in around them?"

"Yeah?"

"Why don't you fix that? Don't you think the air conditioner would work better if it was installed correctly?"

"Probably. But who gives a shit? I just haven't gotten around to it."

"If I was living with you and sharing the bills, would you fix it?"

"Yeah, or get the super or whatever . . . yeah. When did you notice it?"

"Last night, when we were on your bed."

"When we were making love?"

"No, while we were talking."

"So, while I was asking you to go steady, you were preoccupied with my badly installed air conditioner and worried that it was a metaphor for something much larger and more heinous about my character?"

"Yes."

"Okay."

"But as I said, it's still 90/10. The good things still far exceed the bad."

"So you do or don't want to go steady?"

"Well. I need to be honest about something . . . " *Oh, my fucking god. I don't believe it. I knew this girl was crazy but I really didn't think she was "I-need-to-be-honest-with-you-about-something" crazy.*

" . . . there's this guy who I dated for two weeks a year ago, and he's been e-mailing me for the last month saying he made a big mistake and wants me back." *I could not believe my ears.*

"And I owe it to him and you and myself, if I'm going to commit to you, to just see him and see if there's anything there there." *She's even* using her little cute sayings? "*Anything there there?*" Carrie-fucking-Bradshaw. The metamorphosis was complete.

"So let me get this straight. You're in love with me, which is the first time you've been in love with anyone in fourteen years, and haven't had sex with anyone the way you had with me last night in fourteen years, but you just want to see if this guy you went out with for *two weeks a year ago* is better than me?"

"I don't look at it that way, but—"

"Well, if you're not telling him to fuck off because you're in love with someone and willing to see if there's 'anything there there' with him, then you're saying ultimately that if there is something there, you'll choose him over me."

"You still may be a forty-four-year-old narcissist; I don't know." Okay, her material was so fucking stale at this point, I couldn't even get mad about it. It was just sad and pathetic.

"Go out with the guy and let me know what you decide after."

"I can't talk to you until I see him? That might not be for a week. I haven't even e-mailed him back yet, telling him I would see him."

"Whatever. I'm not going to go out with you when this shit is hanging over my head. You see him, see if there's 'anything there there,' and call me after. I'm getting off the phone now."

"Okay. I really still hope it works out with us."

"Good-bye." I hung up. I really hadn't expected that and was in shock. I sat on the couch and then realized this was bullshit. I e-mailed her.

You've treated me with disrespect the entire time. I hope you find what you're looking for. Don't ever contact me again. Namaste, E

And I meant it. It was hard and really sad, but I knew in my heart, as I had all along, this girl was dangerous.

I realized that she had been having this e-mail thing with this guy the entire time she was seeing me, yet she thought until the day before that we were exclusive. It was completely fucked up. It would have been one thing if she thought we weren't exclusive. And the argument that I had been the advocate of seeing other people—well, you know what, I changed my mind and retracted that and only wanted us to see each other. You don't tell someone you're in love with them if you want to see other people, but I wasn't in love with April. I didn't even really like her. I liked what I hoped she could become. In forcing my hand, she had a wisdom I didn't have. She knew I wouldn't go for her seeing this other guy, even for coffee, so she was, in essence, ending it without doing it herself. A cowardly move but, you know what, I'm not proud of it, but I've done it before myself. In fact, with the last girl I dated, so instant karma. Thank you. Get it out of the universe's system right away so it's not hanging over my head.

As with the previous two breakups, there were a few days of April and me independently telling Lexi how much it sucked and how we missed each other, but this time I wasn't going to make a move. It was up to April to come to me if she wanted me back, and, even then, after all the things she had said and done, I wasn't sure I would sign up again.

A week later, I was having one of those really hard postbreakup days when the drama and anger are gone. You're lonely and having euphoric recall and believe you can work it out and really want to see the person. I was about to go straight to her house with a bushel of Brussels sprouts. Maybe I would leave them with the doorman and sit across the street waiting for her to get them and, when she did, rush over and just kiss her. Or leave the Brussels sprouts with a note. Or forget the Brussels sprouts, I'd just go to her house and kiss her. I was working myself into a frenzy. I was nervous and scared that I might really do it. Half of me wanted to and the other half was screaming, *NO, YOU IDIOT! THE HARD PART IS OVER! YOU GOT OUT! STAY OUT! SHE'S FUCKING CRAZY AND WILL KILL YOU!*

BUT I REALLY WANT TO! SHE'S GREAT! YOU'RE FORTY-FOUR AND ALONE ON SATURDAY NIGHT AND SHE'S FUCKING GREAT! SHE'LL CHANGE AND BE NICER! SHE WAS COMING AROUND! AND YOU CONTRIBUTED TOO! JUST GO GET HER BACK!

I grabbed my yoga mat and headed downtown on the express. Her stop was one past yoga. I had until the last second to make the call. The battle raged all the way downtown.

By Seventy-second Street, I was going to her house.

Changing to the NRWQ at Times Square, I was going to yoga.

As the R stopped at Thirty-fourth, to her house. Twenty-eighth Street, her house.

I prayed hard. Twenty-third Street, her house.

Union Square was the yoga stop. The doors opened with a DINGGGGG. People got off. People got on. "Next stop, Eighth Street. Stand clear of the closing doors, please," said the Indian conductor. I suddenly jumped off, changing my mind at the last instant. The yoga mat strapped to my back got caught in the closing door behind me. DING-DING. The door opened, freed me, and then closed again. Was God, in the person of the train doors clutching me, trying to tell me I had made the wrong decision and should have stayed on the train and gone to April's house? If it had been the computer man making the announcement about what stop was next, I might have stayed on the train, but something about the real, live conductor, Indian no less, made me jump off and opt for yoga. I remember how horrified I was a few years ago when the computer announcement man started replacing the real people on the subway. Now, the only way I can find pleasure in it is to silently mouth the announcement along with the computer man, moving my mouth up and down like a ventriloquist's dummy, never contorting my face to annunciate the words. It makes me laugh and therefore allows me to handle our world's slow death with a little more grace and even muster the energy to fight it.

Anger exhausts me. If I'm smiling, I have a chance.

I felt calm and resigned about my decision to go to yoga, yet I still had a ton of April energy buzzing around me as I navigated the lookie-loos at the farmers' market that takes over Union Square on Saturdays. I usually love looking at the fruits and vegetables, too, but today I was rushing to get to yoga, so I had to be stealthy and move through the crowd with alacrity. I passed the statue of Ghandi across from Coffee Shop on Sixteenth Street, where April and I had eaten sandwiches we had made from individually wrapped Whole Foods cold cuts and multi-grain baguettes on our fifth date, but my resolve wasn't shaken. *Yoga*. I crossed Fourteenth Street and was steps from Jivamukti's new home across the street from the Union Square multiplex where April, her family, and I had gone to see *Superman* a couple of weeks before. Intense April energy all around me. *Yoga*. I opened the door of the nondescript office building. Jiva is on the second floor, though you'd never think it was there. I could feel eyes on me as I held the door for three people to leave. A couple of yogis leaving the noon class, and then a guy with a rolled-up carpet on his shoulder. An idea popped into my head.

The longer you hold the door for people, the nicer day you'll have.

Simple and obvious, maybe, but unfortunately, with my mind, not the first thought that usually comes in. Grace has to deliver it. Luckily, it does more and more as I practice listening for it.

The sweet black security girl watching a tiny portable TV behind the cheap white podium asked me to sign in, and I waited for the elevators with two other yogis. As we got on, I purposely didn't look at the front door of the building so if anybody was coming and wanted us to hold the elevator I could claim I hadn't seen them and absolve myself of being selfish. I mean, I had just held the door for an extra-long time. I'll give someone else a chance to bank some good karma. *Hey, I'm trying*. I got upstairs, paid, and started changing for yoga. I checked my Blackberry one last time before shutting it off for class.

BLINK.

BLINK.

BLINK.

It was a text from a number I knew but couldn't place. I searched my cluttered memory.

FUCK ME! It's April. I had erased her number from my phone when we last broke up, so her name didn't appear anymore.

I pressed the scroller to open the message.

"I almost just got on the elevator with you. Shaking." *Was she going to yoga? SHE was the person I didn't look at coming in? Wow. God, what the hell does this all mean? You gotta help me out here.* I texted her back. "Where are you?"

"Next door. In session." *Wow.* Her normal IMDB appointment was Wednesday at eleven A.M. She must have arranged an emergency weekend one. *She's still into me.*

"If you want me, find me. If not, leave me alone," and I went into yoga. I figured her appointment was an hour; my yoga, a half hour longer. She'd be waiting for me when I got out.

I sat on my mat and felt a loving, rolling, sense of calm and presence. I didn't feel any longer that I had fucked anything up with April. Completely gone was the historic feeling that I had irreparably ruined a gift from God and, as a result, would never be given another. I try very hard to unearth my conception of that kind of God, but it's a challenge. I imagined April in her spiritual practice next door and I in mine here on this mat, and I was free. Free from blame and shame and sadness. I just saw us as two people doing the best we could, trying to love ourselves and the people around us.

That lasted about twenty seconds, and then my mind was off to the races. I distractedly gutted my way through an hour of the class, watching the clock with every breath until I knew she was out of IMDB, and then I left class early. I went straight to the front desk. She wasn't there. Before I even had a chance to check the café around the corner, the girl working the front desk handed me a letter. "She dropped this off for you."

My heart sank. I knew it wasn't good if she had left a letter in lieu of meeting me. I read it while I waited for my "Crown," a smoothie made of coconut water, raspberries, mint, and ginger. It would soothe my stomach after the bad news. It was handwritten in blue pen on the back of two pieces of scrap paper that had crossed-out typing on the original side.

Basically she said I was great, was sorry she hadn't "practiced" on someone she didn't like before me so she was a better "communicator," and would cherish our time together always. She hoped I wanted her there to "cheer me on" when my book came out and was sure it would be a smashing success, signed, "I love you."

I called her. She answered, sounding harried, preparing for her Saturday night plans, probably meeting the "year-ago guy" or some such nonsense.

"What the fuck is this? 'I love you, stay out of my life?'"

"Uh-huh," she said with that same precocious smile in her voice she had when she told me she would have blown me if I was fifteen pounds thinner. I should have hung up right there but instead I did the hard sell yet again, one last time. The luster of it was gone even for me. "Come on, sign up for love . . . You can do it . . . We can do it . . . How often do you meet people you love? Don't give up." She came with her standards, as well as a few closing stabs. She wanted it over, once and for all, and her little play to see if I still cared had worked so well that she knew I was primed for one final wooden stake through the heart to finish me off. "It's too late. I have a date. You opened that door and I walked through it."

"It's too late? You just told me you're in love with me five minutes ago."

"But that doesn't mean it can work."

"After three weeks, you're certain?"

"I just think it'll get worse."

I was over it. She hadn't wanted this from the beginning.

"Well, hopefully you'll find someone who's more of a *value add*,'" I said with obvious unadulterated contempt for the term "value add" and her use of it concerning human beings. And then came the most horrifying April moment of our entire relationship.

"And you will, too." She was being serious. No anger at my judgment of her. In fact, she thought it was an olive branch I had extended, thinking I had finally accepted my fate with dignity and grace and taken the high road, not succumbing to a baser instinct to react with anger or meanness. She hadn't a clue of my sarcasm in my use of her vile term "value add." It was really frightening.

"Good-bye, April." And I hung up.

* * *

That was three weeks ago and, thankfully, nothing since. I might not
have had the strength to stay out of it if she had called. The Brussels
sprouts will be the ending of the movie. I apologize to all of you who
think that'll be a Hollywood-sellout-of-the-integrity-of-the-book
ending, but I'm both a realist and a romantic. Here, I'll be the realist.
In the movie, I'll be the romantic.

I was walking up Amsterdam Avenue with another new friend Mary
on my way to have dinner at my mom's. I was recounting the events
with April, to get a female perspective on all of it. I don't know Mary
that well, but like my other new friend Caroline, she's a genius, that's
obvious. And very, very funny, and very, very deep and crazy, like me.
I trust her implicitly. After listening to the whole story, she said the
most amazing thing.

"If you had a six-year-old son, and this girl treated him like she
treated you, how would you have reacted?"

Fucking sage!

Are you kidding? Can you imagine?

"If you weren't such a fat little boy I would play with you more,
but because you are sickeningly obese already at six, I'm going to
ignore you and lock you in your room alone."

"You don't like to read Dr. Seuss? What do you talk about? I can't
be your friend unless you read more books. Especially Dr. Seuss."

I would grab my son up in my arms and flee straight to the police,
where I would obtain a restraining order against her.

"Yeah," Mary said, "it's easy to see when you look at it that way,
but not so easy when it's you."

That is my new barometer from now on. Along with that other
great question: "If they never changed ONE BIT from how they are
RIGHT NOW, would you stay with them?"

When using those two questions as the criteria for whether April was for me or not, the answer was obvious. A quiet calm came over me. I hugged Mary, thanked her for her amazing counsel, and she split off at Ninety-first Street heading west for Riverside Drive. I grabbed a cab to my mom's.

I banged on her door loudly, over and over again. Of course, the doorbell doesn't work and, on principle, I refuse to call anyone from the hallway to tell them I'm at their front door, but when Mom's in the back bedroom with the AC on and the TV blasting, even with Abner, the silent shelter dog they adopted who never barks, there's no chance they will ever hear me. After three minutes, I broke down and called on my Blackberry.

"Hello?"

"Mom, why won't you get the doorbell fixed?"

"Oh, it works now, honey. They fixed it."

"Can you hear that?"

"Hear what, sweetheart?"

"Right. They haven't fixed the doorbell."

"Yes, they have."

"Mom! I'm ringing it now! I can't hear it, you can't hear it, the dog can't hear it. No one can hear it. It's broken."

"Are you at the front door?" I love her. She is so sweet.

"Yes, Mama. I'm at the front door."

"And you're ringing the doorbell right now?"

"Yes, Mama."

"How strange. Okay. I'll come get you."

After a minute the door opened. She was smiling and happy, as she usually is now.

"Hi, honey! I'm so sorry. I don't know what happened. It was working yesterday. It's not working?" She pressed it a couple of times, apparently not convinced that I was telling the truth.

"Yeah, Mom, it *does* work. This was all just a charade to get you to press the button yourself to make it ring because I know that's fun for you and I want you to embrace your 'fun side' and do more 'fun things'

that make you happy because I know you deprive yourself sometimes."
She started laughing hard. She has a great laugh and is quick to use it.

"Honey, I'm serious. They fixed it."

"How many glasses of wine have you had, Mom?" She smiled
innocently.

"Just one." She was telling the truth and only ever had one a
night, but she would get tipsy from it, especially the later it got. She
would be nodding off by the middle of *American Idol*, for sure (which
wouldn't upset her too much since no one will ever be able to top Clay
in her mind, anyway) and then my stepfather Bill will silently point to
her and we'll smile and wake her up.

"Did I fall asleep?" she'll say and smile. "I love this show."

"But Clay's not on anymore," I'll say, setting her up coyly.

"I know," she'll lament. "I loved Clay. I don't think anyone will
ever be as good as he was."

A minute later, the same routine will happen in reverse. This time
Bill will be the one asleep and my mom will be the one alerting me with
a mischievous point. They never seem to be out at the same time for
some reason. Thank god or the world might stop spinning.

"I'm starving. Is dinner ready?"

"Yeah, we were just waiting for you."

It was my favorite. Lasagne. She made it often when I was a kid.
We ate in what used to be my room but is now the TV and computer
room, the "America room," *America* being a combination of my and
Bill's grown daughter Amanda's name. Although Amanda never even
lived in this house, let alone in my childhood room, being twenty-
one years old and in college when I introduced Bill to my mom, my
mother wanted to be fair and make her feel part of the family. It was
fine with me.

I like Amanda a lot, as do I her father, Bill. I've known Bill for
twenty years, having met him in the spiritual groups I go to. When he
was married to Amanda's mother, they all lived across the street from
my mom's apartment on 104th Street and Riverside. She on the north

side, they on the south. She had never met him. When his marriage broke up in 1991, he stayed on my couch for a couple of weeks until he found another place.

I was making my first short film as part of my AFI film school application, and had cast my mom and Bill as two strangers who accidentally hail the same cab and fall in love. They met on that film and did. I didn't get into film school, but my mother found love, which was an infinitely better reward.

Strangely enough, my father produced his first and only movie in 1961. A small budget independent that never was released. My mother answered an ad in *Backstage*, showed up to audition, got the part, and they fell in love and got married. The marriage only lasted a year, but I was a product of it, so it wasn't all bad. I unwittingly completed the circle by casting her with her next husband in my first movie. It was the least I could do to return the favor of receiving life from her.

This marriage, thirty-five years after her first, has worked out much better for her. They are perfect together and I'm very grateful for their union. Bill looks like a crazy white-haired troll, short and stocky with a small, round belly and a big smile. He's a happy-go-lucky career song-and-dance man who sleeps five hours a night and, when awake, is like a whirling dervish, jacked up on a gallon of Diet Coke. He has a three-second attention span, but a heart of gold. And my mom doesn't hear the doorbell that isn't ringing. They're perfect for each other.

"Honey, don't eat the bay leaves. They're just for flavor."

"I know, Mom. I won't."

"They're very dangerous."

"What do you mean, 'They're very dangerous'?"

"If you swallow them, you could die." She was being dead serious.

"No, you can't," I said, laughing.

"Yes. I'm being serious. You can choke on them and die."

"Mom, I used to shoot heroin and drive drunk on a fifth of Jack Daniels. I think I can survive a bay leaf."

"I don't know."

"When's the last time you heard of a person dying from choking to death on a bay leaf?"

"That's right, you don't. Because they listen to their mothers and don't eat them."

Excellent point, Mom. She has instilled many excellent things in me. My sense of humor. My sense of wonder. But also my sense of worry. And it's getting worse. It's amazing I had a shred of ability not to obsess on the bay leaf thing. I'm usually all too eager to adopt a new pathology I hadn't previously realized was available to me.

"Any word from April?"

"No, Mom. That's over."

"That's good. You didn't deserve to be treated like that."

"You like what your mom did to the apartment?" Bill said, his Coca-Cola–caffeinated bobble head bobbing with excitement.

"What did she do?"

"I decluttered for ten hours today."

"Mom. You've been decluttering for forty years and the house always looks *exactly* the same, except, of course, for the ever-conspicuous absence of my military foot locker–trunk completely filled with baseball cards that you threw out when I was ten, which would have made us all millionaires. God bless your heart, but that's the only thing you've ever thrown away. You have brown paper bags from 1940 that you refuse to throw away." I smiled. She smiled back, a little offended but, deep down, knowing I was right.

"That's not true. Since I've been going to Declutterers Anonymous, that's changed, and I'm willing to throw things out now."

"There is not a Declutterers Anonymous."

"Yes, there is."

"There is," Bill corroborated. "It's helping her."

"Shouldn't it be *Clutterers* Anonymous? instead of *Declutterers* Anonymous?"

"Look. I made a list." She handed me a piece of paper. "There are one hundred and twenty-eight places in the house that need to be decluttered."

"Mom. If you had spent the time decluttering that you spent on making this list, the list would only have, like, forty-two places left. Plus, you've created this piece of paper that at some point will need to, itself, be decluttered. You're such a clutter addict you can't even see that in your attempt to declutter, you're actually making more clutter. You better ask them at the next meeting if there's a decluttering rehab we can send you to." While my mom laughed uncontrollably and Bill suddenly kipped, I checked my Blackberry. No messages. I was hoping for anything. One from April, a new Nerve girl, some surprise gift from God, a girl who got my number from a friend who said we'd be perfect for each other. But I was okay with the silence of the red light. I had my girl. I was with her now.

"I'm gonna go home."

"What? What happened?!" Bill suddenly woke up.

"Eric's going home now. He said I'm only making more clutter."

"That's not true; the kitchen looks great now. She's really making headway."

"Yeah, so we can make another trip with the stuff she's 'throwing away' to the Manhattan Mini Storage, its secondary holding home until we can U-Haul it up to the house in Woodstock?" She started laughing again. "It's been your dream to have a house in Woodstock for forty years, Mom. Why would you blaspheme its birth by only using it as a spillover storage bin for the clutter this apartment and the ministorage can no longer house?"

"That's not true, I'm recycling things from here and using them there, instead of throwing away perfectly good things."

"Mom. An Epson printer from the first computer ever built in 1976 doesn't work with any computer in the world, and you don't even own the computer it did work for. I somehow got brainwashed into taking that thing into my closet at home. How you managed that I still don't know, but I had to wait till you were in the bathroom at the ministorage place to throw the printer away when you couldn't see. That's an example of the things you are 'recycling'?"

"You threw that printer away?" She was shocked. She looked at Bill. "Did you know about this?" Bill looked down sheepishly, "Honey, you were never going to use that printer again," he muttered under his breath.

"I might have at some point."

"Mom, I and your Declutterers Anonymous sponsor need to do an intervention and walk you through this house and force you to throw stuff away."

"No, that's too stressful. Just let me handle it, please." She was getting upset now.

"Really."

"Okay, Mom, don't get upset. Have some Häagen-Daz." She also passed down chocoholism. As with me, it's the great pacifier for her. She was suddenly chirpy.

"Do you want some? We have chocolate and vanilla."

"No, Mom. I gotta go."

"Okay." She was fine now, just knowing chocolate ice cream was coming soon.

"Bye, Mom. Thanks for dinner, it was great. I love you." I reached down to wrap my arms around her as we stood in the hallway, waiting for the elevator.

"I love you, too, honey. You look great."

"Thanks, Mom. So do you. You're going to the gym every day, right?" I asked pointedly.

"I have been. I'm walking on the treadmill for thirty minutes now."

"Good. But you should lift some weights, too."

"I know. But they're heavy."

"I know they're heavy, Mom, but it's good for you. And try a yoga class." The elevator door opened. I got in.

"I don't like yoga. It makes me dizzy." The door started closing.

She waved and smiled, leaning to the right so she could see me for as long as she could until the doors were closed.

"I'll talk to you tomorrow," I said and she was gone. Tears filled my eyes as they often do when I leave her now. I'm so grateful for her and our relationship, which was once so fractured and is now so loving. I know it's the key to all my healing and why, when I do find the right girl, she'll be wonderful.

I wiped my eyes and looked at myself in the brass button panel to the right of the doors. It's always been there even though the yuppies swapped out the beautiful old tin elevator of my youth in favor of this wood-paneled Park Avenue–looking fancy one when the building went co-op. I made strange faces at myself in the reflection. I've been doing it for forty years. It's tradition now. I said good-bye to Jeff, the nice black doorman who took over for Julio after he died of AIDS in the mid eighties. Frank, Abe, and Sanchez were all gone, too. All of the doormen of my childhood had died. The marble floor was the same though. And the heavy iron front door.

I walked up 104th Street from Riverside Drive, diagonally crossed 103rd Street and walked on the east side of West End to 102nd Street. I've taken that route for forty years. I took a left at the brown castle-looking building on 102nd and West End where this exhibitionist guy stands half-dressed in his second-floor window that looks out onto the avenue. He's been doing it ever since I was five, so, for forty years. Clearly I was feeling nostalgic that night, as I have been a lot recently for some reason. No one tells you this shit happens at forty-four. Your mind and body falling apart. You assume it's more like seventy-four, but it's not. It's much earlier. Hair growing out your ear. You sleep wrong, and you can't move your arms for two weeks. Simple acts such as drinking milk out of the carton, things you've done for years without thinking, now take arduous concentration to perform correctly and without spillage. My first glance at parties used to be at pretty girls, now it's at men's bellies and hairlines. Scary but true. And I've been sober since I was twenty and pretty healthy since then. God only knows where I'd be if I wasn't. You'll be lucky if you don't join the "shit people" club by thirty-nine, at the rate you're going. No judgment, friend, just trying to soften the blow if it comes unexpectedly early and maybe provide a little reality check to help you change a few habits, you know what I'm sayin'?

I walked to Broadway and turned right, heading south past Sal and Carmine's Pizza on 102nd Street. They came over from Italy in 1958, and had been on Ninety-fifth and Broadway, next to Symphony Space, until they moved to my block in 1996; they've been there ever since.

They were going to throw out their original hand-painted "Sal's Pizza" sign when they moved, but I asked and they said I could have it. It hung in my apartment on 114th and Broadway for five years but when I moved to 93rd Street, I happened to have a broken arm I had gotten from a fall in a pool in Greece, and couldn't deal with moving it. I took the old vintage Coca-Cola sign that was attached to it, but threw the "Sal's Pizza" part away. I felt at least I was keeping the memory alive by retaining the Coke sign that had been part of the original one. Every time I went in there for years, Sal and Carmine asked me about it.

"How's our sign? You still got it?"

"Of course. I love it." I never felt like I was lying since I did still have part of it, at least.

One day, a few years ago, Sal said in his thick Italian accent, "Hey Eric, you think we could have the sign back?" They realized they had made a mistake in throwing it away.

"Come on, Sal, it would break my heart to give it back. I love it. It's on my wall in my living room."

"We'll pay you for it." These guys have been making the best pizza in New York every day for fifty years. They maybe take a two-week vacation every August, and take Christmas Day and Easter off. That's it. And they have never delivered. That's the magic of Sal and Carmine's.

"I would never take your money. It's your sign." I laughed it off a couple of times but they kept after me. Finally, with my best poker face, I had to call their bluff. I was terrified.

"If you really want it, I won't let you pay me for it, but I'll bring it back tomorrow."

Pause. Carmine blankly looked at Sal. Sal blankly looked back at Carmine and then blankly looked at me . . . "Naaaah! You keep-a dat ol' sign if you like it." *Phew! I had dodged a bullet.* I would have been heartbroken to admit the full truth to them, but they're great guys and I'm sure would have understood.

I continued south on Broadway past the closed down Metro Theater and Oppenheimer's, the butcher who's also been there for fifty years though his son now runs the business since Harry passed away. I hung a left at the first Empire Szechuan on Ninety-seventh and Broadway, which is now, of course, a bank. Legend had it that that huge Chinese restaurant chain was started by Marty Reisman, the only American to meddle in Ping-Pong in the Olympics, a sport dominated by who else, the Chinese. Genius. He also owned a Ping-Pong parlor on Ninety-sixth between West End and Broadway that has long since gone. My mom and I used to play there Sunday nights when I was a kid.

My neighborhood has changed a fair bit but, luckily, because of the projects that are pervasive on Amsterdam and Columbus between 97th and 106th streets, it will never get too gentrified. There's still a wonderful cacophony of ethnicities and classes that intermingle.

I got home to no messages. The downside of having the Blackberry is that I know the score immediately now, so there's no chance of a surprise good message or e-mail when I get home, but I still hold out hope that something may have slipped through the cyberspace cracks. Once in a while there's one, but not tonight.

I decided not to troll for Nerve girls (I got back on a couple of months after retiring, content with not being on the top fifty list after such a long absence, the victory having achieved its purpose, but, much to my dismay, I reentered at number one anyway. It's just the way their site's software works, I guess. Since I left at number one, I reentered at number one. It feels a little creepy, but there's nothing I can do about it.) or Craigslist massage girls or Eros whores. I didn't even want to jerk off, which would at least have made me feel less lonely, having some way to exercise control over my love life. Maybe I would go to a sex addicts' recovery meeting and stop masturbating altogether. Save my chi. The few times I tried sticking to a "plan" (which lasted a couple of months, at best) of no jerking off, no casual sex, no kissing except on a second date, and no sex until a third date, it proved very calming. No judgment on what anyone wants to do as long as it doesn't hurt anyone, but I have found that when I retain that sexual energy and don't dissipate it if I'm not in a relationship, I'm happier. It's always a debate, though, because it does relieve a lot of anxiety to jerk off once or twice a day, and the odd fling is nice, too. Just to feel the physical energy of a woman is important to me. The touching, the affection, the sensuality, the sexuality. Even a booty call relationship holds honest affection and some degree of intimacy, which I need. But ultimately it feels sad and lonely, and drags me into hours of Internet trolling, which I somehow believe sends a message to the universe that's different than the one I want out there. Just for me. For you, it might be different.

I decided to meditate on whether I should be celibate. The answers always come when I sit. I went to my room and sat on my tattered childhood red-and-blue silk blanket that has ship and sea designs on it. My collie, George, used to lie on it and it still smells a bit of her. Even though she died twenty years ago, I still have dreams of her kissing my face and laughing. I miss her terribly. So her old blanket is my seat. My altar is a miniature Pennsylvania Dutch rocking chair I've had all my life. It holds basketball cards from 1969 that somehow escaped my mom's one authentic decluttering episode. Clyde's rookie card sits on top. The cards were bigger then. Longer and wider than the ones today.

Next to Clyde is a fading sepia-toned three-by-two picture of me when I was five years old. I was at my grandmother's in Middletown,

Pennsylvania, where we always went for the holidays and played "family." My fondest childhood memories were of Christmases there. My big bosomed grandmother would bake these amazing chocolate chip cookies that we'd have for dessert after Sunday dinner, which was strawberry shortcake with cream and powdered sugar. You gotta love the Pennsylvania Dutch. Dessert for dinner, dessert for dessert. Although I didn't like that she dragged me to church, I do believe her prayers helped keep me alive when I was an active drunk and drug addict. When I was little, she would tell me that I was such a good boy and I would be even better if I found Christ. But I did get to make out with my three little cousins after services so it was a wash. Uncle Sy and Aunt Judy lived in a trailer by a river. Sy pumped gas and I couldn't think of a cooler job, other than running the service elevator in my building of course. The old manually operated one with the brass lever that would make it go up and down. Judy and Sy were always happy. Always full of life and smiles and hugs. The complete opposite of my family that was always worrying and quiet and scared. Except when my dad was in a good mood some weekends and we would build forts out of the sofa cushions, act out Rocky Raccoon, and then demolish the forts by diving onto them. When I was six years old I asked Judy why she was so happy and she told me it was because of Jesus. Her Jesus seemed much more fun than my grandmother's Jesus so I asked Judy if her Jesus could love me, too. She smiled and said, "of course, he already does." I remember distinctly feeling protected in that moment for the first time in my life. Hopeful that things could be good for me from then on if Jesus was on my side. My father quickly squelched that idea when we were driving back to New York in the car.

"God is for people who need to believe in something to make their lives seem okay, Eric. God doesn't exist." I was heartbroken. But I still loved the trips with my father and Jane to visit my relatives. We'd pile in the Volkswagen station wagon and drive through the night. I loved sleeping in the way back and smelling the gas at the gas station and the muffled sound of the pump when it went in the gas tank. We were driving to family. Driving to love.

It was Easter and I was showing off my new PF Flyers in my grandmother's garden when the picture that I keep on my altar was taken. I keep it on the altar to remind me that I have a history. And a family. Listening to the Beatles does that for me, as well. I always feel safe when I listen to any Beatles song. Like I have an identity. Like everything is going to be okay. I fell asleep to *Revolver* and *Rubber Soul* played over and over from when I was six until I was in Junior High. Also on the altar is a Steuben glass owl given to me by a man I used to help stay sober, who eventually ended up drinking. The wisdom in his soul and in the reminder of how tenuous and blessed sobriety is, is embodied in the owl. The remaining items are a little card with a biblical saying on it given to me by one of the Jamaican women from the first cleansing rehab in the Berkshires. A rosary Helen gave me, some incense, and a plastic Crystal water bottle filled with sand from Tulum, a sacred place I visit a couple of times a year to try to get closer to God. I last went to Tulum three months ago, a week before I met April.

I was doing a yoga retreat with a hundred other people. I went down three weeks before the retreat so I could chill out and get tanned. It's a magical windswept stretch of beach two hours south of Cancún. The sand is very fine; and the water is clear and turquoise in parts of the shallow surf, but dark blue and rocky in other places, so it's not too precious. Saint Bart's it's not, which I like.

Sand-floored bungalows and Swiss Family Robinson tree huts on stilts dot the oceanfront for miles. Thick tropical jungle surrounds them. Until recently, the road wasn't paved, and the deep potholes kept the tourists away. The clientele is mainly backpackers from Europe, wearing faded white braided rope bracelets and dark tans from months of world travel, ex-pats living in old school buses they drove down in the '60s, and yogis from New York who like quiet and funky vacations. If you pay one hundred bucks, you get a bathroom and electricity until the generator goes off at midnight. If you pay forty, you get a bed and a sink in a thatched hut so close to the water so that, in the middle of the night, you can wander a few steps by starlight and pee in the ocean. Although I enjoy that sometimes, I paid the hundred and got the deluxe model.

This time I stayed at Maya Tulum, the Four Seasons of the string of bungalows.

I flew two Nerve girls down a week apart before the yoga retreat started. First, Meirike, an amazing, tall, German ex-ballerina. Twenty-four and hot, she had survived brain cancer at nineteen, and was a wise and wonderful spirit. We had corresponded via e-mail for a couple of months, and then Fred was nice enough to give me a gift of using some of his million Continental miles to fly her to Mexico so we could meet.

We ended up just being friends, which was fine with both of us. It was nice having her company for a few days. She had a sweet and loving energy that calmed me.

After Marieke left, I flew Liz down from Seattle. Based on our e-mail and phone exchanges, I knew she would be a lot of fun and was up for anything, no expectations.

I told her to bring a strap-on and her clown makeup. Say no more.

She brought neither, but we still had three days of hot sex before she went home. Although I liked both of them very much, neither of them were going to end up being my wife, and I wanted the air around me cleared of all romantic energy so that one of the ninety-two yoginis arriving for the retreat might.

I sussed out the possibilities at the first group circle, when everyone meets each other and "declares their intention" for the week. I was honestly on the retreat to get closer to God but if I met my wife in the process, all the better; and the closer I would get to God in finding her.

Unfortunately, this group was not going to yield any prospects. The only girls I found attractive and in my age range were these blond twins, and I just couldn't go there. And they both had boyfriends, anyway, but even if they hadn't it wouldn't have been realistic. They were two of the most fabulous girls I've ever known, but it would just be too sketchy. I wouldn't be able to figure any of it out. I'd want them both and it would get too confusing; it's hard enough dealing with the fantasy of wanting to fuck your girlfriend's sister, let alone if she's identical looking. . . . Just too many issues there. And they were too young, like, twenty-one or something. As much as I try to rationalize the idea of marrying a girl in college—you know, "It's an age-old practice," "They do it in Europe all the time," "If you like each other that's all that matters, the world can go fuck themselves," whatever—the bottom line is this: What are we going to talk about? And even if we find something, we speak different languages. It's hard enough to communicate when speaking the same language, let alone if her reference of a relationship is Britney and KFed and her main news provider is Carson Daly. These girls were way smarter than that and actually wise beyond their years but you get my point.

The rest of the girls were either in relationships, or were nuts. It was fine. I could just focus on my yoga; my union with God.

The retreat was led by Constance. A warm, spiritual forty-year-old ex-model. She had long been investigated. I had asked her out years ago and she had politely declined, but we were fine and friendly. Of course, by "fine and friendly," I mean that I hated her deeply for rejecting me with the lame excuse that she "had just started seeing someone but was flattered." And even if he was so special that she was exclusive with him after date two, they broke up shortly after and she had been with, like, seventeen other guys since him, and never once came to me and said, "Hey Eric, I broke up with that guy I was seeing that precluded me from accepting your sweet date offer, but I am now single and would like to take you up on it if the offer still stands." Whatever. I had forgiven her for not just saying, "Thanks, but I'm not interested in you," which, although smarts for a moment (or a lifetime, depending on the day I'm having) is still preferential to a lie. Anyway, five hours of yoga a day for the next six days would get my head together, which I needed in the worst way as my spiritual life was in free fall and my world myopic.

She started the first practice as she always did, with meditation, chanting, and a talk on something important. The first day's "dharma" talk was about global warming. I was very interested, and concentrating hard on what she was saying. "I saw this movie that Al Gore was in? Did you guys see it? It's about global warming and it's really scary. This is not something that we can ignore anymore, people. We all have to make an effort to"— *Goddamn it, she has beautiful tits.* They were 36Cs, and they were real. On her five foot nine frame, they stuck out as firmly as if she was nineteen and, with her wide shoulders and dancer's body, you just knew without the leotard to hold them there, they would still be rock hard. *Come on! Al Gore, Al Gore.* He was way better than baseball to make my growing hard-on drop faster than losing a fly ball in the midday sun.

"You all MUST see this movie. It's important! Okay, Eric? You'll go?"

"Yes. Al Gore. Al Gore." I actually said out loud although for very different reasons than Constance thought. She laughed. "Pick an intention today and dedicate your practice to it. It can be anything, as long as it's not you. A family member in need. A friend. The world. And devote your efforts today to the well being of that person or thing." I picked world peace.

"Come onto your hands and knees and make your way to downward-facing dog." I could tell I was going to have an excellent, focused practice. "Breathe in . . . " Constance commanded, "breathe out." My intention of world peace was clear in my mind, and I was breathing it in and out with every breath. So far so good.

"Breathe in . . . "

World peace.

"Breathe out."

World peace. Two for two. Who's better than me? Come on, stay focused.

"Breathe in, three."

World peace.

"Breathe out, three."

World peace. Three for three. You're doing great man. Your ego is so dead! You're free!!!

"Breathe in, four."

World peace.

"Breathe out, four."

You are a fat fuck. DAMN IT! World peace.

"Breathe in, five."

Look at that fucking belly. How the fuck did you let yourself get that fat, no wonder those twins think you're disgusting and old. If you weren't so fucking fat you'd have a chance at them.

"And breathe out, five." *Isn't it weird how fat is colder than the rest of your body? It's so demoralizing when after a good work out or a hard yoga class when you bend over to take your sweatpants off and your fat belly touches your hot sweaty chest, it's cold as ice. Like, "Hey fat fuck! I'm still here!"*

WORLD PEACE, DUDE! Not how fat is colder than the rest of your body!

"Walk your hands up to your feet and hang over your legs. Utanasana. Breathe in, one . . . "

How can that guy let his toenails be that long? It's disgusting. Does he not understand how rude that is? To be in yoga where everyone has to see his long, gross toenails?

"Breathe in, two . . . "

Oh, now he's gonna drink water?! Please. I learned in my first week of yoga that drinking water is just a mental exit door when you can't stand to focus on your breath or intention.

"Breathe out, two . . . "

If you can't even stay in utanasana for a couple of breaths without getting distracted and having to pretend you really need water as an out, how do you think you're gonna handle it when your CEO or whatever, the boss of the bullshit, fucking rich job you have tells you that you fucked up your client's account, or whatever? Huh? You might want to start practicing here by just focusing on your breathing and not going for the water as an excuse, buddy. My gift to you.

"And breathe out, five. Where's your intention? Has your mind already wandered?"

Not me, baby. Solid as a rock. World-fucking-peace. Right here. I was so dead. I prayed to God for some help, and I got it. I tried just observing this guy and leaving the story behind. Just labeling him without judgment. *Man drinking water in the middle of class. Woman with too much perfume on. Loud noise outside the yoga hall made by workers.* Instead of listening to the accompanying, *Who the hell are they to be making that racket?! Don't they know we're here on a yoga vacation? If I wanted noise I would have stayed home in New York.* Just stopping it all. Just, *loud noise outside yoga hall.* No drama. No anger. No righteousness. No sense of entitlement.

It was amazing. I was happy. I was able to stay with my intention when distracted momentarily, and not go on a long side trip to fuck-everyone-land. Like two of Ruiz's Four Agreements that my friend and spiritual advisor John is always reminding me of: "Don't assume" and "Don't take anything personally." It really is a recipe for contentment, and then I can spend my energy helping instead of obliterating.

It didn't work every time, but the yuppie guy drinking water turned out to be a lovely man and became a friend, and even though I was lonely and wishing I had someone who I loved and who loved me to share this paradise and my life with, I found many moments of peace and joy while there.

It was sunset, and I took a walk down the beach to Nueva Vida de Ramiro, a stilted-bungalow joint a mile south of Maya Tulum. I've stayed there before with Oscar and Gea, the proprietors of the place, who opened it eight years ago after their son Ramiro miraculously awoke from a six-month coma he'd been in after a motorcycle wreck. He walks with a limp and his motor skills are compromised, but his mind is sharp and he can still play in the sand with his two small sons.

Besides offering a warm and jovial home away from home, Nueva Vida is part of the turtle conservation effort on the beach. They collect the eggs laid in the night by the massive sea turtles and keep them in enclosed pens on the beach so they can hatch without being plundered by birds.

Every few weeks, Oscar, Gea, and anyone who wants to join them, take a bucket filled with baby turtles, small enough to fit in the palm of your hand, to the seaside and set them free with a kiss.

The newborn *tortugas* instinctively scurry, their little legs pushing the sand away, and catapult themselves into the surf. They ride the undertow like an exhale from their mother out into the world. Like a hundred little underwater Raisinettes, they swim out into the ocean trying to make their way to safety.

Only one in two thousand survive. The ones that do will travel forty years to Australia and back to this very stretch of beach where they were born, to lay their own eggs.

I kissed one on the head and, with tears in my eyes, said, "You make it to that reef, little man. You can do it!" and set him free. The reef, a hundred yards offshore, is the first safe haven for them. I thought of the parable about a man who, one dawn, was throwing starfish that had washed up onto the beach back into the sea. A stranger happened upon him and said, "Why are you throwing the starfish back into the ocean?"

"If they're here when the sun comes up, they'll die from the heat."

"But there are a million of them on this beach. You really think you're going to make a difference?"

"It'll make a difference to this one," and he threw the star fish he had in his hand into the ocean.

We let the last baby turtle go, and everyone headed back to their bungalow. The sun had almost set and looked like a perfect piece of red candy. A round fireball sitting on a flat table of blue water. My favorite time on the beach. It was almost empty, and I sat down in the sand. I like when I don't care if I get sand on me, unlike when I'm slathered in oil, tanning, and all about being sand free and smooth. This time of day, when the warm blue water and soft orange sunlight make you feel brown and healthy and thin, you don't care about any of that.

I sat cross-legged in the sand after my evening dip and looked out at the endless ocean, a towel wrapped around me to help with the lovely late afternoon chill. The horizon was interrupted by a jogger. I watched him, panning my head right to left with him as he went. He abruptly stopped, his attention caught by something in the surf. I studied the sea and at first didn't notice anything, but then I spotted a large dorsal fin. A very big fish was thrashing around in the shallow water. *A shark?* I rose excitedly and ran over to where the jogger was.

"It's a dolphin. It's bleeding. See? It must have been hit by a boat," he said. I immediately walked into the surf to get a closer look. He didn't seem too badly hurt, though he was scraped on his back and bleeding from his nose. He was a baby, but still five feet long, at least. He was letting the waves wash him ashore but then would flip around as if he was stuck. I tried to pick him up but he was really heavy, much heavier than he looked, and the waves, though small, were knocking us over whenever I would get a grip on his shiny, hard, slick skin. The jogger helped me pick him up, and we carried him out a few feet and let him slide into the ocean. He could swim and did. He headed out to sea but, after making it past the first set of waves, turned back on his own and washed up again on the beach. *Does he want to die here?* He seemed scared and disoriented, as if he wanted no part of whatever was out there in the deep water.

"I don't think there's anything we can do for him." And with that, the jogger ran off.

I held the dolphin strongly in my arms and sat down in the water so, even though the waves caused me to list, I could keep my head above the water and still hold on to him. It seemed to calm him though he was still breathing sporadically, inhaling and exhaling haltingly with sudden hard bursts of air through his blowhole. His exhale spray hit me in the face, and the salty water was mixed with a little blood. I instinctively turned my face, afraid I might catch HIV, but then realized it was a dolphin and that I was safe. Insane I know, but you're 000 pages into my life, I think you probably called that one yourself. Not even an irrational fear of dying could distract me from the fear of the sadness I would have to endure if this sweet creature died in my arms. I was on my own with God.

"It's going to be okay. We're going to get you some help," I told him over and over.

"I love you." I didn't want him to be scared. He was so alone. Like I was.

After he calmed down, I tried to help him swim out again. He seemed like he might venture into the deep water this time but he just came back in once more. I tried again, and again, and again, and again. Swimming next to him, my arm around him, I tried to encourage him to make it, but the most he wanted to do was to swim along the beach in the shallow water, back and forth, but not swim out alone. Finally, he came back in again and I just sat and held him. I was as out of breath as he was, my clumsy attempts to help him swim having failed, beaten back by the surf. I was unable to negotiate holding on to him to guide him to the deep water while standing on the rocky sea surface below. My feet kept slipping, and as I got into deeper water my motor skills radically decreased. I was living the recurring nightmare I've had my entire life, where I'm running away from someone who's trying to kill me and they're able to run at full speed but I'm only able to run as if I'm running in water up to my waist. Only now I was trying to help someone else from dying rather than keep from dying myself, but it seemed just as frightening and fruitless anyway. I was always a really fast runner and I always won. I wasn't winning now. I was small against this ocean and this dying dolphin. Tiny. I felt destined to fail but I just couldn't accept that. I must make this dolphin live.

Oscar came down, having heard I was in the water with the dolphin, and called the marine biologist from Dolphin World, sixty miles north. He assured me that even though it was a place where they train dolphins to do shows in captivity for the rest of their lives, they treat them well and it was better than his dying on the beach, which seemed ordained if we left him here.

I had yoga in ten minutes and had "committed," as we all had, not to miss any of the classes with the group. Even though I knew they would understand if I missed one for this reason, having Oscar there to stay with him until help arrived in an hour made me feel I could go.

"You're gonna be fine and I'm going to come visit you tomorrow at your new home. I love you," I said to the baby dolphin and then jumped up and raced to my bungalow to change into my yoga clothes, leaving him with Oscar.

When I got back from yoga later that night, Oscar told me the marine biologist had taken him on the truck in the water tank. He had been hit by a boat and had a skull fracture but the doctor said that he would be fine. I was so relieved and couldn't wait to visit him. I felt this dolphin and I were kindred spirits. He was a gift from God and the reason I had come to Tulum. Not to find a girl, but to find him and, in doing so, further find myself.

The next day, I went to the morning yoga class at Maya Tulum. Oscar promised me he would call and get news on the dolphin by lunchtime so I could go visit him after class. I drove the short distance down the newly paved road. It had completely changed the vibe of the place, but still hadn't spelled ruin. It was still a sleepy, funky road in nirvana, just a paved road now. I pulled over outside Nueva Vida and Oscar came up to my car, a greasy engine part and dirty white rag in his hands.

"Did you get hold of them?"

"I have bad news, Eric."

"What?"

"The dolphin died, I'm afraid." I couldn't believe it.

"I thought they said he was going to be okay?"

"He had internal bleeding and died on the truck before they even left Tulum."

"Could they be lying for some reason?"

"No. For sure. I know the doctor well from the turtles. He tells the truth. The dolphin died. I'm sorry." He walked away to fix a boat. I sat in the car and cried. I had forgotten to kiss the dolphin good-bye when I left because I was in such a hurry to get to yoga. What if he had died not knowing how much I loved him? I couldn't bear that thought.

* * *

I used to have a very detailed list describing the woman of my dreams. I looked at it every day, meditated on her, and prayed we'd find each other. In *Return to Love* (which I, of course, didn't read but instead listened to on the beach after the dolphin died), Marianne Williamson talks about how lists are great. We will manifest anything we write on a list, but she suggests we stop seeking our limited ideas of abundance and give it over to God. Allow God's infinite love to guide us to our heart's desire instead of placing our faith in our little ideas on a piece of paper, which can't possibly, if our mind came up with them, *if my mind came up with them*, be nearly as perfect as what God will come up with.

I got home from Mexico and ripped up my list . . . Then came April.

I've since thought about going back to the list system but haven't. Although April didn't turn out to be HER, I still like the idea of leaving it up to God's imagination instead of mine.

My prayer now is simply "Dear God, I pray that I be attracted to the woman of my dreams and that she be attracted to me . . . whoever she may be." I got nostalgic for this girl I dated before April. I never really liked her very much but we had amazing sex so I thought I did and, of course, really wished I would. I looked on her My Space page and through some remedial investigative work tracked her to her new boyfriend. They seem perfect for each other. She was a singer-songwriter. Good but not brilliant. But even mediocre songs can seem great when it's a week before Christmas and you don't have a girlfriend and they were written about you.

I've always wanted to take a train cross country. I think it'd be fun and romantic and feel like being in a 1940s movie. I'm really afraid of flying, and just the idea of staying on the ground is comforting to me. I'm sure once will be enough, but I think I'm going to do it next week. It's time to fast in the desert again. Maybe she'll be on that train, or getting a colonic after me. It would be really nice to finally meet her. But until I do, I'll rejoice in the smell of snow and my mother's smile. How my bare feet feel against dirt and Savasana. The last perfect bite of a bacon cheeseburger and the first perfect bite of the best chocolate cake on earth. Naps, the quiet trance after a good cry, a belly laugh, an icy wind, hands, giving a twenty-one-year-old Pakistani cabdriver an extra fifty dollars because it's his birthday and he's going to AC for the weekend after he drops me off. Long-legged, sexy girls in baby-doll dresses and combat boots walking down Broadway and two-A.M. bad TV and sleeping as late as I want. The memory of the Mets winning the World Series in '69 and '86, and football all day Sunday on the couch and on Monday night and the funny three-year-old kid dancing on the subway, and, and, and, and . . . and the vision of kissing the girl I'm going to marry. I've seen her in my mind my whole life. Hurry up. I'm getting really tired of not having you under the covers as my space heater. Maybe I don't want separate beds, after all. Whatever, we'll work it out. Just come. I'd rather have the sequel to this book be *I Can't Believe I've Been Married for a Year* than *I Can't Believe I'm Still Single at 50.*

That's my wish for you, too, that you find him or her in this lifetime. I know you will. There's a beautiful saying, "Don't give up five minutes before the miracle." As much as I love its sense of hopefulness, the truth is it's impossible to give up before the miracle because the miracle is now. So welcome to the miracle. Oh my god, I forgot to tell you. Guess who e-mailed me this morning? Taudry Hepburn. I shit you not. I guess since I'm the prom King now Miss Prom Queen can take a chance on me. Fuck her, right?! I mean, if I wasn't good enough for her when I was number 47 . . . come on, be real. I have a date with her Friday night. I'll let you know how it goes.